The Elusive African
Renaissance

The Elusive African Renaissance

Essays on Today's Critical Development Issues

Edited by GEORGE KLAY KIEH, JR.

McFarland & Company, Inc., Publishers
Jefferson, North Carolina

LIBRARY OF CONGRESS CATALOGUING-IN-PUBLICATION DATA

Names: Kieh, George Klay, 1956– editor.
Title: The elusive African renaissance : essays on today's critical
    development issues / edited by George Klay Kieh, Jr.
Description: Jefferson, North Carolina : McFarland & Company,
    Inc., Publishers, 2018 | Includes bibliographical references
    and index.
Identifiers: LCCN 2018031327 | ISBN 9781476667744
    (softcover : acid free paper) ∞
Subjects: LCSH: Democratization—Africa. | Nation-building—
    Africa. | Economic development—Africa. | Africa—Politics
    and government. | Africa—Economic conditions.
Classification: LCC JQ1879.A15 E45 2018 | DDC 338.96—dc23
LC record available at https://lccn.loc.gov/2018031327

ISBN (print) 978-1-4766-6774-4
ISBN (ebook) 978-1-4766-3525-5

BRITISH LIBRARY CATALOGUING DATA ARE AVAILABLE

Front cover image © 2018 poco_bw/iStock

Printed in the United States of America

McFarland & Company, Inc., Publishers
  Box 611, Jefferson, North Carolina 28640
  www.mcfarlandpub.com

To the memory of our colleague David N.P. Mburu, who contributed to the success of this volume. Regrettably, he passed away while the volume was being prepared. We will continue to work tirelessly for the fulfillment of David's dream of a democratic and developed Africa in which its constituent states make public investments in the material advancement of the African peoples, including in the critical area of education.

Acknowledgments

We would like to acknowledge the kind assistance of two journals. *The Journal of Safety and Crisis Management* granted permission for Emmanuel O. Oritsejafor to use his article, "Silent Tsunami: The Nexus of Food Security and Rising Oil Prices in Sub-Saharan Africa," Vol. 2, No. 2, 2012, pp. 1–12, as the foundation for his essay "The Nexus of Food Security and Bio-Fuels in Sub-Saharan Africa." Similarly, we would like to thank the *Journal of Developing Societies* for George Klay Kieh, Jr., to use his article "The State and Political Instability in Africa," Originally published in *Journal of Developing Societies*, Vol. 25, No. 1. © 2009 SAGE Publications. All rights reserved. Reproduced with the permission of the copyright holders and the publishers Sage Publications India Pvt. Ltd, New Delhi, as the base of his essay "Political Instability and Development in Africa."

Table of Contents

Preface

GEORGE KLAY KIEH, JR.

Africans greeted the dawn of the 21st century with tremendous optimism and expectations that the labyrinthine of development problems—jobs, education, health care, food security, clean drinking water, acceptable sanitation, democratic governance, and stability, among others—that have bedeviled the continent and the preponderant majority of its constituent states since the post-independence era would be addressed. In this vein, the former president of South Africa, Thabo Mbeki, referred to the emergent millennium as "the African Renaissance."

Interestingly, after almost two decades into the new century, the emerging evidence suggests that while some progress has been made in addressing the African continent's vexatious development challenges, much work needs to be done in order to bring to fruition the "African Renaissance" President Mbeki envisaged. It is in this spirit that this volume was conceived. Specifically, the overarching purpose is to examine some of the continent's critical development issues by analyzing the challenges and building on the progress that has been made by proffering policy-relevant proposals. Two of the overarching proposals that run through the volume are the imperative of reconstituting the neo-colonial African state and jettisoning the failed neoliberal development model and its associated permutations of structural adjustment programs and so-called "debt forgiveness," and "poverty reduction." Undoubtedly, the full realization of the aforementioned projects would require visionary and transformative leadership, and an engaged and activist citizenry throughout the continent.

Undoubtedly, this volume would not have been possible without the invaluable contributions of several persons and entities. First, I would like to thank the African Studies and Research Forum for commissioning the research that led to the writing of this book under its "Book Series." Second, kudos to the contributors for conducting the research that culminated in the

1

writing of their various essays, and for their willingness to revise them against the background of the comments from me and the two anonymous reviewers. Last, but not least, I would like to thank the anonymous reviewers for the feedback they provided. Certainly, it helped to enrich the quality of the essays included herein.

Introduction

Mapping the Development Landscape in Africa

GEORGE KLAY KIEH, JR.

Africa is the region of many paradoxes. For example, the continent is the richest in the world in terms of natural resources—minerals, oil, etc.—but its peoples are in the lowest rung in terms of human development. For example, mass abject poverty and human malaise are prevalent across the continent (United Nations Development Program, 2016). Also, the continent has some of the most fertile land in the world, but millions of Africans are suffering from hunger and malnourishment. Similarly, Africa has several rivers and lakes, but a significant number of Africans lack access to clean drinking water and sanitation. Kutor (2014:14) poignantly summarizes the general African development condition thusly:

> ... [the African] Continent has remained largely underdeveloped regardless of the presence of huge natural resources (gold, cocoa, bauxite, oil, diamonds, timber) and human resource base. Several decades after the end of colonialism, most parts of Africa is [*sic*] still fighting with problems such as high poverty rate, corruption, lack of basic infrastructural facilities in all sectors of the economy, unemployment, high mortality rate, political instability and insecurity of lives and property.

Consequently, the continent has become the object of pity and the subject of ridicule. In the case of the former, for example, in the United States, there are numerous television commercials soliciting humanitarian assistance to Africa, ranging from food to benches and chairs for schools. Particularly, the ads that seek humanitarian assistance often show emaciated and seriously ill children in Africa as the core of their pitch to contributors. In addition, most African leaders have made begging for foreign aid the cornerstone of their states' foreign policies. For example, one of the major pillars of the New Part-

3

nership for Africa's Development (NEPAD) is the continent's collective appeal to the "Global North" for more aid (Kieh, 2003; Ayittey, 2004; Taylor, 2008). Ayittey (2004:26) aptly refers to this phenomenon as "Africa's leaky begging bowl."

There are numerous books, articles in academic journals, articles in magazines, newspapers, blogs, and regular commentaries in various media outlets about the state of the human condition in Africa. A pervasive theme in these literatures is the depiction of the continent as the cesspool of human misery. For example, in his interesting article and book "The Coming Anarchy," Robert Kaplan portrayed the African continent as the bastion of primitive life and unmitigated violence (Kaplan, 1994, 2001). Specifically, in a sweeping generalization, he argued that the continent lacks some of the most basic necessities of life, and is a caudillo of crime and violence. In his own words, "The cities of West Africa at night are some of the unsafest places in the world. Streets are unlit, the police often lack gasoline for their vehicles; and armed burglars, carjackers, and muggers proliferate" (Kaplan, 1994:45). Clearly, Kaplan's account was pivoted on exaggeration and generalization. This is because he used a single case to generalize to the entirety of West Africa.

Importantly, there is no doubt that Africa has major development challenges. However, it is not useful to simply catalogue these challenges. The most useful approach would be to interrogate both the internal and external causes of the African development condition, and to proffer some suggestions for addressing these conundrums. By so doing, the lives of the peoples of Africa could be improved, so that they too could find fulfillment in jobs that pay wages that meet the cost of basic human needs, first-rate health care and education, access to clean drinking water and sanitation, food security, a decent place to live, and public transportation. In short, the utility of any treatise on the African development condition will be determined by whether it provides concrete ideas for helping to ensure that the peoples of Africa enjoy the "freedom from fear, and the freedom from want" (United Nations Development Program, 1994:3; Kaldor, 2007:182).

Against this backdrop, this book is intended to examine the causes of African development conditions, and to offer some suggestions for improving them for the material well-being of the peoples of Africa. In this vein, as the frame for the book, the introduction has several interlocking purposes. First, it provides an overview of the African development landscape. Second, it briefly teases out some of the central elements of the frontier issues that constitute the book. Third, it examines the state of human development on the continent. Fourth, it articulates the book's conceptual framework with the focus on development. Fifth, the theoretical framework that provides the compass for the book is mapped out. Sixth, the objectives of the book are mapped out. Lastly, the major arguments of the various essays that constitute the book are summarized.

The Development Landscape: An Overview

The Crucible: The State

Background

Any examination of the African development landscape must begin with the interrogation of the portrait of the state in Africa. This is because the state sets the parameters within which all societal activities occur. Also, the state is the arena of struggle (Glasberg and Shannon, 2011). That is, the state is the space in which various forces engage in sundry contestations. The portrait of the state conditions and shapes these contestations. Ultimately, the outcomes are determined by the various forces' relationships with the state. In this vein, in this section of the introduction, the foci is on the historical development of the state in Africa, and the resulting portrait.

The Phases of the Development of the State in Africa: A Brief Overview

Historically, the state in Africa has evolved in three major phases: precolonial, colonial and post-colonial. During the pre-colonial phase, Africa, like other regions of the world, had several types of states—ranging from small to large—as well as state forms—empires, kingdoms, etc. Further, these states had divergent systems of governance that could be characterized as democratic, authoritarian and mixed. Importantly, these states represented the historical-cultural experiences of the various groups that occupied them. In other words, these polities were indigenous in terms of their portrait—nature, mission, etc. There were varieties of states with their own peculiarities in Africa during this period; however, these polities had some shared general characteristics. Economically, for example, communalism was the common mode of production in these states. That is, the major means of production—mainly land—was owned and controlled by the state. An individual then had access to the land through his family line. In patrilineal societies, land use was accessed through one's father's bloodline, and in matrilineal-based polities through the mother's family line. Overall, each of these indigenous polities undertook socio-economic development on the basis of its objective conditions—the circumstances that were involved in obtaining it. Naturally, some polities were more developed than others.

The colonial phase began after the Berlin Conference of 1884–1885, which was dubbed the "scramble for Africa" (Pakenham, 1992; Meredith, 2006; Kieh, 2007) because the various major global powers assembled (the United States was an observer) and carved out the territories of Africa, dividing them among themselves. The process was informed by the reports that various European explorers, who were sent to investigate the lay of the land in Africa, provided to their various states. The information gathered, especially about the economic resources of the various areas in Africa, was pivotal to the jockeying for territories by European powers. Ultimately, the station of each of the major powers in the global "division of power" determined the amount of territory it acquired from the negotiation. So, Great Britain and France received the largest number of territories. Thereafter, the colonial powers imposed their rule on Africa through the use of military force (Mbaku and Kimenyi, 1995; Kieh, 2007).

The resulting colonial system was anchored by the "Berlinist state" (Kieh, 2007). Conceptually, the "Berlinist state" was a repressive and negligent construct that, among other things, violated political rights and civil liberties, and refused to provide for basic human needs such as education and health care (Kieh, 2007). Briefly, the "Berlinist state," as Ake (2001:3) observes, was "totalistic." That is, it controlled virtually every aspect of the colony. For example, in the cultural sphere, European cultures were superimposed on the African colonies. Economically, embryonic capitalism replaced communalism as the economic system. The attendant class structure was based on inequalities in wealth and income, as well as the exploitation of African labor and natural resources. Politically, an authoritarian model of governance was established that was anchored on repression and suppression through the instrumentality of force. Socially, the colonial state refused to invest in education, health care and other social services for the colonized Africans. However, the colonial state used the natural resources that were pillaged and plundered from the African colony to help advance the material well-being of Europeans, who were resident in the colonizing countries, as well as the African colonies.

The post-colonial phase began in the 1950s, as the result of a confluence of factors, especially the struggles for independence that were waged by colonized Africans. Africans were excited that they had exorcised the colonial "demon" and were consequently hopeful that the post-independence era would usher in a new era of human-centered democracy and development. Ramsay (1993:3) described the time as "electric." Regrettably, it did not take long for the peoples of Africa to realize that, with few exceptions, independence would not end the crises of underdevelopment that colonialism had bequeathed to the new states. This was because, for example, the post-colonial state, the fulcrum for the promotion of democracy and development, was a replica of its colonial progenitor (Kieh, 2007, 2008a). Hence, the public policies that were formulated and implemented by the overwhelming majority of the governments were similar to the colonial ones (Kieh, 2007, 2008a). To make matters worse, each succeeding generation of African leaders, with few exceptions (e.g., Nkrumah in Ghana and Nyerere in Tanzania), maintained the anti-people, anti-democracy, and anti-development state and its associated policies. For example, by the mid–1980s, Africa was in the stranglehold of social and economic malaise and this prompted observers to refer to the decade as "Africa's lost decade" (Magstadt, 2010:555). Even the imposition of a neo-liberal development model by the Bretton Woods institutions—the International Monetary Fund (IMF) and the World Bank—and the United States and other advanced capitalist states as the panacea to the continent's socio-economic development woes have not led to the improvement of the material conditions of the majority of Africans (Chang, 2015). In fact, the various neoliberal policies such as the structural adjustment programs (SAPs) that have been imposed by the IMF and World Bank have worsened the material conditions of the majority of Africans (Chang, 2015).

The Portrait of the State in Africa

One of the major by-products of the development of the post-colonial state in Africa over the past six decades is the portrait of the construct. This means that the state in various African countries has shared nature, character, mission, and political economy. In terms of its nature, the state in Africa is a foreign construct that was imposed by the colonial powers during the notorious Berlin Conference (Kieh, 2007; Craven, 2015). In other words, the post-colonial state in Africa is "Berlinist" (Kieh, 2007:6). Thus, the post-colonial state in Africa does not represent the cultural and historical experiences of the citizens of various African countries. Another dimension of the nature of the post-colonial state in Africa is that it lacks hegemony and autonomy— relative or otherwise. Hence, it is a weak, dependent and peripheral actor in both the "international division of power" and the "international division of labor."

In terms of its character, it has been described variously as "criminalized," "exploitative," "negligent," and "neopatrimonial" (Agbese, 2007; Kieh, 2007, 2008b, 2009a, 2009b, 2012). In other words, the post-colonial state has a multidimensional character. However, either one or more dimensions became ascendant during a particular historical conjuncture (Agbese, 2007). For example, at a particular time, the post-colonial state's negligent dimension would be dominant, as evidenced by its refusal to invest in education, health care, and food security, among others. However, during this time, the other dimensions of the state's character are present, but latent (Agbese, 2007).

The mission of the post-colonial state is twofold. A key one is to provide an enabling environment in which metropolitan-based multinational corporations and other businesses can accumulate massive profits by exploiting the natural resources and labor of the various African states. The members of the faction or fraction of the ruling class of a particular African state that is ruling the country at a specific time get compensated mainly through the receipt of bribes, and political and military support from the home governments of these foreign businesses. For example, in spite of its pro-democracy rhetoric, the United States government has supported, and continues to support various authoritarian regimes in Africa—Mobutu (Zaire, now Democratic Republic of the Congo), Barre (Somalia), Doe (Liberia), Moi (Kenya), Zenawi (Ethiopia), and Museveni (Uganda), among others—because they served, and are serving the economic and strategic interests of the United States (Petras and Veltmeyer, 2012). The other part of the mission is to provide the members of the fraction or faction of the local ruling class of an African state that is ruling the country at a particular historical juncture the opportunity to engage in the primitive accumulation of wealth through the use of their respective public offices. The most pervasive method that is used by state managers to enrich themselves is through corruption—bribery, extortion, embezzlement, etc. The resulting effect is that the state in Africa has become "akin to a buffet service in which the members of the ruling faction or fraction and their relations eat all they can eat for free" (Kieh, 2009b:10). According to Transparency International, the most corrupt state in Africa in 2016 was Somalia (Transparency International, 2017). The other countries in the top tier (in pecking order) of the most corrupt states included South Sudan, Sudan, Libya, Guinea-Bissau, Eritrea, Angola, Congo, Chad, the Central African Republic, Burundi, Democratic Republic of the Congo, Zimbabwe, Comoros, Uganda, Madagascar, Kenya, Guinea, Cameroon, Mozambique, Mauritania, Guinea and Nigeria (Transparency International, 2017). On the other hand, the least corrupt states in Africa were Cape Verde and Mauritius (Transparency International, 2017).

As for the political economy of the post-colonial state in Africa, it has several major features. A key one is its peripheral capitalist mode of production. That is, African states are essentially the producers of raw materials such as agricultural products—coffee, cocoa, and rubber—minerals—diamonds, gold, etc.—and oil. However, they are marginal players in making the decisions regarding the prices of these commodities. This means that they are on the periphery of the "international division of labor," and are victims of the "system of unequal exchange" (Kieh, 2003). Another element is the relations of production or the class structure. Under this arrangement, there are three major class clusters: the ruling or *bourgeois* class consists of the owners of the foreign-based multinational corporations and other businesses that have investments in various African states (the external wing), and the members of the faction or fraction of the local ruling class—state managers, local entrepreneurs who are relatively well-off economically, and foreign merchants, who are resident in the various African states (the local wing). The *petit bourgeois* class is comprised of intellectuals and entertainers. The lower classes consist of the workers, the farmers, the unemployed, and the *hoi polloi*. Furthermore, there are three major models of governance: democratic, authoritarian and hybrid. According to Freedom House, there were 10 democratic states in Africa in 2016, 22 authoritarian states, and 22 hybrid states (Freedom House, 2017). Cumulatively, there were more non-democratic states on the continent (44) than democratic ones (10). Also, the public policies in the various sectors often reflect the interests of the members of the ruling class. However, a few countries, like Mauritius, are making efforts to democratically reconstitute the post-colonial state.

Problematizing Some of the Frontier Development Issues

Background

In this section, the frontier issues that constitute the foci of the book's essays are briefly examined in order to provide a summative context for the subsequent detailed analyses provided by the essays. The overview of these frontier issues sets the stage for the in-depth examination that each essay provides regarding the nature and dynamics of the challenges, as well as policy relevant suggestions for helping to address these challenges.

Democratization in Africa

The struggle for democracy has been an enduring feature of the socio-economic and political landscape of Africa. During colonialism, for example, Africans from divergent regional, ethnic, class, religious and gender backgrounds, united under the auspices of various nationalist movements to wage struggles against European colonialism—"the first wave of democratization" (Kieh, 2007). These struggles yielded the primary dividend of decolonization, and the resulting independence of African states (Kieh, 2007). In this vein, Africans entertained the hope that the "first wave of democratization" would have led to the establishment of democratic states across the continent (Ramsay, 2003; Kieh, 2007).

However, the end of colonialism and the dawn of the era of independence, with few exceptions (e.g., Botswana and Mauritius), did not yield the desired results (Ramsay, 1993; Kieh, 2007). Frustrated by the failure of the "first wave," Africans organized themselves into various organizations with the shared objective of struggling for democracy against the pantheon of authoritarian states that adorned the continent's landscape—"the second wave of democratization." However, these collective pro-democracy struggles did not yield the desired dividend, due to various internal and external factors—e.g., the hijacking of democratic struggles by the proliferation of military coups, and the support for authoritarian regimes by the United States, the Soviet Union, and their respective allies.

Undaunted by the setbacks of the "second wave of democratization," pro-democracy forces in Africa continued their struggles against both civilian and military-led authoritarian regimes on the continent. Dubbed the "third wave of democratization," or "Africa's second liberation" (Huntington, 1993; Osaghae, 2005: 1), this phase of the pro-democracy struggles has been shaped by both domestic and external factors, including the resilience of pro-democracy groups, and the end of the Cold War. After almost three decades, the "third wave" has experienced both successes and challenges. In the case of the former, for example, the number of democratic states increased from two (Botswana and Mauritius) in 1990, to ten in 2016 (Freedom House, 2017). However, much work needs to be done, especially since the majority of African states—44—are undemocratic (Freedom House, 2017). Another major challenge is that political democratization has not led to improvement in the material conditions of the majority of ordinary Africans (United Nations Development Program, 2016). For example, democratic states like Benin are in the lowest rung in terms of human development (United Nations Development Program, 2016).

The Economies of African States

The economies of African states have certain shared structural characteristics. For example, most of them have a peripheral capitalist mode of production. This entails that the major means of production—especially capital and the limited technology—are owned and controlled by the suzerains of international finance and industrial capital based in the "Global North" (the developed states). Also, African states have monocrop economies and are thus dependent upon a single major commodity—agricultural products, oil and minerals—as the "lifeblood" of their economies. These commodities are ostensibly produced to feed the industrial and manufacturing complexes of the "Global North." In turn, African states depend upon the "Global North" for manufactured goods. Under the "system of unequal exchange," African states are paid less for their goods, but are required to pay more for the manufactured goods from developed states. One of the resulting adverse consequences of African states' monocrop economies is their vulnerability to the vicissitudes of the "Global North"–controlled and dominated global economy: when the prices of these raw materials go up, the economies of African states experience a temporary boom; but, when the prices go down, there is a bust or decline. Further, African states are marginal players in the global economy. Accordingly, they do not play a major role in the formulation of the norms that govern global economic interactions like trade. One of the major resulting negative consequences is that collectively African states reap minimum benefits from international economic interactions, since, as has been discussed, African states are paid less for their raw materials, but are required to pay more for the manufactured goods, especially from the "Global North."

Another shared feature of the economies of African states is their foreign investment dependence. According to fDi Intelligence, "Africa is the world's fastest growing region for foreign direct investment" (Fingar, 2015:1). For example, in 2014, the African continent received a total of $87 billion in foreign direct investment (Fingar, 2015). Of this amount, about $33 billion was invested in the oil and gas sector. In addition, since the dawn of the 21st century, a foreign investment race in Africa has commenced between China, the new imperialist power, and the United States, France, the United Kingdom and the other older imperialist powers. Aptly dubbed as "The New Scramble for Africa" by Carmody (2011:v), "once marginalized in the world economy, the past decade has seen Africa emerge as a major supplier of crucial raw materials like oil, uranium, and coltan." In this vein, China has invested about $75 billion in various African states over the last 10 years (Burnett, 2015). Not to be outdone, the Obama administration announced in 2014 that American companies have "committed to invest $14 billion in Africa" (Burnett, 2015:1).

On the policy formulation front, ultimate economic decision-making rests with the Bretton Woods institutions—the World Bank and the International Monetary Fund. For example, it was these "Global North"–dominated international financial institutions that designed and implemented the notorious "Structural Adjustment Programs" (SAPs) that devastated the economies of several African states and worsened social conditions (Mkandawire, 2001; Kieh, 2003). With the failure of SAPs, the Bretton Woods institutions under American suzerainty then designed other economic policy schemes for various African states, including the Heavily Indebted Poor Countries Initiative (HPCI) and the Poverty Reduction Strategy (PRS). The former is supposedly designed to forgive the debts qualified African states owed to the Bretton Woods institutions and the countries in the "Global North." The reality is that heavily indebted African states have already paid the principals for these debts many times over through the periodic payment of the interest.

As for the PRS, it is more of a public relations gimmick, because it has done nothing to reduce poverty in the various African states where it has been implemented (Malahuan and Guttal, 2006).

Microfinance

Microfinance has gained appeal as an innovative approach to addressing the scourge of poverty in Africa. In 2011, about 415 million Africans or about 42 percent of the continent's population were living on less than $1.25 day (Chandy, 2015:1). Amid the failure of the neoliberal development model as a suitable pathway to the improvement of human welfare on the African continent, and the resulting exacerbation of mass poverty, hunger, and the broad labyrinthine of human development problems, microfinance was adopted as a useful approach to help address the socio-economic malaise. At the core of microfinance is "the idea of lending or giving very small sums of money to poor [as credit for undertaking various small business ventures]" (Hamam and Schwank, 2015:22).

Like any undertaking, microfinance has had successes and challenges. In the case of the former, the successes have included giving poor people access to financial credit on a small scale that they would otherwise not have; a channel for savings; insurance; pensions; as money transfer centers; helping to spur economic growth; adaptability to the nature of the environment; and service to traditionally under-serviced rural areas (United Nations, 2013; Hamam and Schwank, 2015). On the other hand, the challenges include governance issues or what the United Nations calls "structural fragility" (United Nations, 2013:xiv); the inadequacy of the credit that is needed to meet the growing demand; the lack of incentives for medium and long-term loans; the over-indebtedness of borrowers; high interest rates approaching the level of loan sharks; and the weak regulatory framework (United Nations, 2013).

The HIV/AIDs Pandemic

The HIV/AIDs epidemic continues to ravage the population of some African states. For example, in 2013, 24.7 million people were living with HIV in Sub-Saharan Africa. Further, there were 1.5 million newly affected people during the same period. Sadly, about 1.1 million people died from AIDS as well. These stark statistics make the Sub-Saharan African region the most HIV/AIDS affected area in the world (Avert, 2014:1). Of the region's constituent sections, "Southern Africa is the worst affected region, and is widely regarded as the 'epicenter' of the global HIV epidemic" (*ibid.*). In terms of the individual states, "Swaziland has the highest HIV prevalence of any country world-wide (27.4 percent), while South Africa has the largest epidemic of any country—5.9 million people are living with HIV" (*ibid.*).

There are two major dimensions of the HIV/AIDS epidemic: crisis and systemic challenge (Commission on HIV/AIDS and Governance in Africa, 2008). The crisis dimension is reflected in the rapidity with which HIV has spread both across the African continent and within states. The systemic challenge is much broader and more pernicious, "because it impacts most heavily on the most productive sectors of African economies, namely prime-aged adults" (Commission on HIV/AIDS and Governance in Africa, 2008:2).

Significantly, the HIV/AIDS epidemic continues to adversely affect Africa's development in several major ways. At the socio-cultural level, the epidemic has devastated families due to the death of relatives, especially heads of households, from AIDS. In turn, this has led to the affected families experiencing economic hardship due to the loss of their respective "bread winners." In terms of public health, the treatment of HIV and AIDS-related diseases has resulted in enormous cost for various African states. Economically, the epidemic has contributed to the precipitous decline in the supply of labor, as well as labor productivity, because the number of the eligible members of the workforce has been declining. In addition, AIDS-related illnesses have led to the affected workers missing several days of work.

Higher Education in Africa

Higher education in Africa is facing several major challenges, and these need to be addressed if higher education is to successfully play its pivotal role in the development of African states. A major challenge is the proliferation of new universities in some countries. In some cases, new universities are being established without provision for adequate funding, personnel, and other resources on a sustained basis. In other cases, as Goolam Mohamedbhai, the former Secretary-General of the Association of African Universities, observes, "At the same time, in several African countries an effort has been taken to rapidly set up new universities that are almost copies of the existing ones" (Mohamedbhai, 2011:21). This development has had several adverse consequences. One of which is the "depleting of the staff of the existing institutions and transferring them to new ones" (Mohamedbhai, 2011:21).

Another major challenge is the inadequacy of the instructional infrastructure—qualified lecturers, libraries, laboratories, and research (Munene, 2013). At the heart of this multidimensional challenge is the critical issue of the lack of adequate funding for public universities. For example, in 2012, spending on higher education accounted for less than 0.5 percent of the GDP of African states (ICEF Monitor, 2015:1). To make matters worse, the number of college students has been growing across the continent—in 2012, there were about 10 million college students (ICEF Monitor, 2012).

Faced with inadequate funding, public universities have resorted to increasing student fees as an alternative revenue stream. Clearly, this places strain on students and their families, who are facing major challenges in adequately meeting their basic needs. As Cooper-Knock and Cheeseman (2015:1) lament, "African students get a raw deal: In some cases, they pay higher fees than their counterparts in Europe, but get less in return."

Further, there is a disconnect between higher education and employment opportunities for graduates. Historically, African universities have trained students to work in the public sector, the main source of employment in the majority of African states (Friesenhahn, 2014). However, one of the major effects of neoliberalism has been the downsizing of the public sector. This then means that employment opportunities in the public sector are dwindling. So, in light of this emergent reality, African universities would need to incorporate the training of their students for employment in the private sector in their curricula (Friesenhahn, 2014).

Food Security in Africa

Food security is another major frontier issue on the African development landscape. Several major challenges need to be addressed to help arrest the rising tide of food insecurity and its resulting adverse consequences for human well-being on the continent. The major challenges include: insufficient production of food; inadequate supply or availability of food; access; affordability; and nutritional value of the available food that is consumed. In addition, these major challenges are mediated by several factors, including mass abject poverty, drought and other problems that result from climate change.

In terms of the adverse effects, hunger and the attendant malnourishment are among the major ones. For example, in 2016, about 233 million people in Sub-Saharan Africa were classified as hungry (Food and Agricultural Organization, 2016:1). In 2015, an estimated 218 million people in Sub-Saharan Africa were undernourished (Food and Agriculture Organization, 2015:1).

Addressing the major challenges to food security would require the confluence of several factors. Among these are: the need for improved governance; the restructuring of the economy; and the formulation and implementation of agricultural policies that emphasize adequate food production, availability, access, affordability, and high nutritional quality. In the case of governance, the focus needs to be on improving the material conditions of Africans, including the issue of food security.

Political Instability

Although political instability has become a major issue on the African continent, it is not idiosyncratic to the region (Kieh, 2009b), as other regions of the world, including Europe, have experienced and continue to experience the phenomenon. Political instability is neither a novelty in Africa nor any other region of the world. It has been an enduring feature of the twin processes of state-building (the design and implementation of institutions, processes and rules for building a country, as well as the formulation and implementation of public policies in various spheres—cultural, economic, environmental, political, security, and social, among others), and nation-building (the design and implementation of modalities for developing a common sense of national identity and belonging).

Nonetheless, since the post-independence era, Africa has experienced various forms of political instability, spanning from violent demonstrations to civil wars. The central cause of this is state failure (the unwillingness of the custodians of the state to formulate and implement policies that would address the cultural, economic, environmental, political, religious [in some cases], security and social needs of the majority of their citizens). The overwhelming majority of African states have failed to invest in job creation, and the provision of quality public education and health care for their citizens, especially the subalterns (United Nations Development Program, 2016). However, on the other hand, the overwhelming majority of African states have privileged the members of their respective ruling classes, as evidenced by their substantially higher standards of living (United Nations Development Program, 2016).

The State of Human Development in Africa

Background

The ultimate measure of development in Africa is the well-being of the citizens of the various states. Accordingly, in this section of the introduction, the material well-being of Africans is examined using various indices of human development—employment, health care, education, access to clean drinking water and food security.

The Indices

The unemployment data for Africa do not capture the depth of the jobs problem on the continent. According to the International Labor Organization

(ILO), in 2014, the total unemployment rate stood at about 8 percent (International Labor Organization, 2014:1). For the youth, the figure was about 12 percent (World Economic Forum, 2015:1). The crux of the problem is that unemployment statistics do not reflect vulnerable employment (unpaid workers and those who are in the employ of family owned businesses). In 2014, vulnerable employment was 77 percent (International Labor Organization, 2014).

One of the major resulting consequences of the precarious employment situation on the African continent is abject mass poverty. For example, in 2014, 75 percent of the world's poorest countries were located in Africa (Packtor, 2014). In addition, the top 10 countries with the highest proportion of residents living in extreme poverty (living on less than $1.25 a day) were in Sub-Saharan Africa (Packtor, 2014).

Another measure of economic inequality in Africa is the skewed distribution of wealth. In 2014, for example, "the combined wealth holdings of high-net-worth individuals—those with net assets of $1 million or more—in Africa totaled $660 billion" (Sedghi and Anderson, 2015:1). In contradistinction, during the same period, about half of the population of the continent lived on less than $1.25 per day (*ibid.*).

In terms of health care, the statistics are numbing. For example, in 2014, women in Sub-Saharan Africa were over 230 times more likely to die during childbirth or pregnancy than their counterparts in North Africa (*ibid.*). To make matters worse, of the 738 million people who lack access to clean drinking water globally, 37 percent were living in Sub-Saharan Africa (*ibid.*). Thus, over 500 million people living in Africa, or about half of the continent's total population, suffered from waterborne diseases like cholera (*ibid.*).

As for education, there are a plethora of problems. One of the major challenges is the woeful inadequacy of the educational infrastructure. Specifically, there is a dearth of trained personnel, including teachers and school administrators. This problem is exacerbated by the very poor salaries and benefits for teachers. Furthermore, there are inadequate instructional materials, equipment and supplies. Cumulatively, these challenges have negatively affected the quality of education. Placed in the context of development, educational institutions on the continent are not producing high-caliber skilled individuals who would provide the technical, managerial and administrative skills that are imperative for national development.

Food insecurity constitutes a major development challenge as well. For example, in 2015, about 220 million people in Africa were undernourished (Food and Agricultural Organization, 2015:i)—a by-product of the inadequacy of food production. That is, a significant amount of African states is not making the required investment in food production for domestic consumption. Consequently, a significant amount of people does not have enough food to eat, and lack a balanced and nutritious diet.

Overall, the state of human development (the human development index is based on three major indicators: life expectancy at birth, being knowledgeable and having a decent standard of living) in Africa is very poor. In 2016, only five African states had high levels of human development. In terms of medium levels of human development, there were 13. The overwhelming majority of the African states—36 of the 54—were ranked in the lowest rung of human development (United Nations Development Program, 2016), meaning that the majority of residents are living precariously in terms of basic human needs in 67 percent of the African states.

The Focus of the Book

The focus of the book is twofold. First, it is intended to examine some of the major frontier development issues in Africa, such as political instability, democratization and democracy, the economy, microfinance, the HIV/AIDS pandemic, higher education and food security. Specifically, each frontier development issue is examined in terms of its nature and dynamics, including the forces and factors that shape them.

Second, the contributors then proffer some policy-relevant suggestions for addressing these frontier development issues. The intent is to transcend the realm of simply identifying and cataloguing the development conditions in Africa by offering suggestions for tackling the challenges. It is hoped that doing so will help provide ideas to policy-makers for the formulation and implementation of policies that can improve the material conditions of Africans, especially the members of the subaltern classes—workers, farmers, the unemployed, and *hoi polloi*.

The Theoretical Framework

The book uses a mixed theoretical framework of development. The various essays reflect diverse disciplinary backgrounds; hence, interdisciplinarity requires an analytical framework that draws from various theoretical approaches to development. Briefly, the framework is based on several interlocking contours. A major tenet is that development is multidimensional—cultural, economic, environmental, political, and social. Cultural development concerns issues such as ethnic pluralism, while political development focuses on issues such as the respect for political rights and civil liberties—the right to vote, the right to run for public office, and the freedoms of assembly, association, press, and speech, among others.

Development is framed, conditioned and shaped by both domestic and external systems and actors. At the domestic level, the systems are economic (capitalism, socialism, mixed, etc.), and political (liberal democratic, social democratic, authoritarian, totalitarian, and hybrid), among others, and their associated power relations. Also, the domestic actors consist of governmental officials and institutions and non-governmental entities such as local non-government organizations, civil society organizations, social movements, classes, and ethnic groups, among others. At the external level, the overarching system is the world capitalist system, which has two major subsystems: the "global division of power," which has a broad scope, and "the division of labor," and its "system of unequal exchange," which concerns the assignment of production roles between the "global north" and the "global south," and the resulting pricing of goods and services in the unjust and unfair international trading order. Further, the actors are global powers such as the United States, metropolitan-based multinational corporations, the IMF, the World Bank, the World Trade Organizations, semi-peripheral states such as South Korea, and peripheral states, including African countries that constitute the majority. Under the world capitalist system, the global powers and their multinational corporations and the global economic institutions, which they (the global powers) dominate, control the various modes of economic interactions.

Also, the outcome of development—success, failure or mixed—must be determined by the state of the human condition. Evaluative criteria should revolve around issues such as ethnic pluralism, the distribution of income and wealth, poverty, employment, education, health care, food security, political rights and civil liberties. Each African state's level of development can be evaluated both sectorally (cultural, economic, political, social, etc.) and generally (composite).

The Organization of the Book

In this collection's first essay, E. Ike Udogu explores the travails of democratization and democracy in Africa. He begins by mapping out the philosophical debate about democratization and democracy. This is followed by a discussion of the struggle for democratization and democracy in Africa during both the colonial and post-colonial eras. He concludes by suggesting specific policy actions for helping to institutionalize democracy on the continent, including the rule of law, transparency, addressing corruption, political participation, the promotion of human rights, human development and sustainable economic opportunity.

Next, Johnson W. Makoba examines the challenges of leadership and the management of the economies of African states by their respective governments. He argues that generally, the economies are mismanaged through corruption and sundry forms of graft. The major resulting effects are recurrent economic crisis. Consequently, some African states have turned to the IMF and the World Bank for loans under their notorious "Structural Adjustment Programs" (SAPs) to address their economic woes. Frustrated by the deleterious effects of SAPs, African states have turned to sub-regional and regional initiatives such as the New Partnership for Africa's Development (NEPAD), as the panacea to the continent's perennial economic problems. While these initiatives have made some major strides, Makoba argues that there are major challenges, including dependence.

Samuel Wai Johnson, Jr., goes on to tackle the emergent important issue of microfinance as a modal approach to addressing mass poverty in Africa. He begins by probing the linkages between microfinance and financial inclusion. Specifically, he argues that the kernel of the nexus centers on the provision of financial services to the segments of the population in various African states that are impoverished and economically marginalized. As for the structural arrangements, he argues that the lending architecture for microfinance is dispersed and framed by a variety of policies. In terms of the impact of microfinance on poverty reduction on the continent, he concludes that the results are mixed.

Samuel Zalanga examines the enduring challenge of the HIV/AIDS pandemic in Africa in the following essay. He begins by probing the debate about the origins of the pandemic, and then interrogates the two dominant approaches—biomedical/epidemiological and political economy—to study the pandemic. Next, he probes the impact of the pandemic on Africa's socioeconomic development. In this vein, he identifies several adverse effects, including declining life expectancy, declining human productivity, and increasing poverty. Zalanga then locates the pandemic within the context of neoliberal globalization and argues that the thrust of neoliberal globalization is the commodification of everything, including health services. In turn, this is a major impediment to addressing the pandemic.

David N.P. Mburu next deciphers the travails of higher education in Africa. His central premise is that higher education is indispensable to development in Africa, because it is the arena for training the human resource pools that are critical to the socio-economic and political transformation of the continent and its constituent states. He then identifies the three major challenges confronting higher education on the continent: access, quality and funding. He concludes by making several major recommendations for improving higher education on the continent, including the need for African governments to focus their scholarship programs on disadvantaged students, establish affirmative action initiatives to help increase the number of female students, provide incentives for private institutions to lower their tuitions, narrow the urban-rural divide, and the centrality of quality assurance, particularly against the backdrop of the increase in cross-border educational activities.

In the next essay, Emmanuel O. Oritsejafor examines the critical issue of food security in Africa. His central argument is that bio-fuels could be used to address the critical issue of growing food insecurity in Africa. In this vein, he suggests several major policy options. One is for African governments to offer food and transportation vouchers to citizens. Another is to establish or expand school feeding programs. Cash transfers that can be used to purchase food could also pay a major role in tackling the problem of food insecurity. Finally, the pursuance of a comprehensive educational model could provide the overarching framework for designing ways in which biofuels could be used to address the continent's food security challenges.

George Klay Kieh, Jr., then interrogates the nature and dynamics of political instability, and the ramifications for development in Africa. Specifically, he begins by probing the causes of political instability on the continent. His central argument is that the peripheral capitalist state in Africa is the epicenter of political instability on the continent. Next, he examines the consequences or results of the phenomenon, including coups and civil wars. Third, he suggests some solutions to the phenomenon, including the deconstruction and democratic rethinking of the post-colonial state in Africa.

Finally, George Klay Kieh, Jr., writes again to draw from the lessons and insights from preceding essays and argues that development needs to be rethought on the continent. First, he argues that the state, the crucible of development, needs to be democratically reconstituted so that it can ultimately have a pro-people and pro-development orientation. Next, he provides suggestions for addressing some of the major frontier issues analyzed in the book, such as the economies of African states, the HIV/AIDs epidemic, and political instability.

Conclusion

Undoubtedly, African states are faced with major development challenges, spanning from peripheral economies that are appendages of the world capitalist system, to epidemics like HIV/AIDS. The *sine qua non* for understanding the nature and dynamics of each of the major development challenges is the interrogation of the neo-colonial state. Since the neo-colonial African state is designed to serve the interests of the dominant states in the international system and their respective ruling classes, the development of the African continent is subordinated to the interests of the United States, France, Britain, China, and other powerful states and their dominant classes. Africa's abundant natural resources are primarily used to feed the industrial-manufacturing complexes of these dominant states. Thus, the resources that African states need for their development are used for the continual development of the dominant states. In this vein, there is a dialectical tension between underdevelopment in Africa and development in the dominant states. As Frank (1969:9) aptly observes, the two processes are "two sides of the same coin."

To make matters worse, the overwhelming majority of African states are ruled by local ruling classes that are subservient to the promotion of interests of dominant states and their ruling classes. In return, the members of the various local ruling classes in African states receive rewards for their service to the dominant powers and their respective ruling classes—ranging from accepting bribes to military-security protection. In sum, the African state is Janus-faced and performs two major contradictory functions: it creates favorable conditions for the ruling classes and their external patrons to reap maximum benefits that enable them to live prosperous lives but, on the other hand, it visits mass abject poverty and social disorder on the majority of Africans.

Finally, the custodians of various neo-colonies in Africa are unwilling to invest state resources in addressing the constituent states' various development challenges. The state of human development in Africa is horrendous, and this is clearly reflected in the fact that the overwhelming majority of Africans lack the basic necessities of life—jobs, health care, etc.—which results in mass abject poverty and vulnerability to disease. Further, the severity of poverty on the continent makes substantial portions of the citizenries in various African states quite dependent on remittances from diaspora Africans in the United States, Europe, and Canada, among others.

REFERENCES

Agbese, Pita Ogaba. 2007. "The Political Economy of the African State." In George Klay Kieh, Jr. (ed.). *Beyond State Failure and Collapse: Making the State Relevant in Africa*. Lanham, MD: Lexington Books, pp. 33–48.
Ake, Claude. 2001. *Democracy and Development in Africa*. Washington, D.C.: Brookings Institution Press.
Avert. 2015. *HIV and AIDS in Sub-Saharan Africa. Regional Overview, 2014*. www.avert.rg. Accessed December 14, 2017.

Ayittey, George. 2004. "NEPAD and Africa's Leaky Begging Bowl." *Global Dialogue.* 6(3 &4), pp. 26–36.
Burnett, John. 2015. "China is Besting the U.S. in Africa." *Economic Intelligence.* March 24, p.1.
Carmody, Padraig. 2011. *The Scramble for Africa.* London: Polity.
Chandy, Laurence. 2015. "Why is the Number of Poor People in Africa Increasing When Africa's Economies Are Growing?" *Africa in Focus.* May 4, pp. 1–2.
Chang, Ha-Joon. 2015. "The Failure of Neoliberalism and the Future of Capitalism." In Satoshi Fujii(ed.). *Beyond Global Capitalism.* Tokyo: Springer, pp. 19–34.
Commission on HIV/AIDS and Governance in Africa. 2008. *The Socio-Economic Impact of HIV/AIDS.* Addis Ababa: UNECA.
Cooper-Knock, Sarah-Jane, and Nick Cheeseman. 2015. "Higher Education in Africa: Four Key Challenges." *OXPOL.* November 3, pp. 1–3.
Craven, Matthew. 2015. "Between Law and History: The Berlin Conference of 1884–1885 and the Logic of Free Trade." *London Review of International Law.* 3(1), pp. 31–59.
Fingar, Courtney, 2014. "Foreign Direct Investments in Africa Surges." *Emerging Markets.* May 19, p.1.
Food and Agricultural Organization. 2015. *Regional Overview of Food Insecurity in Africa.* Accra, Ghana: FAO.
Food and Agricultural Organization. 2016. *International Fund for Agricultural Development.* www. Fao.org. Accessed on September 6, 2017.
Frank, Andre Gunder. 1969: *Latin America: Underdevelopment or Revolution?* New York: Monthly Review Press.
Freedom House. 2017. *Freedom in the World: Historical and Comparative Data, 1972–2016.* Washington, D.C.: Freedom House.
Friesenhahn, Irene. 2014. "Sub-Saharan African is Struggling to Produce More and Better Trained Graduates." *SciDev.Net.* June 25, pp.1–2.
Glasborg, David and Deric Shannon. 2011. *Political Sociology: Oppression, Resistance and the State.* Thousand Oaks: Sage Publications.
Hamam, David Mehdi and Oliver Schwank. 2011. "Microfinance: What Role in Africa's Development?" *Africa Renewal.* August 2011, pp. 22–23.
Huntington, Samuel. 1993. *The Third Wave: Democratization in the Late 20th Century.* Norman, OK: University of Oklahoma Press.
ICEF Monitor. 2015. "African Summit Calls for Major Expansion of Higher Education." March 16, pp. 1–2.
International Labor Organization. 2014. *Global Employment Trends.* Geneva: ILO.
Kaldor, Mary. 2007. *Human Security: Reflections on Globalization and Intervention.* London: Polity.
Kaplan, Robert. 1994. "The Coming Anarchy." *The Atlantic Monthly.* February, pp. 44–76.
Kaplan, Robert, 2001. *The Coming Anarchy: Shattering the Dreams of the Post-Cold War Era.* New York: Vintage.
Kieh, George Klay, Jr. 2003. "Africa, the New Partnership for Africa's Development and the International Capitalist Order." *Journal of Comparative Education and International Relations in Africa.* 5(1 &2), pp. 111–127.
Kieh, George Klay, Jr. 2007. "Introduction: The Terminally Ill Berlinist State in Africa." In George Klay Kieh, Jr. (ed.). *Beyond State Failure and Collapse: Making the State Relevant in Africa.* Lanham, MD: Lexington Books, pp. 3–22.
Kieh, George Klay, Jr. 2008a. "Political Corruption and Violence in Africa." In Michaelene Cox(ed.). *State and Corruption, State of Chaos.* Lanham, MD: Lexington Books, pp. 143–163.
Kieh, George Klay, Jr. 2008b. "The State in Africa." In George Klay Kieh, Jr. (ed.). *Africa in the New Millennium.* Trenton, NJ: Africa World Press, pp. 53–85.
Kieh, George Klay, Jr. 2009a. "Reconstituting the Neo-Colonial State in Africa." *Journal of Third World Studies.* 26(2), pp. 41–55.
Kieh, George Klay, Jr. 2009b. "The State and Political Instability in Africa." *Journal of Developing Societies.* 25(1), pp. 1–25.
Kutor, Senanu Kwasi. 2014. "Development and Underdevelopment of African Continent: The

Blame Game and the Way Forward." *Research on Humanities and Social Sciences.* 4(7), pp. 14–20.

Magstadt, Thomas. 2010. *Nations and Governments: Comparative Politics in Regional Perspective.* Boston, MA: Cengage Learning.

Malahuan, Jenina Joy Chavez and Shalmah Guttal. 2006. *Poverty Reduction Strategy Papers: A Poor Package for Poverty Reduction.* Working Paper. Focus on the Global South.

Mbaku, John Mukum and Mwangi Kimenyi. 1995. "Rent-Seeking and Policing in Colonial Africa." *Indian Journal of Social Sciences.* 8(3), pp. 277–306.

Meredith, Martin. 2006. *The Fate of Africa: A History of Fifty Years of Independence.* New York: Public Affairs.

Mkandawire, Thandika. 2001. "Thinking About Developmental States in Africa." *Cambridge Journal of Economics.* 25(3), pp. 289–313.

Mohamedbhai, Goolam. 2011. "Higher Education in Africa: Facing the Challenges in the 21st Century." *International Higher Education.* 63, pp. 20–26.

Munene, Ishmael. 2013." 'University Is ISO: 9000:2008 Certified': Neoliberal Echoes, Knowledge Production and Quality Assurance in Kenyan State Universities." *Journal of Higher Education in Africa.* 11(1 &2), pp. 161–182.

Osaghae, Eghosa. 2005. "The State of Africa's Second Liberation." *Interventions: International Journal of Postcolonial Studies.* 7(1), pp. 1–20.

Packtor, Jordanna. 2014. "Top Ten Poverty Countries in Africa Facts." *The Bergen Project.* November.

Pakenham, Thomas. 1992. *The Scramble for Africa: The White Man's Conquest of the Dark Continent From 1876 to 1912.* New York: Harper Perennial.

Petras, James, and Henry Veltmeyer. 2012. *Beyond Neoliberalism.* Aldershot, UK: Ashgate Publishing.

Ramsay, Jeffress. 1993. "Introduction: Africa: The Struggle for Development." In Jeffress Ramsay(ed.). *Global Studies: Africa.* Guilford, CT: McGraw-Hill/Dushkin, pp. 1–3.

Sedghi, Ami, and Mark Andersen. 2015. "Africa Wealth Report: Rich Gets Richer Even as Poverty and Inequality Deepen." *The Guardian* (United Kingdom). July 31

Taylor, Ian. 2008. *Toward Africa's Development or Another False Start?* Boulder, CO: Lynne Rienner Publishers.

Transparency International. 2017. *Corruption Perceptions Index, 2016.* Berlin: Transparency International.

United Nations. 2013. *Microfinance in Africa.* New York and Midrand, South Africa: Office of the United Nations Special Adviser for Africa and the New Partnership for Africa's Development.

United Nations Development Program. 1994. *Human Development Report.* New York: United Nations Development Program.

United Nations Development Program. 2016. *Human Development Report, 2015.* New York: United Nations Development Program.

World Economic Forum. 2015. *The Challenge of Youth Unemployment.* www.weforum.org/community/global-agenda-councils. Accessed December 4, 2017.

Democracy in Africa

Fiction or Fact in the 21st Century?

E. IKE UDOGU

No one nation ever attains a worthwhile goal [democracy] designed for the benefit of the entire people in one fell swoop without courting irreparable or prolong disaster for the people.
—Obafemi Awolowo [Falola and Ihonvbere, 1985:254]

Introduction

The preceding citation is meant to set the groundwork for my contemplation on the question of democracy in Africa: fiction or fact, against the backdrop of critical development issues in Africa. Specifically, the essay examines whether the character and exercise of democracy within the first 35 years or so of African independence was a "fiction." This was due in part to social, economic and political instability on the continent. As an outcome of the preceding issues, the operation of democracy during this period was problematic in terms of providing enabling political environment for development. Following the collapse of communism in the Union of Soviet Socialist Republics and Eastern Europe democracy, with a few exceptions, became the dominant political ideology worldwide. It also became the way of life in Africa, too. Further, the essay, *inter alia*, argues that because democracy is a fact—the zeitgeist in Africa today—it provides the condition for significant development as the continent continues to deepen, institutionalize and consolidate democracy in this millennium.

Let it suffice to say that the historical and philosophical trajectory of democracy from antiquity to the present is quite confounding to many students of democracy. This is the case because of the way in which it has morphed and currently imagined by scholars. Thus, the nature of democracy and its developments in Africa inform the descriptions in the excerpt of the late Nigerian statesman—Awolowo—that I quoted above. Even so, many past sages and contemporary scholars of democracy have explained the character of democracy in various unique ways possibly to highlight this complex governance system and why it has maintained its resiliency.

The Debate

Even though Plato and Aristotle were advocates of the philosophy of democracy, it is instructive and yet perplexing that they, as members of the intelligentsia in ancient Greece, were not generally enthusiastic about the practice of democracy (i.e., people's rule). This observation and manner of thinking in those days were perhaps based on the political and social disposition of their society. Possibly, the rationale for advancing this thought at that time could be adequately elucidated in Machiavelli's exposition in *The Prince*. Here he, among other things, expressed the view that an uninformed majority in political terms were not, in the main, rational about affairs of the state because they were not well-informed enough to comprehend the complexities of political issues. Apropos the foregoing thesis, ordinary citizens tended to fall victim to highfalutin promises that political actors make to attract citizens' electoral support. Indeed, my preceding suppositions are *mondial* but especially common in the current quadrennial and quinquennial political elections in many developing nations (Udogu, 2010:103–104).

Thomas Hobbes' arguments and preference for a monarchical system of govern-ance in his volume *Leviathan* never endeared students of democracy to his philosophy; nevertheless, the rationale for his position could in part be explained and also understood against the background of the claim of "divinity" by Kings who had powers over life and death matters of their subjects in the past. In short, arguably, his writings were subjected to—and even prejudiced by—the politics of his time.

Jean-Jacques Rousseau, John Stuart Mill, Edmund Burke and other philosophers affirmed their reservations about the practicality of democracy as a governance genus in a polity. In their discourses on democracy, some equivocated in their opinions on the efficacy of democracy as a valid governance technique for a society. Put in another way, they argued that although democracy had the propensity to further political stability and "the good political life," they questioned its soundness in the governance of a society. This was because of the character of the trustees of the state who frequently pursued their self-interests above those of the nation-state (Houngnikpo, 2003:197–210).

Samuel Huntington averred—and rightly so—that democracy did not always produce a desired result since "government produced by elections may be inefficient, corrupt, shortsighted, irresponsible, dominated by special interests, and incapable of adopting policies demanded for the public good [that is the good political life for a majority of the population]. These qualities may make such a government undesirable but they do not make it undemocratic" (Huntington, 1991:10). Remarkably, Huntington's caricature is spot on with respect to the character of democracy in many African states in the first 35 years or so after independence.

Larry Diamond also avowed that:

> it is symptomatic of the international momentum of democracy in the world that so many kinds of regimes strive (and strain) to define themselves as democracies and that democracy is the term used to signify so many different visions of the 'good' society... [Diamond, 1988:142–143].

Moreover, to rephrase Sir Winston Churchill's dictum "democracy is a problematic system of governance except that humankind has yet to come up with a better model" (Udogu, 2010:105).

In any case, the foregoing brief and peculiar theoretical discourses on democracy may be helpful in explaining why an application of democracy and its principles in the governance of African societies immediately following home-rule has been slippery. But why has the trajectory of democracy and democratic consolidation in the continent's post-colonial history been topsy-turvy and thus impeded an impressive growth agenda? In view of the current relatively positive democratic trends in Africa, could it be argued that democracy is a fact of life that is essential for promoting Africa's development? Answers to the above queries will be attempted in the following discussions and analysis within the context of this region's historic antecedent.

Colonial and Post-Colonial Africa

Analogically, it is said that the comprehension of a family's medical history by a physician can help a doctor probe into a patient's ailment and provide medication to heal the sick. My above allegorical allusion to medical history relates to how some students of African politics have approached the question of democratic development in Africa in order to explain the area's difficulties with democratization and to proffer solutions.

The effect of the autocratic colonial governance method on African leaders has been a main source of the problem and discourses among scholars on the democratic progress in the continent. A sketch of the nature of the state bequeathed to African political chiefs at independence is summed up in the following terms:

> Colonial state, as the term signifies, was a creation of the colonial powers for their purposes. As such, it exhibits specific characteristics that are not found in the metropolitan state. These are (1) an imposition from outside [of their own constructed values]; (2) a contrivance meant to administer not citizens but colonial peoples or natives—i.e. to administer not subjects but objects; (3) not accountable to those who are administered but to itself and ultimately to the metropolitan power; (4) arbitrary use of power and lack of transparency; (5) highly extractive, especially with regard to the peasants; and (6) disregard of all civil liberties in the colony [Mafeje 2002; Uwizeyimana, 2012:146].

My contention is that the preceding form of governorship inherited by African chiefs, or bequeathed to African leaders, at the end of colonial rule has endured in post-colonial Africa principally by way of education and political socialization. In other words, it was difficult for African nationalists carefully schooled and socialized in the governance methods of the colonial overseers to suddenly peel off the authoritarian character imbibed during colonial rule. Put bluntly, Western imperial powers governed autocratically but imposed on its successors a liberal democratic constitution and form of government; it was an impossible mission, many scholars have argued, for Africa's new leaders who mimicked their colonial administrative ancestors with panache to change. They loved their inherited authority and displayed it on their compatriots who were expected to treat them with the same quality of respect as they did to the colonial superintendents.

The problems after the granting of self-rule to African states that arose were how to free African leaders from their authoritarian ways, and how to superimpose autocratic rule with the principles of liberal democracy such as:

- Free and fair elections
- Rule of law
- Protection of minority rights
- Separation of powers
- Due process of law
- Existence of more than one political party
- Existence of an [efficacious] constitutional document or documents
- Government accountability
- Freedom of the press
- Independent judiciary [Fatton, 1990:455–473].

The issue confronted by Africa's trustees of the state in adopting and implementing liberal democracy has led some scholars to suggest that democracy in Africa is a myth at least during the first 35 years or so of independence. Slow economic growth, the problematic nature of democratic development and the lack of adequate knowledge of the new political elites—not to mention the massive ordinary citizens—on how the bequeathed Western democratic genus worked led to different forms of experiment.

As long ago as 1982, Richard Sklar, in his presidential address to the 25th annual meeting of the influential American African Studies Association identified five variations of democracy in Africa. These were (1) liberal democracy; (2) guided democracy; (3) social democracy; (4) participatory democracy; and (5) consociational democracy (Sklar, 1982:12–18).

Briefly, liberal democracy was the genre of democracy handed down to African states by the colonial administrators. In this type of democracy power was limited by law and citizens were free to form political parties and to compete for office in open elections at regular intervals—that is either in quadrennial or quinquennial elections (Sklar, 1982: 12). Achieving liberal democracy remains the major objective of African countries while the other forms were merely experimental (Young, 1994:241; Lijphart, 1967:1; Udogu, 2010:110–116).

What is the significance of my reference to these democratic typologies? It is that Africa's leaders immediately following their political freedom were unsure of what system would be best suited for them. Moreover, many rulers in post-independence Africa, as for example, Julius Nyerere of Tanzania, Kwame Nkrumah of Ghana and Jomo Kenyatta of Kenya, disavowed multiparty democracy, an important attribute of liberal democracy, as inconsistent with African traditions—not least the countries they governed (Ahluwalia, 2001:56). These political captains contended that a system of one-party government without opposition was more appropriate for Africa (Ahluwalia, 2001:56) because it could promote impressive development. Thus, their vision of African democracy was one founded on one-party rule that they and their political associates would control. Political factions may exist among civic groups but are not to indulge in political activism aimed at threatening the ruler's power and party (Uwizeyimana, 2012: 140; Udogu, 2016).

Some factors—such as acquisition of personal power and wealth, military coups—have made the deepening of democracy and economic development a fiction. Historically, these features have also stifled the propensity to advance Africa's development plans at least until about 1989/1990 when communism collapsed in Eastern Europe. Indeed, in support of the above important forces (power and wealth) in a polity, and how they have afflicted the character of leaders, democratic consolidation and African development, I quote significant postulations of three political philosophers and theorists.

These are Thomas Hobbes, Claude Ake and Arthur W. Lewis:

Borrowing from his classic book, *Leviathan*, Hobbes discussed the character of human nature from the standpoint of the individual whose *raison d'être* is the acquisition of force [or power]. He avowed: "I put for a general inclination of all mankind a perpetual and restless desire for power after power that ceases only in death. And the cause of this is not always that a man hopes for a more intensive delight than he has already attained to, or that he cannot be content with the moderate power, but because he cannot assure that power and means to live well [i.e. wealth] which he has ... without the acquisition of more (Schneider, 1958, Ch. 11; Green, 1993; Tannenbaum and Shultz, 1998; Udogu, 2010:4).

For Claude Ake, the quality of the post-colonial state did not change significantly at independence [and after] since with few exceptions, the colonial state was inherited rather than transformed. Like the colonizer before them most of the national leaders regarded the state as the instrument of their will. They privatized, and exploited it for economic gain and used it oppressively to absolutize their power. Even after independence, the state in Africa has not become a reassuring presence but remains a formidable threat to everybody except the few [political and economic oligarchs] who controlled it (Ake, 1994:7).

Insofar as Arthur W. Lewis was concerned no politician will admit that he suppresses his political opponent primarily because he wants to stay in power [e.g., Mugabe of Zimbabwe, Biya of Cameroon, Mubarak of Egypt, etc.]; he will more usually say that their [politics, policy and tactics endanger the country as with arap Moi of Kenya]. ...But it would also be mistaken to forget that much of what is going on in some of these countries is fully explained in terms of the normal lust of human beings for power and wealth [with negligent attention paid to the consolidation of democracy, national development and plight of ordinary citizens] [Lewis, 1965:30–32; Udogu, 2010:5].

Democracy: Is It Fiction or Fact?

Within the context of the preceding notional discourses on the political development in Africa many scholars, especially Afro-pessimists, have expressed concerns on the slow democratic trajectory that mitigates the economic development scheme in Africa. First, some Afro-pessimists have pointed to the ubiquity of military *coups d'état*, as illustrated in the table below, as obstacles to the consolidation of democracy on the continent and its concomitant obstacle to major growth schemes. Indeed, military rule literally blanketed the region between the 1960s and 1990s. In several countries, too, coups took place multiple times.

List of Coups
and Coup Attempts in Africa

Country	Years
Algeria	1962; 1965; 1992
Benin	1963, 1965; 1967; 1972; 2013 (failed)
Burkina Faso	1966; 1980; 1983; 1987; 2014

Country	Years
Burundi	1966; 1976; 1987; 1996; 2015
Cameroon	1984 (failed)
Chad	1975; 1982; 1990
Congo-Brazzaville	1963; 1968; 1979; 1997
Congo-Kinshasa	1960; 1965; 1997
Egypt	1952
Equatorial Guinea	1979
Ethiopia	1974; 1977
Gambia	1994
Ghana	1966; 1972; 1978; 1979; 1981
Guinea	1984
Guinea-Bissau	1980; 1999; 2003
Ivory Coast	1999
Lesotho	1986; 1990; 1991
Liberia	1980
Libya	1969
Madagascar	1972
Mali	1968; 1991; 2012
Mauritania	1978; 1979; 1980; 1984
Morocco	1971 (failed)
Niger	1974; 1996
Nigeria	1966; 1975; 1983; 1985; 1990
Rwanda	1973; 1994
São Tomé & Principe	1995
Seychelles	1997
Sierra Leone	1967; 1997
Somalia	1969; 1991
Togo	1963; 1967
Tunisia	1957; 1987
Uganda	1966; 1971; 1980
Zanzibar	1964

Sources: List of Coups d'État and Coup Attempts by Country https://en_wikipedia.org/wiki/list_of_coups_d'etat_and_coup_attempts_by_country; List of Coups and Coup Attempts in Africa http://www.systemicpeace.org/africa/ACPPAnnex2b.pdf

Second, Afro-pessimists have also argued that democracy at this juncture on the continent is a fiction. In part, the pessimism expressed by these scholars flows from the truism that post-colonial African leaders constructed nation-states that they run in a "corporatist" manner to further their insular interests and those of their cohorts. In short, these powerful guardians of the state (such as Felix Houphouet-Boigny of Ivory Coast, Paul Biya of Cameroon, Robert Mugabe of Zimbabwe, etc.) converted the nation-state into their private fiefdoms (Udogu, 2010:6). Therefore, the masses see very little reason to promote the political legitimacy of a system that marginalizes them. Ironically, these are states in which leaders claim to be democrats but act autocratically (Chazan, 1988: 119). Such a development probably prompted Catherine Newbury to contend that: "Perhaps the most salient feature of democratic openings in Africa is their fragility. Though in some cases political liberalization, multi-party politics and elections have led to regime change, we cannot assume that this will necessarily result in broadened participation and representation... (Mewbury, 1994:7)." This uncertainty and nature of the weak state in Africa has, arguably, led to the emergence of what some scholars have dubbed a cyclical model whereby because of state's fragility vacillates between despotism and democracy (Huntington, 1984:210). Despite the above pessimism, however, Robert H. Jackson and Carl G. Roseberg have expressed a view that Africa cannot be said to be indifferent to democracy even when its leaders seem nonchalant about democracy. Nevertheless, an observer is troubled by the painful tendency not to institutionalize democracy, significant for Africa's robust economic growth agenda, where the seed of democracy has been planted (Jackson and Rosberg, 1985:293). Perhaps this confusion in the development of democracy in many African societies provoked Dominique E. Uwizeyimana (2012:139–161) to write a critical essay titled: "Democracy and pretend democracies in Africa: Myths of African democracies."

Also, writing on the "Bleak Horizon for Democracy in Africa," Jibrin Ibrahim historicized and expressed anxiety at the development of democracy in Africa especially after the death of communism in the Union of Soviet Socialist Republics (USSR) and the triumphalism of democracy in its wake. It would be recalled, he noted,

> that between 1989 and 1990s, 43 African countries hitherto under one party rule or military dictatorship switched to multiparty democracy. Subsequently, even the Organization of African Unity (now African Union), which [until now] had been a cozy club for African dictators made the 2002 Durban Declaration in which they resolved that henceforth Democratic Elections are the basis of the authority of any representative government; regular elections constitute a key element of the democratization process and therefore are essential ingredients for good governance, the rule of law, the maintenance and promotions of peace, security, stability and development [Ibrahim, 2015].

Indeed, Article 4, of the *Declaration on the Principles Governing Democratic Elections in Africa,* provides a salient template for institutionalizing democracy. These provisions have the propensity for creating enabling milieus critical for genuine electoral process capable of advancing democratic consolidation and Africa's development project:

Elections: Rights and Obligations

We reaffirm the following rights and obligations under which democratic elections are conducted:

1. Every citizen shall have the right to participate freely in the government of his or her country, either directly or through freely elected representatives in accordance with the provisions of the law.

2. Every citizen has the right to fully participate in the electoral processes of the country, including the right to vote or be voted for, according to the laws of the country and as guaranteed by the Constitution, without any kind of discrimination.

3. Every citizen shall have the right to free association and assembly in accordance with the law.

4. Every citizen shall have the freedom to establish or to be a member of a political party or Organization in accordance with the law.

5. Individuals or political parties shall have the right to freedom of movement, to campaign and to express political opinions with full access to the media and information within the limits of the laws of the land.

6. Individual or political parties shall have the right to appeal and to obtain timely hearing against all proven electoral malpractices to the competent judicial authorities in accordance with the electoral laws of the country.

7. Candidates or political parties shall have the right to be represented at polling and counting stations by duly designated agents or representatives.

8. No individual or political party shall engage in any act that may lead to violence or deprive others of their constitutional rights and freedoms. Hence all stakeholders should refrain from, among others, using abusive language and/or incitement to hate or defamatory allegations and provocative language. These acts should be sanctioned by designated electoral authorities.

9. All stakeholders in electoral contests shall publicly renounce the practice of granting favors, to the voting public for the purpose of influencing the outcome of elections.

10. In covering the electoral process, the media should maintain impartiality and refrain from broadcasting and publishing abusive language, incitement to hate, and other forms of provocative language that may lead to violence.

11. Every candidate and political party shall respect the impartiality of the public media by undertaking to refrain from any act which might constrain or limit their electoral adversaries from using the facilities and resources of the public media to air their campaign messages.

12. Every individual and political party participating in elections shall recognize the authority of the Electoral Commission or any statutory body empowered to oversee the electoral process and accordingly render full cooperation to such a Commission/Body in order to facilitate their duties.

13. Every citizen and political party shall accept the results of elections proclaimed to have been free and fair by the competent national bodies as provided for in the Constitution and the electoral laws and accordingly respect the final decision of the competent Electoral Authorities or, challenge the result appropriately according to the law (OAU/AU, 2002).

Despite the foregoing impressive declaration, however, most African countries have on paper maintained the principle of regular elections that are still to be fully free and fair (Udogu, 2016). And, as such, they do violate a fundamental tenet of liberal democracy—free and fair election—that invariably creates political instability and conflict (Ibrahim, 2015) that retards Africa's development trajectory. One of the persistent antinomies of the democratic process in Africa is the emergence of incumbent leaders who are determined on staying in power by hook or by crook having thoroughly enjoyed the privileges of a political throne. This seduction of power has become pathological in a few cases; and some scholars have referred to this phenomenon in a leader as Hubris syndrome—i.e., a form of mental disease that makes it difficult for a leader to acknowledge his or her destructive policies (social, economic and political) in a polity. This nature of leadership in a society has also led to violent conflicts and civil wars with their disastrous consequences for ordinary citizen in many societies (Ibrahim, 2015).

In some cases, African leaders have been in power since independence and have used their power in office to maneuver the democratic process so that they could stay in power ad infinitum (Udogu, 2016). Some of such past and present leaders were and are: Yahya Jammeh (21 years in The Gambia); Yoweri Museveni (29 years in Uganda); late Omar Bongo (44 years in Gabon); Robert Mugabe (35 years in Zimbabwe); Paul Biya (33 years in Cameroon); Obiang Nguema (36 years in Equatorial Guinea); Jose dos Santos (36 years in Angola); and Isaias Afewerki (23 years in Eritrea). What these men have in common is that they have been despotic leaders and their genus of leadership was and is anathema to democratic solidity in Africa (Ibrahim, 2015). And this is not to mention leaders who abrogate or have attempted to change provisions in the constitution so that they could run for reelection for more terms than the constitution stipulates. President Olusegun Obasanjo of Nigeria and President Blaise Compaore of Burkina Faso, for example, attempted it and failed. President Pierre Nkurunziza altered the constitution notwithstanding violent protests to this act in Burundi in 2015. Such behavioral patterns of leaders result in political unstableness. This political instability is caused by opposing political actors who engage in fights to replace them. These struggles disturb economic development and have made democracy on the continent look like fiction.

In North Africa, on December 17, 2010, the so-called Arab Spring about what was believed to be an uprising of democratic opening happened. Although this revolt has faced resistance from the establishment, many students of democracy are optimistic that democratic renaissance will endure. Reflecting on this popular struggle in African Maghreb and Egypt, Thabo Mbeki, a former president of the Republic of South Africa, mused as to the overall character of societies that emerged out of such rousing insurgency. A question was whether the democracy movement in the Maghreb and Egypt will survive, and like a wild fire engulf the Middle East with its embers and transform this region's authoritarian tradition and regimes into an oasis of democratic states, or if the democratic rebellion would come to a cul-de-sac? Accordingly, he wondered whether democratic development in this region would lead to

- A reassertion of the right of the African masses to determine their destiny and the recover of their democratic right to govern;
- A resumption of the struggle for the victory of the national democratic revolution;
- A rebellion against the abuse of power by ruling elites to enrich themselves at the expense of the people [Mbeki, 2015].

Unfortunately, in the short term, the outcome of the vivacious Arab Spring in North Africa did not produce the desired result of advancing democratic consolidation that promotes national economic development. It swept into power the Muslin Brotherhood under the leadership of Mohamed Morsi in Egypt. But his reign as president was short-lived as his regime was suffocated and then dislocated by a society that was uncomfortable with his form of despotism. He was replaced by a military officer turned politician, General Abdel Fattah el-Sisi, in keeping with an Egyptian political culture dating back to the accession to power of Gamal Abdel Nasser following his coup in 1952.

In Tunisia, the democratic fervor before the Arab Spring was unsteady after so many years of authoritarianism since self-government; predictably, the fight for democratic revival and survival in the Maghreb and Egypt will continue in spite of its temporary setback.

In sub-Saharan Africa and North Africa what the democratic metamorphosis suggests is that consolidated democracy in this region of the world is still morphing at this moment in African political history. Thus, I contend that democracy will become a *fait-accompli* and way of life in part because democracy has had an inimitable and special cultural and traditional root in Africa. Added to my supposition is the fact that the push toward democratic consolidation is, indeed, the zeitgeist globally! Consequently, the struggle for democratic solidity is not an illusion or fantasy in Africa; the democratic trajectory in African countries has been evolutionary as was the case in Britain, France, the United States and elsewhere (Udogu, 1996:14). Accordingly, I contend that the outcome of the current democratic trends and its consolidation in Africa will usher in an impressive development in the 21st century beyond our wildest imagination.

Democracy Is a Fact: The Debate

My thesis and contention that democracy is a fact in Africa flow partially from a belief by some scholars and Afro-optimists that the introduction of "liberal democracy" into Africa some five to six decades ago marked the beginning of a slow process that is not unlike the development of democracy in the Occident. In fact, my proceeding postulations are informed by Awolowo's allusions to the fact that the process of imbibing the attributes of democracy, liberal democracy, for example, is an incremental process with occasional missteps, and that requires patience. Nevertheless, once sufficiently established it could advance the development scheme.

Also, within the context of my above assumptions, I concur with the observation that the development of democracy—especially consolidated democracy—is one that continues to baffle and frustrate scholars concerned about its practice in Africa (Kieh: 101–103) Even so, Richard Sklar, an Afro-optimist, remained optimistic about its resiliency. Little wonder, then, that he contended persuasively that: "Democracy dies hard…. It stirs and wakens from the deepest slumber whenever the principle of accountability is asserted by members of a community [as in the Arab Spring in North Africa]…" Democracy cannot be destroyed by a *coup d'état,* it will survive every legal assault upon political liberty (Sklar, 1982:11). This is true in part because political freedom tends to create peace and to provide a catalyst for economic growth in a polity.

But, why are democracy and its consolidation a fact in Africa within the context of my argumentations in this essay and volume? The existence of democracy has always been a way of life in Africa because democracy in its various forms flourished in different regions on the continent before the arrival of European powers first to trade and later to colonize it. It was also factual as Leslie Rubin and Brian Weinstein have argued that owing to ethno-centrism, the colonial hegemonies and many political scientists "failed" to recognize and consequently refused to distinguish the peculiar genus of democracy practiced in pre-colonial/colonial Africa because what they saw and read about African democratic practices were not identical to, and did not resemble, the system in Europe (Rubin and Weinstein, 1977: 8).

In fact, Ali Mazrui has argued that within the Tiv society in colonial and post-colonial Nigerian society, democracy thrived. Tiv polity had no rulers. Accordingly, the elders met when necessary to debate village concerns and issues. In Tiv democratic culture, accountability was and still is a critical canon. Discourses amongst these "wise men" could be boisterous as they talked and talked until they could come to a consensus. At the end of a very prolonged debate, they would take a solemn oath to abide by the decision arrived at—as an indication of democratic centralism of sorts—thus giving the motion its legitimacy (Mazrui, 1985).

In addition to the above Tiv's genre of democracy, Chinua Achebe noted: "In my Igbo community in Nigeria, there is a heated discussion when [problems facing the inter-est of the public] are happening. If you [as a member of the society don't participate in the discourse, it's your own fault]; nobody stops you. So, the notion that [Africans] are learning something new [democracy] is absurd" (Dialogue with Achebe, 1992:11). What the foregoing references imply is that attributes and values of democracy are not novel to Africa, as noted previously. Thus, the failure of some African leaders to inculcate the ideals and traditions of democracy has a lot to do with what the trustees of the state see as the immense rewards accruing from their hold onto power; therefore, they are unwilling to play by the rules of the democratic game. Thus, many fix, rig and manipulate the electoral system with the connivance of their cohorts in order to retain their position of privilege in society (Udogu, 2016). But this political behavior is under attack as was the case in the Gambia, following the 2016 presidential election.

A relatively contemporary understanding of the trajectory of democratic solidity in Africa situates its renaissance on two major European events. The first was the tearing down of the Berlin Wall that demarcated Western Europe from Eastern Europe following the end of World War II. The second was the implosion of the USSR that led to the balkanization of its vast Empire. The collapse of communism is a major cause of the democratic revival in Africa that created an enabling environment for advancing the development agenda on the continent. Indeed, it transformed African Marxist-Leninist leaders into "born again" democrats. This development followed their political epiphany that was brought about by the above political revolution in the Soviet Union and its rippling effect. Immediately following this political tsunami, democracy became the vogue globally and African states that resisted this change did so at their own peril—isolation.

Writing on the democratic wave in Africa, Julius O. Ihonvbere made references to some of the major forces that influenced the process. These were the following:

- The *end of the Cold War* which witnessed a drastic reduction in military and financial support for Africa's dictators...
- The imposition of *new political conditionalities* by Western nations, as well as by multinational organizations, credit clubs and other donors and international organizations forced African leaders to accommodate new political demands and embrace political pluralism...
- The *delegitimization of the state,* its custodians, and institutions contributed significantly to the democratization process. It could not pay salaries, repair roads … and maintain security...
- The *deepening economic crisis* in Africa was, in several respects, and in spite of the pains it has caused, a blessing in disguise. The UN Economic Commission for Africa (ECA) declared the 1980s as Africa's lost decade...
- The *emergence of new leaders*, political parties, organizations, and

pro-demo-cracy movements also invigorated the struggle for
democracy...
- The *reinvigoration of civil society-based movements...*
- The *emergence of new intellectual discourses on democracy and
democratiza-tion* [Ihonvbere, 1999:46–49].

What the above penetrating list of the challenges and opportunities toward
a process of giving substance to the quest for democratic consolidation in
Africa implies is that the instrumentalities for moving the process forward
exist; and, so are the modalities for Africa's development agenda today when
compared to or with the situation in early post-colonial Africa with its weak
democratic tradition and economic underdevelopment. What is important
at this juncture is that politicos, donor countries, civil society, the mass media,
are pressing for democratic consolidation and accordingly making democracy
the fact of life on the continent in this millennium. The role of civil society
in promoting the democratic course and *a priori* economic growth plan will
be examined later in this essay.

However, it might be useful to sum up President Muhammadu Buhari's
speech at Chatham House, London, United Kingdom in 2015 on the trajectory
of democracy in Africa that gives zing to its solidity and the development
enterprise. The President affirmed that before 1989 when most independent
African countries were only 29 years old, just four countries held multi-party
elections. By 1993, according to Freedom House, the number of electoral
democracies rose to 10 and then to 18 by 1995. Between 2005 and 2006, the
number of electoral democracies catapulted to 24. Strikingly, *New York Times*
reported that 42 of the 48 countries in sub-Saharan Africa organized and
carried out multiparty elections between 1990 and 2002 (Buhari, 2015:3).

Additionally, the *New York Times* wrote that between 2000 and 2002,
incumbent political parties in four African countries, viz. Senegal, Mauritius,
Ghana and Mali peacefully transferred power to victorious opposition parties.
Moreover, the proportion of African countries that are labeled not free by
Freedom House's assessment fell drastically from 59 percent in 1983 to 35
percent in 2003 (Buhari, 2015:3). This is a reassuring signpost of the weight
given to democratic consolidation and the fruits of development that could
come in its wake.

Bearing in mind the positive and current state of democratic revivalism
and the political history of the continent Buhari opined:

But the growth of democracy on the continent has been uneven. According to Freedom House, the number of electoral democracies slipped from 24 in 2007/2008 to 19
in 2011/2012; while the percentage of countries categorized as "not free" assuming for
the sake of argument that we accept their definition of "free" increased from 35% in
2003 to 41% in 2013. Also, there have been some reversals at different times in Burkina Faso, Central African Republic, Cote d'Ivoire, Guinea, Guinea Bissau, Lesotho,

Mali, Madagascar, Mauritania and Togo. We can choose to look at the glass of democracy as either half full or half empty... [Nevertheless], it is globally agreed that democracy is **not an event, but a journey**. And that the destination of that journey is **democratic consolidation** [that validates a state] where democracy has become so rooted and so routine and widely accepted by all actors.... With this important destination in mind, it is clear that though many African countries now hold regular elections, very few of them have consolidated the practice of democracy [Buhari, 2015:3].

Why is it that some scholars and political observers are so bold in predicting that the practice of democracy will remain a fact of life in Africa in this century? How should Africa continue with her movement toward democratic consolidation that is crucial for the continent's development agenda? I argue that the inspiring tenets of the African Charter on Democracy, Elections and Governance and the Mombasa Declaration and Code of African Leadership, *inter alia*, contain manifestos that will further democratic consolidation in Africa in this millennium. In fact, the practice of the precepts contained in these declarations will make democracy and its consolidation an inspiring way of life on the continent in 21st century Africa. And, I shall argue my case in a terse discussion on the role of civil society in advancing democratic solidity, as a fact of life, and its importance in promoting development. My analysis will be followed, in the conclusion, by some additional factors that could serve as important engines that could further democratic consolidation—a useful fillip to the continent's growth agenda.

Civil Society and Democratic Consolidation

According to the Governance Resource Center (GRC) of the UK Department for International Development (DFID), civil society is "a domain between the state and the market-place. It can be linked to the media in that both play important roles in holding the state accountable.... They continue to be fundamentally important to making government work better for poor people as they provide the basis for collective action" (GRC, 2015). Moreover, the British Library defined civil society in the following terms:

1. For some observers, it only includes political activity engaged in through nonprofit organizations such as NGOs. At the other end of the spectrum, some observers include all forms of voluntary participation;
    Civil society includes not just the individual who participates but to the degree that those institutions are large and powerful [Hauss, 2015].

Larry Diamond identified seven types of civil society of which his 7th is most germane to my analysis. That is civil society groups are "civil organizations that are generally non-partisan organizations devoted to improving the political system and making it more democratic through human rights monitoring, voter education and mobilization" (Diamond, 1994:5).

That there exist a plethora of competing and conflicting definitions and explanations of the activities of civil society groups depending on the rationales for their formation is instructive. Even though some critics—both scholars and politicians—see some good in the presence and actions of civil society organizations, other scholars have mixed feelings about these groups' activities and efficacy (Udogu, 2007:127–128). They argue that civil society groups are unlikely to implement their objectives because of their *raison d'être*. For instance, some civil society groups are critiqued on the following points: "lack of accountability; … reliance on donors and their agenda; often dubious legitimacy as representatives of wider society; ambiguous relations to the state, particularly in the case of weak states" (Jega, 1997:8).

On the other hand, the following salient queries have been posed to counteract the views of opponents of civil society groups and some of their activities:

> Who critiqued and resisted transnational corporations, International Monetary Fund, the World Bank and miss-guided Strategic Adjustment Program/policy? Who provided the energy for resistance to the 'big man' syndrome in Africa? Who organized the hundreds of political demonstrations in Egypt, South Africa, Kenya, Nigeria and elsewhere for multi-party democracy [Ihonvbere, 2002:9].

Moreover, in Francophone Africa, Celestin Monga noted that political parties did not initiate the agitation for democratic opening that resonated across Africa. This role was carried out by vibrant civil society organizations using their special networks of communication [as in the case of USA/Africa Dialogue series moderated by Toyin Falola, of the University of Texas, Austin] (Monga, 1995:365).

All the same, I contend that the activities of civil society organizations (and the activities of the mass media) in their efforts to improve the political and social conditions in African societies have been phenomenal. They have been especially formidable in dismantling apartheid in South Africa, iconoclastic in pulling down the military bulwark in Nigeria, Ethiopia, Sudan, Burkina Faso and elsewhere that aborted the path toward democratic consolidation. In short, they have been in the firing line in the promotion of the democratization project on the continent useful for promoting a general development project. These achievements notwithstanding, civil society groups, as engines for democratic consolidation, must remain vigilant constantly monitoring this process that creates the climate for advancing Africa's development plan (Udogu, 2007:128–129).

It is within the context of my foregoing suppositions on the importance of civil society in promoting political change in Africa that I posit the theory that "professional" Africans in the Diaspora, as a civil society group, could also contribute substantially to democratic consolidation in Africa and uphold democracy as a fact of life in this century. My thesis on the possibility of Africans in the Diaspora supporting and sustaining democratic solidity in the continent is informed, *inter alia*, by the following factors: 1. they are not beholden to a national government; 2. they are not paid by their governments in Africa; 3. they tend to be less inclined to partisan politics; 4. they are less likely to be settled by political actors; 5. they feel safe in critiquing inadequate policies and to offering possible solution/s; 6. unlike those politicians and entrepreneurs who invest their wealth overseas, they contribute significantly to the economic growth of Africa through remittances (Darko, 2002:5; Udogu, 2007:116); 7. they are stake-holders in African societies due to the fact that they contribute their talents and expertise to improving education and other aspects of development; 8. Africans in the Diaspora are recognized by the African Union as a force to be reckoned with in Africa's development agenda.

How might Africans in the Diaspora, as a powerful international civil society group, enhance or boost democratic consolidation and *a priori* institutionalize it as a fact of life on the continent in this millennium? Given the immense talent and wealth, that collectively surpasses those of many countries in the region, Africans in the Diaspora could use their untapped influence, among other things, in promoting the following:

- Popular participation.
- Transparency and accountability in public affairs.
- Organization of free and fair elections.
- Monitoring of elections in Africa to make sure that they are not fixed.
- Promoting the respect for the rule of law.
- Calling for international sanctions on leaders and countries that fail to live up to the constitutional provisions on elections.
- Recognizing and rewarding exemplary leaders who operate within the rule of law [UN-NGLS, 2015; Udogu, 2007:141].

The foregoing recommendations are strategies that will promote democratic solidity and make it a permanent way of life. Also, the institutionalization of democratic consolidation could further political stability and peaceful co-existence. Such concretization of democracy, and the dividend of peace that will flow from this situation, is what Africans need in this century to advance the current relatively impressive growth process on a continent endowed with tremendous natural resources.

Conclusion: Looking Ahead

Although the struggle for sovereignty from the colonial powers was started during the early 1900s by the influential Pan-African Congress and movement, the clamor for self-rule only reached its crescendo following the end of World War II (Udogu, 2010:59–69). After the 1960s many African countries were granted independence. Some were granted freedom on a "platter of gold" and others took up arms against the colonizer as in Algeria, Kenya, Mozambique and Angola, for example. In granting self-government to their colonies, the colonial overseers imposed their governance techniques on their former colonies without adequately educating and preparing the natives to govern their societies democratically. The practice of democracy was accordingly frail in part because the states were weak and so were their economies.

In Kenya, as in Zambia, several British administrators continued with their administrative functions after emancipation simply because these countries lacked sufficiently trained manpower at the time of independence (Branch, 2011:39). Thus, the period within which to carefully study and adapt to the European parliamentary system was relatively short; this failure explains partially why democratic development and consolidation in Africa has been wobbly and why the general development process has been particularly weak. In some cases, political confusions and wanton corruption in nation-states have resulted in military interventions thereby aborting the democratic procedure. Uncertainties in the democratic trajectory, and slowness in economic growth since independence, have led some scholars and Afro-pessimists to contend that the operation of democracy in Africa was a fiction. Other catalysts to the political quagmires in Africa are economic woes brought about by poor leadership, mismanagement of resources in one of the world's richest continents, and ethno-political conflicts. So, how should African states exculpate themselves from the preceding quandaries to deepen and strengthen democracy critical for advancing the development scheme in this millennium? Whereas answers to this query are numerous and vary, I shall briefly examine two overlapping templates. These are Mo Ibrahim's "Index of African Governance (IIAG)" and Robert I. Rotberg's and Rachel M. Gisselquist's "Strengthening African Governance."

Mo Ibrahim, a Sudanese business tycoon, has developed an important index of African governance intended for measuring and promoting the following factors significant for moving the continent forward developmentally and solidifying democracy as a fact of life in Africa. These are: 1. safety and Rule of Law; 2. participation and human rights; 3. sustainable economic opportunity; and 4. human development (Ibrahim, 2015). Coincidentally, Rotberg and Gisselquist in their impressive project on Strengthening African Governance referred, among other things, to Ibrahim's indices (Rotberg and Gisselquist, 2009). Ibrahim and Rotberg/Gisselquist templates will be briefly and eclectically examined with a view to providing possible stratagems for deepening democracy and institutionalizing it for the purpose of development.

Rule of Law, Transparency and Corruption

The rule of law, definitionally, refers to a legal framework that accentuates the supremacy of the law and limits the discretionary power of public officials. Additionally, the rule of law safeguards individual rights from the arbitrary interference of government and nongovernmental agents. It is said to provide the foundation for democratic constitutionalism (Plano and Greenberg, 1985:23; Fatton, 1995:67–99) essential for furthering political steadiness. Commonly, it entails a full protection of all forms of human rights including those of ordinary citizens and minorities (Udogu, 2005:180).

Apropos the rule of law, it is critical that the judiciary should be independent and efficient (Rotberg and Gisselquist, 2009:97–129). Judicial independence implies that the courts and judges must not succumb to the vagaries and control of politicians—especially the president and governors of states who appoint the judges and chief justices. Very often in African politics judges are beholden to the president and when, as in Ivory Coast, the problem of electoral democracy was brought before the court, the judge nearly always ruled in favor of the incumbent president even when the judge was aware of electoral malfeasance (Udogu, 2016). This was so because the chief justice was strategically chosen from the ethnic group or region of the president. So, decision made on the outcome of a rigged political competition in favor of an incumbent president is frequently greeted with skepticism. Conflictive elections often lead to political mayhem. Accordingly, I contend that political upheavals impede the progress toward democratic consolidation even though democracy is a fact of life in much of Africa today. Thus, it is imperative that judicial independence should be respected and guaranteed to further democratic consolidation essential for economic development.

Although a practice of the rule of law subsumes transparency and accountability, it is worth noting that the lack of transparency and accountability in the activities of governments also nourishes the allure of corruption. Transparency suggests that policies that are made, and their implementation in a polity, are carried out in such a manner that sticks to rules and regulations laid down by the system. Accountability entails, among other factors, the readiness of policymakers and those in political power to present a re-port on their stewardship to tax payers and those whom they swore to serve whenever such a request is made. The criticality of transparency and accountability in advancing political stability and economic development in a society is a given in democratic theory; yet, many politicos are reluctant to subject their activities to auditors for fear that their "corrupt practices" could be detected. It is necessary to undertake periodic inspections of accounts of government agencies by experts to reduce corruption and to increase the system's legitimacy and opportunities for economic growth.

Corruption as I have noted elsewhere is an ogre and an impediment to African renaissance (Udogu, 2007:134). Moreover, John Mukum Mbaku has argued that preponderant research conducted on this issue in Africa during the last 50 years or so has shown that this "monster" has a significant negative impact on economic growth as well as political development (Mbaku, 2000:9–54). Furthermore, the extent to which corruption has affected the progress toward democratic consolidation is manifested in electoral malpractices. If elections are not free and fair because bribery, suppression of votes of opposition parties, and the balloting process is rigged such a victory by a leader of a party will create national angst and mitigate state's legitimacy; it is the lack of support for a regime from opposition parties that has in part decelerated the pace toward democratic consolidation needed for stability and development.

For example, so serious is the issue of corruption in Nigeria that President Muhammadu Buhari stated forcefully: "unless Nigeria kills corruption, corruption will kill Nigeria (Sahara Reporters, 2015)." Accordingly, he has declared War against Corruption (WAC) in this republic. I suggest that since democracy is a fact of life today—especially among members of the informed public—African leaders should emulate President Buhari WAC policy. This strategy is vital at all levels (local, state and national) of a polity. This policy is critical for speeding up democratic consolidation, political stability and economic growth on the continent.

Political Participation and Human Rights

It is crucial in the contemporary democratic consolidation project in Africa to open up the political space so that all qualified citizens can take part in the electoral system as a way of life in this century. Even so, there are many instances in which political activists apply nefarious tactics to disenfranchise those constituencies that are unlikely to vote for their candidate/s. Such practice is commonplace, and it violates the human rights of individuals as in Article 2 (1) of the Universal Declaration of Human Rights (UDHR). It states that: "Everyone has the right to take part in the government of his country, directly or through freely chosen representative." This act of vote suppression is frequently resisted on the streets with violence because some governments have a knack for unleashing the police and other state security forces against demonstrators fighting for their rights to the poll.

It was to this end that Rotberg and Gisselquist suggested the following as strategies for moderating and alleviating electoral violence and its concomitant effect of slowing down the progress toward institutionalizing democratic consolidation: 1. free, fair, and competitive elections; 2. opposition participation in executive elections; 3. free and fair legislative elections, and 4. opposition participation in legislative elections. As to human rights, they suggested, *inter-alia*, the following: 1. respect for physical integrity rights; 2. respect for civil rights; 3. press freedom; 4. women's rights; and 5. economic rights (Robert and Gisselquist, 2009:133–154).

Suffice it to say that adherence to the preceding recommendations could further the legitimacy of a victorious party in electoral contestations. A political culture in which opposition parties could supersede an incumbent political faction with minimal crisis promotes democratic consolidation and solidifies democracy as a way of life. This situation is somewhat similar to the case of Nigeria's presidential and legislative elections of 2015 when the incumbent President Goodluck Jonathan of the People's Democratic Party (PDP) was defeated by the All Progressives Congress (APC). The transfer of power to President Muhammadu Buhari, leader of the APC, was velvety. It paved the way for concretizing democracy as a fact of life in this country and improved the conditions for peace needed to provide opportunities for economic development.

Human Development

Human development stresses the importance of education at all levels from the elementary to the tertiary level in a polity (Rotberg and Gisselquist, 2009:221–276). A theory that the more educated a society is the more likely that society will develop is not lost in this contemplation and analysis. Citizens that are well educated are more likely to demand their rights in a political system and to query government policies that are inadequate in the governance of the society and to demand improvement. Educated citizens are more likely to participate in the electoral process than uneducated compatriots— all things being equal. They could change the government by voting out of power an inept political leader and replacing him or her (and party) with another party whose platform addresses their needs and those of the society. Educated cadres are savvy in their use of social media to inform and educate others about the political activities in a country and to coordinate ways to change the system. The use of social media was displayed effectively in the so-called Arab Spring and revolt against the incumbent government in Tunisia and Egypt, for example. This process, arguably, illustrates the fact that democracy is a way of life in "modern" Africa.

Moreover, statistics suggest that education helps to reduce poverty and to close the gap in inequality in most societies. Once such is the case, it mitigates the possibility of pent-up frustration that could be combustible in a society. For democracy to fully become a fact of life, and for economic growth to happen, human development issues must be tackled. To paraphrase Jerry Rawlings, a former president of Ghana, a hungry person has minimal interest in democracy or a democratic process if survival is at the forefront of his or her daily life (Democracy, 1994:15).

Sustainable Economic Opportunity

Africa is possibly the richest continent in the world because its untapped natural re-sources are in abundance. Yet, developmentally, it ranks behind the other regions of the world. A reason for this, when one controls for the exploitation of the continent's natural resources by European colonial powers, is that the fruits of its raw materials are still to be reaped in this century. Where-as the process has already begun, the need for the creation of wealth is critical (Rotberg and Gisselquist, 2009:171–218). In this way, the struggle for scare resources will not lead to civil wars amongst ethnic groupings (as in South Sudan) seeking their fair share of the national pie. A consolidated liberal democratic genre could reduce the chances of ethno-political uprising and create an environment for sustainable development.

The objective toward permanently making democracy and democratization the way of life in Africa today demand that Africa's economy remains resilient and that the activities and clamor of marginalization by ethnic groups and other factions in a nation-state are less centrifugal. Moreover, when politics is not the only game in town because citizens are doing well economically, the political system is strengthened and peaceful coexistence furthered.

In sum, because democracy is a fact of life in contemporary African politics the recipes provided in this essay for advancing democratic consolidation critical for development are inspiring. It is equally comforting to observe that the African Union, civil society groups and policy makers are addressing some aspects of the preceding templates. Their positive actions toward making democracy and democratic solidity the way of life essential for peace, stability and development in the 21st century are inspiring.

REFERENCES

Ahluwalia, P. 2001. *Politics and Post-Colonial Theory: African Inflictions*. Abingdon-on-Thames: Routledge.
Ake, Claude. 1994. *Democratization of Displacement in Africa*. Port Harcourt, Nigeria: CASS Occasional Monograph No. 1.
Branch, Daniel. 2011. Kenya: *Between Hope and Despair, 1963–2011*. New Haven, CT: Yale University Press.
Buhari, Muhammadu. 2015. "Full Text of Buhari's Speech at Chatham House, London, United Kingdom," *Daily Post* [Nigeria] (February 26, 2017). http://dailypost.ng/2015/02/26/full-text-of-buhari-speech-at-chathan (Retrieved 8/8/17).
Chazan, Naomi. 1988. "Ghana: Problems of Governance and the Emergence of Civil Society." In Larry Diamond, Juan J. Linz and Seymour M. Lipset (eds.), *Democracy in Developing Countries: Africa II*. Boulder, CO: Lynne Rienner.

Darko, Kwaku A.. 2002. "Pitfalls in the African Brain Drain Discourse. http://www.arts.uwa. edu.au.MotPluriels/MP2002kad.html (Retrieved 8/10/17).

"Democracy: No Mean Achievement." 1994. *West Africa.* January 10–16, p. 15.

"Dialogue with Chinua Achebe." 1992. *Emerge.* 4(3)(December), p. 11.

_____. 1994. "Rethinking Civil Society: Toward Democratic Consolidation in Africa." *Journal of Democracy.* 5, pp. 4–17.

Diamond, Larry. 1988. "Beyond Authoritarianism and Totalitarianism: Strategies for Democratization." *The Washington Quarterly.* 12(1), pp. 141–163.

Falola, Toyin and Julius O. Ihonvbere. 1985. *The Rise and Fall of Nigeria's Second Republic, 1979–1984.* London: Zed Books.

Fatton, Robert, Jr. 1995. "Africa in the Age of Democratization: The Civic Limitation of Civil Society," *African Studies Review.* 38(2), pp. 67–99.

Fatton, Robert. 1990. "Liberal Democracy in Africa." *Political Science Quarterly.* 105(3), pp. 455–473

GRC. 2017. Exchange-Political Systems: Civil Society. http://www.grcexchange.org/g_themes/ politicalsystems_civil.htlm (Retrieved 8/9/17).

Green, Arnold, W. 1993. *Hobbes and Human Nature.* New Brunswick, NJ: Transaction Publishers.

Hauss, Charles C. 2017. Civil Society. http://www.intractableconflict.org/m/civil_society.jsp (Retrieved 8/9/17).

Houngnikpo, Mathurin C. 2003. "Pax-Democratica: The Gospel According to St. Democracy," *Australian Journal of Politics and History.* 49(2), pp. 197–210.

Huntington, Samuel. 1991. *The Third Wave: Democratization in the Late Twentieth Century.* Norman, OK: University of Oklahoma Press.

_____. 1984. "Will More Countries Become Democratic?" *Political Science Quarterly.* 99(2), pp. 193–218.

Ibrahim, Jibrin. 2015. "Bleak Horizon for Democracy in Africa," *Premium Times* [Nigeria]. July 13. http://blogs.premiumtimesng.com/?p-168126 (Retrieved 8/6/17).

Ibrahim, Mo. 2015. "Index of African Governance." https://en.wikipedia.org/wiki/ibrahim_ index_of_African_Goverance (Retrieved 8/11/17).

Ihonvbere, Julius O. 1999. "Africa in the Twenty-First Century: The Challenges and Opportunities." In John Mukum Mbaku (ed.). *Preparing Africa for the Twenty-First Century: Strategies for Peaceful Coexistence and Sustainable Development* (Aldershot, UK: Ashgate Publishing Company, pp. 45–60.

_____. 2002. "Civil Society, the State and the New Politics in Africa." A Paper Presented at the Conference on State in Africa: Beyond False Starts, Grand Valley State University, Allendale, Michigan, held April 11–14.

Jackson, Robert H., and Carl G. Rosberg. 1985. "Democracy in Tropical Africa: Democracy Versus Autocracy in African Politics." *Journal of International Affairs.* 38, pp. 293–305.

Jega, Attahiru. 1997. "State of the Civil Society: Strengthening the Options and Strategies for Change. *Strategic Planning Workshop on Democratic Development in Nigeria, Report and Proceedings.* London: Center for Democracy and Development Publication.

Kieh, George Klay. 1996. "Democratization and Peace." *Journal of Asian and African Studies.* 31(1–2), pp. 99–111.

Lewis, Arthur W. 1965. *Politics in West Africa.* Oxford: Oxford University Press.

Lijphart, Arendt. 1967. *Democracy in Plural Societies: A Comparative Exploration.* New Haven, CT: Yale University Press.

Mafeje, Archie. 2002. "Democratic Governance and Democracy in Africa: Agenda for the Future." A Paper Presented at the African forum for envisioning Africa, Nairobi, Kenya. http://www.uneca.org/itca/governance/documents/ArchieMafeje2.pdf   (Retrieved 8/31/17)

Mazrui, Ali. 1985. "A Legacy of Lifestyles." The Africans: An Annenberg/CPB Project.

Mbaku, John Mukum. 2000. *Bureaucratic and Political Corruption in Africa: The Public Choice Perspective.* Malabar, FL: Krieger Publishing Company.

Mbeki, Thabo. 2015. "Uprising but no Re-Awakenings." http://www.iol.co.za/sundayindepend ent/uprisings-but-not-reawakenings-1.1880574#.VZupzHqqpHv (Retrieved 8/7/17).

Monga, Celestin. 1995. "Civil Society and the Democratization in Francophone Africa," *The Journal of Modern African Studies*. 33, pp. 359–379.

Newbury, Catherine. 1994. "Paradoxes of Democratization in Africa." *African Studies Review*. 37(1), pp. 1–8.

OAU/AU. 2002. Declaration on the Principles Governing Democratic Elections in Africa—AHG/Decl. 1 (XXXVIII). July 8. http://www.au2002.gov.za/docs/summit_.council/qaudec2.htm (Retrieved 8/6/17).

Plano, Jack and M. Greenberg. 1985. *The American Political Dictionary.* New York: Holt, Rinehart and Winston.

Rotberg, Robert and Rachael M. Gisselquist. 2009. Strengthening African Governance: Index of Africa Governance Results and Ranking: A Project of the Program on Intrastate Conflict and Conflict Resolution at the Kennedy School of Government, Harvard University and the World Peace Foundation. www.nher.org/iag/iag2009.pdf (Retrieved 8/11/17).

Rubin, Leslie, and Brian Weinstein. 1977. *Introduction to African Politics: A Continental Approach.* New York: Praeger.

Sahara Reports. 2015. "Buhari Blast Akpabio, Others, Says Corrupt APC, PDP Members Must Face Trial," Premium Times [Nigeria]. August 10. http://saharareporters.com/2015/08/10/buhari-blast-akpabio-others-says-corrupt-apc-pdp-members-must-face-trial (Retrieved 8/12/17).

Schneider, H.W. 1958. *Thomas Hobbes, Leviathan.* New York: Bobbs-Merrill Publishers.

Sklar, Richard. 1982. "Democracy in Africa." *African Studies Review*. 26(3 & 4), pp. 11–24

Tannenbaum, Donald G. and David Shultz. 1998. *Inventors of Ideas: An Introduction to Western Philosophy.* New York: St. Martin's Press.

Udogu, E. Ike. 2006. *African American Politics in Rural America: Theory, Practice, and Case Studies from Florence County, South Carolina.* Lanham, MD: University Press of America.

_____. 2007. *African Renaissance in the Millennium: The Political, Social, and Economic Discourses on the Way Forward.* Lanham, MD: Lexington Books.

_____. 2005. "Building a Sustainable Democracy and Political Stability in the New Millennium." In E. Ike Udogu (ed.). *Nigeria in the Twenty-First Century: Strategies for Political Stability and Peaceful Coexistence.* Trenton, NJ: Africa World Press.

_____. 2010. *Confronting the Challenges and Prospects in the Creation of a Union of African States in the 21st Century.* Newcastle-upon-Tyne: Cambridge Scholars Publishing.

_____. 1994. "Democracy, the Two Party System and the Transition Imbroglio in the March Toward Nigeria's Third Republic 1985–1992." *Scandinavian Journal of Development Alternatives.* 13(1–2), pp. 205–220.

_____. 1996. "Incomplete Metamorphic Democracy as a Conceptual Framework in the Analysis of African Politics: An Exploratory Investigation." *Journal of Asian and African Studies.* 31(1–2), pp. 5–20.

_____. 2016. *Leadership and the Problem of Electoral Democracy in Africa: Case Studies and Theoretical Solutions.* Newcastle-upon-Tyne: Cambridge Scholars Publishing.

UN-NGLS Non-Governmental Liaison Services. 2015. Voices from Africa. http://www.unsystem.org/ngls/documents/publications.en/voices.africa/number (Retrieved 8/10/17).

Uwizeyimana, Dominique E. 2012. "Democracy and Pretend Democracies in Africa: Myths of African Democracies." *Law, Democracy & Development.* 16, p. 139–161.

Young, C. Crawford. 1994. "Democratization in Africa: Contradiction of a Political Imperative." In Jennifer A. Widner (ed.), *Economic Change and Political Liberalization in Sub-Saharan Africa.* Baltimore: MD: John Hopkins University Press.

African Leadership and the Management of African Economies

JOHNSON W. MAKOBA

Introduction

Following the attainment of political independence in the 1960s, political leaders in virtually all African countries accepted the critical role of the state in the achievement of economic growth and the improvement in the well-being of their populations (Makoba, 2011; Shivji, 2005; and Tangari, 1985). Development strategies pursued by Sub-Saharan African countries in the 1960s through the 1970s, led to what Arrighi (2002:11) has characterized as "perverse growth:, also known as "growth without development." This is largely because they did not pay "adequate attention to the agricultural productivity and industrial competitiveness" (UNCTAD, 2001:49). As a result, once the global environment deteriorated from the late 1970s onward, African economic growth could not be sustained. Indeed some scholars contend that conditions of most Africans had declined by 2014 and that they were worse than in the 1970s (Bush and Harrison, 2014). Furthermore, the focus on Structural Adjustment Programs (SAPS) from the 1980s by the World Bank and the International Monetary Fund has not delivered sustained economic growth either. In this essay, we explore new initiatives started in the 2000s by a new generation of African leadership aimed at improving economic growth and peoples' well-being.

Initially, economic development as a theme became central to the efforts of the immediate post-colonial African leaders. However, over time, these leaders and their successors became preoccupied with corrupt practices of personal accumulation and enrichment (Muazu, et al, 2015) as well as the promotion of the interests of social classes or ethnic groups they were affiliated with. In this way, the political elite used state resources at their disposal for personal use or to attract allies and reward supporters of the regime at the expense of the general population. Rather than improving the well-being of the general population, public resources have been used (or misused) to organize and sustain political patronage.

This essay argues that initially, virtually all African leaders tried to control and manage their economies in order to promote rapid economic development, but over time, they abandoned this position as they became preoccupied with personal enrichment and promotion of the interests of their supporters. The efforts by African leaders failed to deliver economic development in part due to corruption and economic mismanagement (Bagire and Namada, 2015). As a result of economic failure, African leaders lost control and responsibility over their respective economies starting in the mid–1980s to international financial institutions, particularly the World Bank and the International Monetary Fund (IMF). Finally, the essay considers collective political efforts at regional and continental levels aimed at regaining control and responsibility over African economies. The essay is divided into five sections as discussed below.

The Post-Colonial African Leadership and the Economy

During the immediate postcolonial period, the African leadership in general appeared to be genuinely concerned about promoting rapid economic development and improving the well-being of their people. Although the leaders possessed power and responsibility, they quickly realized they could not achieve the twin goals of promoting economic development and improving the well-being of the population without attaining economic and managerial control over their respective economies. In order to champion accelerated economic development, it became clear that the state or government had to play an important role in economic activity.

African leaders in the 1960s and 1970s (whether they believed in market or state-led development), saw state control of the economy as essential to achieving rapid economic development (Makoba, 2011; Shivji, 2005; Tordoff 1984; and Makoba 1998). In countries such as Tanzania or Zambia, the governments used policies of nationalization, Africanization and import substitution through public enterprises to bring their economies under state control and strengthen economic planning and management..

At the time, public enterprises (or parastatal organizations) were conceived as the best vehicle to control foreign capital and to promote rapid economic development. The policies of nationalization and Africanization (also called indigenization) pursued in the late 1960s and 1970s were heavily influenced by political or ideological considerations of the African leaders (Makoba, 2011). For example, Nationalization (pursued by Tanzania under the 1967 Arusha Declaration) or the desire for economic nationalism (outlined in Zambia's 1968 Mulungushi economic reforms) sought to prevent continued domination and exploitation of African economies by foreign capital or transnational corporations (Makoba, 1998). Africanization stressed the replacement of foreigners in the public or government sector with indigenous personnel. And in some countries such as Kenya, Nigeria or Zambia, Africanization or indigenization meant the systematic transfer of small to medium size businesses owned by foreigners to the local bourgeoisie in these countries. Overall, these policies were intended to promote economic and managerial control and to put the public sector at the center of the development process. In many African countries the import substitution strategy undertaken by newly established public enterprises was expected to achieve rapid industrialization and transformation of the largely agrarian economies into predominantly manufacturing ones.

In effect statist development strategies were used by the African leadership to promote control of their economies and increase indigenous access to economic activities as well as to create or enhance their political legitimacy. Because African leaders inherited weak and fragile authority from the departing colonial power, they relied on the public sector to achieve both political and economic control and to reward regime supporters through employment opportunities. Through such hegemony, the African political leadership was also able to incorporate its development agenda into a national development strategy embedded in five-year national development plans. Development planning (a legacy of the former Soviet Union) administered by the state or its institutions was often equated to promoting rapid economic development. The question facing African leaders in the 1960s and 1970s was not whether to engage in central planning or not, but rather what kind of national planning to adopt. Most African governments "adopted controlled planning within a mixed economy, though the mix between the public and private sectors ... [varied] substantially between one state and another..." (Tordoff 1984:145). Regardless of such variations, the state was engaged in centralized planning, managing and executing the development process, primarily through the public enterprise sector or parastatals. As a result, such centralized planning tended to accord the state and the public enterprise sector greater control over the implementation of development programs or projects designed to achieve overall economic growth.

Both national development plans and the policies of economic and managerial control failed to deliver the expected economic development. National

Development Planning (NDP) failed due to four major reasons. First, the plans tended to set unrealistic targets for both the public and private sectors. This happened as the private sector was not consulted, while the potential of the public sector was often overstated. Second, lack of discipline or commitment by implementing agencies (whether located in the ministries of planning and development, finance or the offices of the Prime Minister or President) to aggressively pursue agreed upon priorities and targets in the plan. Third, lack of involvement of the top political leadership in the planning process tended to undercut the legitimacy of the plans that did not contain the political priorities of those in control of government. Fourth, was a lack of adequate management capacity to bring about sustainable development (Bagire and Namada, 2015).

The economic crises of the late 1970s and early 1980s, forced African governments to seek loans from the International Monetary Fund and the World Bank. The International Monetary Fund (IMF) is responsible for short-term anti-inflationary macroeconomic stabilization policies, while the World Bank handles medium-term market-oriented structural adjustment programs (SAPs). The implications of both Bretton Woods institutions on African economies are considered later (Sundaram et al, 2011). As we discuss later, the terms and conditions of such loans undermined sustainable economic development efforts as politically driven government priorities were incompatible with the conditionalities of the international financial institutions. Since the 1990s to the present, African countries that continue to engage in planning stress short-to-medium term planning and are often compelled by the World Bank and IMF to set specific and realistic targets that are subject to periodic review and adjustment.

The policies of economic and managerial control adopted by many African countries failed to deliver sustainable economic development. The failure was due primarily to widespread corruption, economic mismanagement (Muazu, et al, 2015) as well as inadequate capital and lack of skilled local personnel to effectively implement the policies. Nationalizations of foreign-dominated enterprises contributed to the rapid expansion of the public sector, thereby exerting pressure on the meager resources and capabilities of African states to manage. On the other hand, Africanization failed to produce sufficient local personnel with necessary skills and expertise. As a result, Africanization intended to empower Africans to manage the government bureaucracy (i.e., civil service) and the parastatal sector instead ended up contributing to demands for more expatriates or management agents to help manage an expanded public sector (Makoba 2011). The overall performance of the public enterprise sector was disappointing, as the sector increasingly became a burden on the state finances. Despite their substantial contribution to both ouput and employment, public enterprises were blamed for both inefficiency and corruption (Makoba, 2011). The political leadership used these enterprises primarily as employment agencies (for their cronies) and denied them the necessary autonomy to make operational or investment decisions. As we discuss later in this essay, the World Bank and Western governments seized upon the issue of widespread poor public enterprise performance in Africa to recommend the privatization of public enterprises and the liberalization of African economies in the 1980s. In the section below, we consider the economic consequences of personal rule, corruption and economic mismanagement.

Personal Rule, Corruption and Economic Mismanagement

Apter and Rosberg observe that postcolonial African leaders "performing at low levels of efficacy ... quickly sought to concentrate power by controlling whatever levels of power might be available, a situation leading ... to the evolution of personalized and authoritarian regimes" (1994:24). As Ogbazghi (2011:3) points out: "The political dynamics of personal rule, ..., promotes personalized state-society relationships rather than institution—based on practices of governance." As a result, "personal rule is based on loyalty to the president as opposed to institutions, which are constantly monitored and controlled to ensure that they will not achieve any balance of power that could threaten the system." In such systems, "personal decisions take precedence over formal institutions mainly due to lack of distinction between personal rulers and their formal institutions" (*ibid.*, 3). Thus personal rule resulted from the concentration of power in the hands of a single, political party, military junta or dictator. Over time, African personal rulers not only controlled political power and economic resources, but "came to represent the law and the state" (Apter and Rosberg, 1994:25 and Makoba, 2001:7–8). Above all, such authoritarian leaders or governments tend to be unaccountable to the public since their legitimacy no longer rests with the general public (as was the case soon after political independence). In addition, personal rule is characterized by a lack of a development ideology that goes beyond loyalty. Hence, statist ideologies tend to symbolize a development ideology instead. This stands in sharp contrast to authoritarian leaders in South East Asia (i.e., South Korea, Singapore, Hong Kong and Taiwan) who sought their legitimacy in a combination of economic growth and equity in the economy (Makoba, 1998). In addition, the leaders of these "four tigers" "did not follow an economic ideology, but [rather] a policy of pragmatic [and incremental] adaptations to changing [global] conditions" (Nürnberger, 1988:147).

The postcolonial African state variously called "soft," "overloaded," "vampire," "over-centralized," "predatory," "autocratic patrimonial," or simply "authoritarian," "has been detached from society and failed to deliver economic development" (Makoba 2001:8). This holds true of most African countries, irrespective of their political or ideological orientation (i.e., whether socialist or capitalist oriented). No doubt, Africa's poor economic performance has been affected by external factors such as the huge foreign debt burden, poor terms of trade, the oil price shocks of the 1970s and the world recession of the 1980s (Sundaram, et al, 2011). Among the external factors, the debt burden is the most severe constraint to Africa's economic recovery and development (Mubangizi, 2010). However, despite the impact of the debt burden and other external factors, we argue that economic mismanagement and widespread corruption have contributed to the severe economic crisis experienced in Africa since the mid–1980s to the present (Muazu, et al, 2015; Mbaku, 1996).

Personal rule breeds nepotism, patronage and corruption, often with devastating implications for the economy. This occurs as there is no distinction between state and ruler and state resources are considered an extension of the ruler's fiefdom (Ogbazghi, 2011). As a result of political and economic control exercised by the postcolonial elite, African rulers enriched themselves and their political associates at the expense of the population (Apter and Rosberg, 1994). African leaders increasingly engaged in the appropriation of state resources for personal aggrandizement or individual accumulation. At the same time, they redirected government opportunities and resources into the service of familial, ethnic and sometimes class interests. Resources used for patronage ensured that political allies of the regime were attracted and supporters handsomely rewarded. Inevitably, nepotism, patronage, clientage and corruption have become enduring features of personal rule in Africa (whether the regime is authoritarian or quasi-democratic). In addition, personal rule engenders a politics of survival rather than the advancement or commitment to achieving civil, community or socioeconomic goals (Ogbazghi, 2011; Apter and Rosberg, 1994).

As a result of constant political instability and actual or potential civil strife, many African rulers have focused their attention on consuming state resources and transferring abroad for safekeeping millions of dollars they could not spend locally within their own countries. Apter and Rosberg observed that "so much have mismanagement and corruption compromised African political systems that it is estimated that $40 billion in African private assets are held [in bank accounts] in industrial states" (1994:26). It was reported, for example, that by 1984 alone, former and late President Mobutu Sese Seko of Zaire (now Democratic Republic of Congo, or DRC) had accumulated personal wealth of $5 billion in western bank accounts. A recent report on how the rest of the world profits from Africa's wealth concluded that: "African countries received $161.6 billion in 2015—mainly in loans, personal remittances and aid in the form of grants. Yet $203 billion was taken from Africa, either directly—mainly through corporations repatriating profits and by illegally moving money out of the continent..." (Honest Accounts 2017 Report:1).

It is unlikely that such "hidden wealth" was unknown to either the Western countries or the World Bank, that continued to provide aid or political support to the Mobutu regime until its downfall at the hands of rebel forces led by the late Laurent Kabila (succeeded by his son as current President of DRC). By condoning or tolerating the twin-problems of corruption and clientelism (i.e., political patronage), personal rule has greatly undermined the viability of most African states and tarnished the image of most African leaders (with the notable exceptions of former and late President Julius Nyerere of Tanzania and former (and late) President Nelson Mandela of South Africa). Beyond failing to deliver economic development, personal rule has been characterized by political instability and even civil strife. Despite efforts to concentrate power and authority in the hands of the personal ruler, authoritarian African regimes have been subject to frequent political instability and regime change through coups detát. Extreme cases of the breakdown of authority in such varied countries as Somalia, Sierra Leone, Liberia or the Democratic Republic of the Congo (former Zaire), have seen authoritarian regimes violently replaced by the "warlordism" of the tribal past. Increasingly, many of these countries are referred to as "failed states."

It is evident that most African leaders use the decaying or unstable authoritarian state to serve their political and economic interests to the detriment of national economic development (Falton, 1992). Ayittey (1998) blames Africa's economic crisis and political chaos on what he calls the "vampire state" and the bad leadership of the elite who control that state. He considers economic problems of corruption and mismanagement as having political underpinnings (Ayittey, 1998). According to Ayittey, bad leadership in Africa is responsible for a long list of internal problems that include:

> Corruption, economic mismanagement, repression or violation of human rights, political instability or military coups detát, senseless civil wars, states with diminished capacity, exploitation and oppression of the peasantry ... and capital flight or lack of both foreign and domestic investment [1998:342].

Thus, personal rule and the political choices of African leaders that favored the appropriation of state resources have combined to undermine economic development and the well-being of the population.

Africa's economic problems are compounded by a crisis of governance. As has been observed, "Africa's economic crisis is as much political as economic" (Callaghy, 1994). Instead of providing a mechanism of economic growth and development, African personal regimes have generally presided over economic decline and political decay. According to Decalo, the autocratic patrimonial state has:

> provided presidential authoritarianism of varying degrees of repression, and *defacto* domination by whatever ethnic group 'possesses' the Presidency; it has been instrumental in plundering the economy, directly or indirectly; it resulted in the disdain for civil and human rights, and with few exceptions has paid minimal attention to agrarian or rural population ... (1992:12). [He adds], Africa is not only marginalized, but scores at the bottom of every criteria of development (Decalo, 1992:15).

As a result of failure to deliver economic development, African states have come under intense pressure and scrutiny from both internal and external forces to undertake political and economic reforms. Though not discussed here, political and democratic reforms that characterized the 1990s have either been slowed, halted or in some cases, reversed. In the section below, I consider demands by international financial institutions (especially, the World Bank and the IMF) and Western governments to link development aid to economic reforms in Africa and the consequences on economic performance. Beginning in the 1980s, the World Bank and the IMF with the backing of Western governments, tried to scrutinize, criticize and impose conditions for development aid to Africa. As we discuss below, the World Bank and Western governments seized upon the issues of corruption and widespread poor public enterprise performance in Africa to call for the privatization of public enterprises and the liberalization of African economies.

African Economic Crisis and Structural Adjustment Programs

It has been argued that the economic crisis that engulfed Africa in the mid–1980s led to the demand for economic reform programs devised by the IMF and World Bank with the support of Western governments. By and large, it is the failure of African government policies of economic development pursued in the 1960s and the 1970s, that contributed to the imposition of IMF-World Bank policies beginning in the 1980s and continuing to the present. As stated earlier, "whether pursuing radical or market-economy development strategies, African states have grafted the worst traits of both, not pursuing cost-effectiveness nor harnessing state sectors to productive ends" (Decalo 1992:16).

The World Bank's Berg Report (1981), "Towards Accelerated Development in Sub-Saharan Africa," blamed the state and government policies for the poor economic performance in the 1960s and the 1970s (Heidbures and Obare, 2011). Supporters of World Bank policies contend that by linking development aid to economic reforms and good governance, African leaders were for the first time being held accountable for the adverse economic conditions of their own economies by the World Bank and its Western backers (Apter and Rosberg, 1994). Before discussing the IMF-World Bank policies and their implications on the African political economy, we need to consider the political, ideological and theoretical contexts that gave rise to the emergence of these policies.

Liberal economic theory as presented by neoclassical theorists argues for either the reduction or elimination of state involvement in any economic activity (Makoba, 2011). Such a theory considers economic growth to result from the efficient allocation of resources by the market forces, or the "invisible hand." Therefore, neoclassical economists view sate involvement in economic activity as either irrelevant or an obstacle to the development process. State or government involvement in economic activity is perceived as an obstacle because it allegedly imposes unnecessary and unacceptable social costs. Such social costs are believed to generate excessive and unproductive bureaucratic activity. It is said this happens as government actions "create incentives for non-productive activities which tend to maximize political advantages rather than economic production" (Makoba, 1998:19). The Central message of neoclassical economic theorists is that for African and other Third World countries to achieve economic growth, they must reduce or eliminate the role of the state or government in their economies. Throughout the 1980s, Western political leaders (especially, Margaret Thatcher of Britain and Ronald Reagan of the United States) believed in the neoclassical criticisms of excessive costs of government involvement in the economy. Both leaders also strongly believed in the "invisible hand" of the market forces to allocate resources efficiently and in the capitalist "trickle down" doctrine to spread benefits from the rich to the poor. The IMF and World Bank that promote these neoclassical economic perspectives and have wholly embraced criticisms of excessive costs of government intervention in the economy in order to aggressively push for structural adjustment programs and their attendant conditionalities in Africa and other Third World countries.

Finally, it is important to note that the collapse of centrally planned economies of Eastern Europe and the former Soviet Union in 1992 enhanced the legitimacy, credibility and power of the "invisible hand" of market forces in allocating scarce resources and promoting economic growth (Makoba, 1998). As a result of the end of the cold war and pressing financial needs in developed industrialized countries, pressure on Third World countries including those in Africa, by the international donor community to promote independent, market-oriented economies intensified (Makoba, 2001 and Makoba, 1998).

Simultaneous with Africa's economic crisis and the end of the Cold War, "came powerful international demands for 'better governance' (and an end to corruption), more democratization (civic and human rights), and ultimately, a free [market] economy" (Decalo, 1992:18). It is said that former World Bank President Barber B. Conable, Jr., expressed his "fear that many of Africa's leaders have been more concerned about retaining power than about long-term development interests of their people" (Decalo, 1992:18–19). Such a mood of fear and frustration expressed at the highest levels of the World Bank is said to have galvanized pressure from the international donor community starting in the late 1980s through most of the 1990s. As a result, France in collaboration with the World Bank, IMF and the United States, demanded "political change as a condition for further loans to Africa" (Decalo, 1992:19).

Interestingly, the World Bank in its own assessment of Africa's economic growth prospects argued that Africa had no chance of achieving any meaningful economic growth and development unless it undertook governance that included political accountability, participatory politics and a market-oriented economy. According to the World Bank and IMF, the causes of Africa's economic crisis include:

> ...a combination of overexpansion of industry [based on import substitution strategy] relative agriculture, overextension of public ownership relative to private sector, overinvestment in import-substituting industries relative to export industries, overinvestment in final good production compared to raw material processing, intermediate and capital goods industries and the usage of excessively high-import and capital-intensive technology relative to the comparative advantage of using local resources and labor [cited in Stein, 1992:84 and 93].

Both the World Bank and IMF (heavily influenced by the ideas of neoclassical economic theorists) believe strongly that the causes of Africa's economic crisis are exacerbated by government intervention in economic activity. As a result, both Bretton Woods financial institutions call for a reduced role of the African state in the economy, while enhancing the role of the market in promoting economic growth and development. Scholars discussing causes of the African economic crisis tend to make a link to the political crisis, as manifested in autocratic personal rule, corruption and economic mismanagement, all of which are considered to be pervasive (Lancaster, 1991; Apter and Rosberg, 1994; and Ayittey, 1998).

The most urgent problem facing several African countries in the late 1970s and early 1980 was the great need for additional external financing. African leaders were desperate for new loans and additional foreign aid, in spite of the heavy external debts their countries had already incurred. In order to secure additional external financing, "creditor governments required that [African] governments negotiate a stabilization agreement with the IMF before they would agree to debt rescheduling" (Lancaster, 1991:90). Hence an

IMF stabilization agreement became the price for both debt rescheduling and receiving new loans. The IMF was empowered to make loans conditioned on the borrower's willingness (not capacity) to implement the following politically risky policies: "currency devaluations, reductions in government deficits (either through increased tax revenues, reduced government expenditure, or both), and restrictions on domestic credit creation" (Lancaster, 1991:91). Furthermore, IMF loans were disbursed in tranches so that each additional disbursement was dependent on a review by the IMF of the borrowing government's compliance with agreed policy changes.

By 1983, it was clear that most African countries were simply unable to fully repay their loans from the IMF. However, the IMF could not stop lending to African countries, including those unable to repay. In addition, it was clearly evident "that IMF stabilization programs alone were not the solution to Africa's economic crisis" (Lancaster 1991:92). Indeed, such programs were seen as part of the problem. Following criticisms of the IMF stabilization programs, the World Bank stepped in aggressively "advising African governments on economic reform, in financing reform programs directly, and in coordinating developed country financing for African reform programs" (Lancaster, 1991:92). The World Bank offered structural and sectoral adjustment programs, collectively referred to as Structural Adjustment Programs or SAPS. The loans given under SAPS tended to be on soft terms (i.e., 10 years grace, 40 years to mature and often with small administrative charge) and targeted economic reforms either at sectoral level (i.e., agriculture, industry, finance or education) or at the whole economy. The requirements for the World Bank's structural adjustment loans include: "increases in producer prices; reduction or elimination of subsidies, prices, wage and credit controls; trade liberalization; revisions in investments regulations; privatization of state-owned enterprises; and reductions in the size of the civil service" (Lancaster, 1991:93).

The structural adjustment programs were conditioned on the prior existence of a stabilization agreement and program with IMF. It is argued that even though "World Bank loans seldom included the quantitative performance criteria typical of IMF…, the conditions of Bank loans tended to be more numerous and often more intrusive than those of the Fund" (Lancaster, 1991:93). The World Bank's model of bringing about economic recovery and renewed growth assumed that:

> borrowing governments would implement policy changes intended to improve the efficiency of government operating and to reduce government controls or engagement in the economy. With incentive prices and fewer impediments to private economic activity, existing producers, agricultural or industrial, would expand their production and investment. The increased inflow of aid loans and grants would ease import constraints on consumption, production, and investment and further speed recovery and growth [Lancaster, 1991:93].

The economic reform programs in Africa began with governments nego-tiating a stabilization program with the IMF, followed by adopting a World Bank sectoral adjustment program (often beginning with rehabilitation of the agricultural export sector), culminating in the implementation of a macroeconomic structural adjustment program with the bank. As a result, between 1990 and 1991 nearly 30 African countries had embraced or been compelled to accept World Bank structural adjustment programs and various IMF economic "fixes" (Lancaster, 1991 and Apter and Rosberg, 1994). Thus policies implemented by various African governments moved "from an early emphasis on reducing unsustainable deficits in the balance of payments to promoting long term growth through improving economic efficiency, reduc-ing the role of the state in the economy, and encouraging an increase in private investment" (Lancaster, 1991:87).

The effects of combined World Bank and IMF economic reform pro-grams in Africa at best show "mixed" results, and at worst, are perceived to have made the economic situation even worse. Critics contend that World Bank—IMF imposed reforms have made Africa's economic decline worse.[1] According to the Economic Commission for Africa (ECA), "those countries implementing IFI–sponsored reform programs have faired worse economi-cally than those without such programs" (Lancaster, 1991:86). Furthermore, the critics maintain that the new World Bank—IMF policy contained implicit tenets of a neo-colonial nature designed to recolonize the continent by impos-ing Western values (Decalo, 1992; Ayittey, 1998; and Lancaster, 1991). Radical scholars who have criticized these policies and African leaders who have resisted them concur that the economic reforms have proven painful for many Africans and contributed to loss of control over economic policy (Lan-caster, 1991). The mandatory budget cuts, once implemented, have often been politically risky for African governments. Besides contributing to declining standards of living, budget cuts have often fed political discontent and some-times outbreaks of violence, popularly known as "IMF riots" (Olamosu and Wynne, 2015).

Economic restructuring due to structural adjustment programs and pri-vatization have contributed to the retreat of the African states from their twin responsibilities of promoting economic development and providing basic social services (Dicklich, 1998). Furthermore, the fiscal impact of such 'unthinkable' budget cuts is considered by critics to be trivial compared to escalating interest payments African countries have to make on their ever ballooning national debts. As Ndegwa points out the structural adjustment programs "have strained the ability of the African states to provide services and has attracted more NGOS to cushion the adverse short term effects of adjustment programs, such as by providing affordable healthcare services" (1996:2). There is some consensus regarding the growing social costs of structural adjustment programs, even from the World Bank itself (Lancaster, 1991). Above all, the continued involvement of "international financial institutions (IFIs) in economic policy-making in Africa has generated deep resentment among many Africans who, with some justification believe that policies affecting their lives are decided abroad once again" (Lancaster, 1991:87). Indeed some African leaders and radical scholars have gone to the extent of viewing World Bank—IMF economic reforms "as conspiracies to recolonize Africa …" (Decalo 1992:16). Increasingly, African leaders appear to possess authority and responsibility, but without the power to influence the direction of economic policy within their own countries.[2] More importantly, it seems African leaders tend to make policy decisions without sufficient understanding of their implications (Kase kende, 2014).And African governments that resist or reject World Bank-IMF policies may be starved of foreign exchange, denied aid and not be allowed to reschedule their debts.

The most sympathetic scholars and policy makers (including those within and outside of the World Bank) of World Bank-IMF economic reforms in Africa tend to view them either as providing limited improvement (Decalo, 1992) or as offering "no clear-cut successes [even] where reform programs have led to economic recovery and sustained growth" (Lancaster 1991:88). At best, the proponents of these policies seem to agree that the economic reforms offer "mixed" results (Bird, 2001), even in countries such as Uganda and Ghana that are often hailed/cited as "models" of economic success.

According to the World Bank, "…countries implementing reform programs have enjoyed greater economic progress in recent years than those without economic reform programs" (Lancaster, 1991:86). It is reported, for example, that "between 1985 and 1987, the economies of countries with strong reform programs grew an average of 3.8 percent per year, while those with weak or no reform programs grew by only 1.5 percent" (Lancaster, 1991:95). The two countries in Africa most often cited as economic success stories based on the World Bank-IMF economic policies are Uganda and Ghana (Sharer et al, 1995 and Lancaster, 1991). Since the 1980s both countries have consistently experienced impressive economic growth rates. However, as the Ugandan case discussed below demonstrates, its economic performance over the past two decades has resulted from increased aid flow and disbursements of multilateral institutions, rather than increased agricultural or industrial production, foreign investments or domestic savings. Increased aid flows have inevitably contributed to a huge external debt with serious debt servicing difficulties. Sharer et al (1995) report that: "over the seven years 1987/88–1993/94, Uganda achieved stabilization and adjustment with growth. During this period, economic growth averaged almost 6 percent; inflation dropped substantially; and the fiscal deficit was steadily reduced" (1995:5).

Although Uganda's improved macroeconomic outlook is attributed to stabilization and structural adjustment programs, in reality it "relied to a large extent on disbursements by multilateral institutions" (Sharer et al, 1995:6). As a result of massive aid inflows, Uganda's "external debt grew from $1.3 billion in June 1987 to $2.9 billion at the end of June 1994" (Sharer et al, 1995:6). Over the same period, Uganda's debt-service ratio rose from 54 percent in 1986/87 to a peak of 128 percent in 1991/92 before beginning a falling trend to 56.5 percent in 1993/94. During this period, Uganda's coffee exports declined due to lower world prices, causing serious difficulties in servicing the huge external debt. Furthermore, Uganda's foreign investments and domestic savings did not significantly increase as envisaged under the stabilization and structural adjustment programs (Sharer et al, 1995:41–2). In Uganda, and several other African countries considered economic success stories by the World Bank, improved economic performance has been mostly a consequence of "more external financing to bring about ... benefits including additional aid loans, grants and debt relief..." (Lancaster, 1991:102). However, since the net outflow of funds to the IMF and World Bank exceed capital inflows from the private international or bilateral sources (Stein, 1992), sustainable growth cannot easily be achieved, even in the so-called successful countries such as Uganda or Ghana.

The World Bank and proponents of its economic programs maintain that African countries implementing its policies have experienced greater economic progress than those without such programs. However, when the Economic Commission for Africa (ECA) recalculated annual growth rates of African countries using a longer time period (between 1980 and 1987), the results indicated that "those countries with strong adjustment programs actually had the poorest growth rates, while those with no adjustment programs enjoyed the highest rates of growth" (Lancaster, 1991:96). Such contradictory or inconclusive evidence on the impact of structural programs may be attributed to two factors. First, "structural adjustment programs and other IMF "fixes" attest to the temporal and limited nature of any improvement" (Decalo, 1992:17). To achieve sustained economic growth and development African countries need committed national leadership and increased agricultural and industrial production, foreign private investments and domestic savings. Foreign private investments have not contributed to filling the capital resource gap in Africa since Africa is perceived by international investors as being highly risky. As a result, "in 1999, Africa attracted only $10.3 billion, or 5 percent of the total flow of $207.6 billion in foreign direct investment (FDI) to developing countries" (Mathews, 2001:136). Hence "it will take more than aid and reform to restore Africa to economic health" (Lancaster, 1991:102). The second possible explanation for contradictory or inclusive evidence is that the World Bank and proponents of structural adjustment programs tend to focus on the macroeconomic outlook rather than performance at the sectoral levels. According to Amin, such "studies have mostly delt with macro-economic aspects neglecting sectoral issues relating to ... exports and food crops" (1999:178). Evidence gleaned from sectoral studies indicates that the World Bank—IMF policies tend to "deindustrialize the existing manufacturing base in many African countries without encouraging any significant replacement" (Stein, 1992:83). In addition, neoliberal policy prescriptions pursued by the World Bank and IMF tend to stay away from promoting structural transformation of Africa's agricultural sector (Senbet and Simbanegavi, 2017).

It is reported that in vast areas of rural Africa, both "structural adjustment and market liberalization policies have triggered a widespread erosion of local peasant economies and social communities" (Bryceson, 2002:737). This occurs as the World Bank/IMF policies contribute to a decline in import substitution manufacturing and public ownership, without replacement by export-oriented or resource processing industry (Stein, 1992). Furthermore, the deindustrialization process forces African countries to rely more on agricultural exports that are often susceptible to demand and price fluctuations on the global market. This situation could be reversed if the focus was on increased productivity of the rural sector including agro-processing or value addition (Yeboah and Jayne, 2017).

For example, when the Government of Cameroon launched its Structural Adjustment Program (SAP) in the export agricultural sector in 1988, it expected to achieve significant productivity, investment and export growth in this sector (Amin, 1999). The World Bank and other proponents of Cameroon's SAP:

> believed that the policy distortion in the input and output prices affect the structure of incentives facing the agricultural (export) producers. Hence by liberalizing both input and output markets, distortions could be removed, incentives increased, consequently increasing agricultural output [Amin, 1999:177].

However, it is reported that despite the comprehensive policy reform in Cameroon's export agricultural sector, there was no significant increase in productivity and exports had little or no value added (Amin, 1999). Furthermore, "low producer prices resulting from low world prices, late payment and little institutional support (in cocoa and coffee) ... [were] a disincentive to producers of these crops since they are supply responsive..." (Amin, 1999:182).

The analysis of the impact of stabilization, liberalization and structural adjustment programs does not only apply to Uganda, Cameroon or Ghana, but could easily relate to all African countries in general. Worrell argues, for example, that "after nearly two decades of pursuing IMF/World Bank Structural Adjustment Programs almost half the population of the African continent lives in grinding poverty" (2001:45). The analysis reveals that economic improvement, if any, tends to be limited or not clear-cut, even for African countries often cited as successful cases (Heidhues and Obare, 2011 and Olamosu and Wynne, 2015). This conclusion calls for the inevitable exploration of an alternative policy framework for future economic development in Africa. The section below considers current perspectives for promoting regional or continental economic development in Africa.

Perspectives for Regional or Continental Economic Development in Africa

According to Ayittey, "there is consensus that reform in Africa must be internally generated, that is, must come from within" (1998:344). Bryceson (2002) concurs with Ayittey (1998) by saying that "future development policy [must be] spearheaded by African countries" (Bryceson, 2002:725). But the major challenge is where the impetus or motivation to reform would come from since African leaders in general are neither capable of nor interested in economic and political reform. More than a decade ago, Olusegun Obasanjo, former President of Nigeria and then leader of the African Leadership Forum (ALF) he helped establish, had wondered how ALF could influence African leaders to engage in forums concerning economic development or nation-building on the continent. Obasanjo had openly lamented that" ... calling them [African leaders] to a conference, trying to have great economists, [or] great leaders talk to them will not work" (1991:102). However, in a recent book on Africa in which Obasanjo is one of several co-authors, the call is to improve "Africa's capacity for economic growth and job creation" (Mills, et al, 2017:ix).

According to Lancaster (1991), "Africans began to recognize the growing seriousness of their economic plight when their heads of state signed the Lagos Plan of Action, discussed at the Organization of African Unity (OAU) ... meeting in 1980" (1991:88). The Lagos Plan of Action not only described economic problems facing Africa, but more importantly "proposed several solutions, including increased aid flows and the creation of sub-regional and, later, continent-wide common markets to stimulate trade, investment, and industrial growth" (Lancaster 1991: 88). The Lagos Plan of Action "strongly favored agricultural demand-led, industrialization approach and replacement of ISI strategy by export oriented trade strategy taking into account industry related requirements" (Mehta, 2002:66–7).

Furthermore, it is said that the 1981 World Bank report titled, **Accelerated Development in Sub-Saharan Africa**, "marked a watershed in thinking about development in Africa, both in the region and abroad" (Lancaster,

1991:88). Prior to the publication of this report, African leaders had attributed poverty and lack of economic development to the colonial legacy, a hostile international donor community and an unfriendly economic environment. However, the 1981 World Bank report blamed poor government policies for the widespread poverty and economic crisis in Africa. The report called for policy change not more aid, if Africa's economic health was to be restored. Initially, the report generated severe criticism from African leaders, but over time "African officials [at different levels of government] began to echo the analysis of the report" (Lancaster, 1991:89). As a result of such self-reflection "African leaders associated themselves with the ECA/OAU submission ... [to the 1986 Special Session of the UN General Assembly on Africa's economic and social crisis]..., which affirmed the view that economic policies were in need of reform throughout much of the region" (Lancaster, 1991:89). It was widely accepted that in order to promote economic growth and development in Africa, external funding be linked to political and economic reform. But as discussed previously, World Bank/IMF policies which conditioned additional external funding to economic reform in Africa, failed to bring about the desired economic performance. Furthermore, both ECA and international institutions (IFIs) agreed on the need for economic reform and increased production through more efficient use of national resources, but vehemently disagreed over the role of the African states in effectively managing their economies. ECA's African Alternative Framework to Structural Adjustment Programs (or AAF-SAP) envisaged a central role for African states in promoting economic development (Mehta, 2002), while the World Bank and IMF under SAPS sought to reduce and even marginalize the states' role in economic activity.

Africa's persistent economic crisis and political chaos have generated widespread negative images in the media and African scholarship. However, such negative images notwithstanding, "a new generation of enlightened African leaders has now decided to stake Africa's claim to the twenty-first century" (Hope, 2002:387). This new African leadership—which included former President Thebo Mbeki of South Africa as the leading voice—has been calling for the establishment of collective regional or continental institutions to promote economic growth and development throughout the continent in the twenty-first century. The optimism of such leaders which builds upon the 1980 Lagos Plan of Action, rests on the assumption that "despite the poor performance ... there is significant potential for sustained growth and development in Africa" (Mathews, 2001).

There is a new pragmatism among many African leaders in analyzing the region's problems and renewed interest and commitment to collective action and accountability. El Mansour Diop contends that "across the continent, Africans declare that we (sic) will no longer allow ourselves to be conditioned by circumstance" [and adds] "we will determine (sic) our own destiny and call on the rest of the world to complement our own efforts" (2001:2). As a result, "an emerging consensus among African leaders on a common vision for the future is increasingly accompanied by efforts to harmonize and integrate their actions and to assert ownership of their development processes" (Mathews 2001: 124). African leaders themselves are increasingly taking regional or continent-wide development initiatives. It is reported that: "in 1995, they adopted the Cairo Agenda, which identified a number of regional priorities. In May 2000, they reached the long desired goal of establishing an African Union" (Mathews, 2001:125).

Since the 1990s, there have been several initiatives launched by a new generation of African leaders (such as former South African President, Thabo Mbeki, and Paul Kagame, President of Rwanda), with the support of international organizations, especially the United Nations and its various specialized agencies. Regional unity, integration and cooperation "is seen as an answer to the continent's deep and prolonged economic and social crisis" (Worrell, 2001:49). The African Economic Community (AEC) treaty signed in Abuja, Nigeria, in June 1991, sought to achieve a Pan-African Economic Community by the year 2025. According to Worrell (2001):

> The AEC treaty pledged (i) to establish and promote economic, social and cultural development and the integration of the African economies, in order to increase economic self reliance and promote an indigenous and self-sustained development; (ii) to establish on a continental scale, a framework for development, mobilization and utilization of the human and material resources of Africa in order to achieve a self-reliant development; and (iii) to promote cooperation and development in all fields of human endeavor, in order to raise the standard of living of the African peoples, maintain and enhance economic stability, foster close and peaceful relations among member states and contribute to the progress, development and economic integration of the continent [49–50].

Though the Economic Community of West African States (ECOWAS) was established in 1975, the spirit of "new regionalism" manifested itself in … the adoption of a revised treaty of the (ECOWAS) in 1993 and the creation of the Union Economique et Moine Taine Quest Africane in 1994" (Worrell, 2001:50). The new spirit of regionalism also witnessed the reestablishment in 2001 of the defunct East African Community (EAC) and efforts to strengthen the Southern African Development Community (SADC). Worrell (2001) correctly observes that "while the regional integration project has not realized the benefits hoped for, the idea of regional integration has remained more prominent and more strongly asserted in Africa than in any other developing area" (2001:50).

There has been a strong sentiment among African leaders that an effective economic community requires the establishment of a continent-wide political union. This explains why the June 1991 Abuja Treaty establishing the AEC also called for "the creation of an African Union (AU) ... established on May 26, 2001 (Mathews, 2001:xviii). Increasingly, it is asserted that "the only solution for Africa to reverse its marginal status is the self-reliant continental approach in the form of a Pan-African Union Government" (Worrell, 2001:57).

The newest and best known initiative[3] launched in October 2001 by a new generation of African Leaders aimed at spurring growth and reducing poverty on the African continent is the New Partnership for Africa's Development (or NEPAD). The NEPAD initiative is a product of a new generation of enlightened African leaders who consider it as the "road map" for Africa's development or renewal (Taylor, 2002 and Mayaki, 2011). It "seeks to build on and celebrate the achievements of the past, as well as to reflect on the lessons learned through painful experience, so as to establish a partnership that is both credible and capable of implementation" (El Mansour Diop, 2001:6). NEPAD represents "a call for a new relationship of partnership between Africa and the international community, especially the highly industrialized countries, to overcome the development chasm that has widened over centuries of unequal relations" (El Mansour Diop, 2001:2). It also challenges the peoples and governments of Africa to look at development as a process of empowerment and self-reliance. Through this initiative, "Africans are appealing neither for further entrenchment of dependency through aid, nor for marginal concessions" (El Mansour Diop, 2001:2). Rather, the new generation of African leaders want Africans to determine their own destiny and call on the international community to complement their efforts (Makoba, 2011). Thus NEPAD seeks to "move the continent forward from its current state of crisis to one of renewal, bringing with it a better life for all Africans" (Hope, 2002:338). According to Hope, NEPAD "is couched within five core principles-good governance; entrenchment of democracy, peace and security; and domestic ownership and leadership-which are seen as the preconditions for Africa's renewal" (2002:387). These same principles are internationally accepted and recognized as preconditions for renewal and sustainable growth and development.

Beyond the core principles, the initiating/sponsoring African Presidents proposed several programs and projects that were to be undertaken in collaboration with international development partners. Programs identified for fast-tracking include: communicable diseases—HIV/AIDS, malaria, tuberculosis; information and communications technology (ICT); debt reduction and market access (El Mansour Diop, 2001). In addition, a number of projects in agriculture, the private sector, and regional infrastructure were conceived to strengthen national and regional development and to help jump-start "the road towards [Africa's] Renaissance" (Mbeki, 2001:178). In order to assess the required needs or action in the priority areas identified, it was recommended that a needs assessment be undertaken, "progressing from the national level, to the sub-regional levels" (El Mansour Diop, 2001). The NEPAD, known previously as the New African Initiative (or NAI), is a synthesis or hybrid of the following policy proposals:

> ...the Millennium Partnership for the African Recovery Program (MAP), which had its driving force in Presidents Mbeki of South Africa, Bouteflika of Algeria and Obasanjo of Nigeria, and the Omega Plan for Africa which was conceived and sponsored by President Wade of Senegal. [NEPAD] also draws on the **Compact for African Recovery: Operationalizing the Millennium Partnership for the African Recovery Programme** which was prepared by the United Nations Economic Commission for Africa following a request emanating from the African Ministers of Finance Conference held in Addis Ababa in November 2000 [Hope, 2002:388].

It is stated that "the NEPAD ... represents a pledge by African leaders, based on a common vision and a firm and shared connection that they have a pressing duty to eradicate poverty and to place their countries, both individually and collectively, on a path of sustainable growth and development, and at the same time, to participate actively in the world economy and body politic" (Hope, 2002:389). It is a strategy aimed at reducing Africa's marginalization in the global economy, while raising the quality of life of most African people.

In an effort to effectively implement the five core principles of NEPAD, outlined above, several challenges have emerged. The first and most important challenge is the inherent bureaucratic intransigence and institutional in fighting. According to Hope, "too many African initiatives in the past have failed [or performed miserably] as a result of bureaucratic subterfuge and the unchecked egos of political leaders" (2002:398). Many regional initiatives in the past have failed because of a bureaucratic and political leadership that was more concerned with self-promotion (i.e., personal power and prestige) rather than regional interests. To avoid or minimize such behavior or conduct, it is recommended that a neutral monitoring organization be created within civil society that would oversee the successful implementation of the NEPAD. The second implementation challenge is NEPAD's ability/capacity to respond to demands emanating from African countries individually or collectively and from the development partners. In this respect, both the NEPAD Steering Committee and its Secretariat Staff need to "ensure that they are not duplicating what other regional or international organizations have been previously mandated to do nor pursuing country actions that are of low priority in the regional context and [that] may be considered a squandering of resources" (Hope, 2002:399). The third implementation challenge concerns the issue of capacity building. In order to achieve economic growth and sustainable development within the NEPAD framework, capacity building in terms of a mix of human skills, management information systems (MIS) and organizational or institutional development, is very critical. There is a need to build institutional capacity and harmonize institutional arrangements to effect program actions. Development partners working with African countries and leading institutions in these countries should strengthen the capacity at both the human resource and institutional levels. The link between the human resource and institutional level is key to effective implementation of the NEPAD programs and projects. As Hope correctly points out, "both the development and the performance of institutions are functions of human resource capacity, given an environment where institutional development is regarded as beneficial" (2002:399).

The fourth implementation challenge relates to "building continent-wide priorities into national poverty reduction programs and coordinating international support" (Hope, 2002). The NEPAD Secretariat is expected to work closely with various international development partners and national governments to accelerate implementation of the Poverty Reduction Strategy Program (PRSP) and the debt relief under the enhanced Heavily Indebted Poor Countries (HIPC) initiative. The PRSP principles complement the five core principles of the NEPAD as preconditions for Africa's renewal (Hope, 2002:401).

The final implementation challenge concerns domestic ownership and leadership. Ownership is crucial because it facilitates the acceptance of implementation and accountability at the national and local levels. In the case of NEPAD, the perception is that only the African elite and donor partners that participated in its creation. The ordinary Africans or their organizations within the emerging civil society were not consulted during the formulation of NEPAD. Taylor contends that "until a strategy is grounded ... in the ordinary citizens and is founded on basic human needs, any project for renewal is subject to a wide variety of destabilizing forces, not least when elites seek to duck out of the commitments they themselves have made" (2002:411).

One of the earliest efforts to assess NEPAD's achievements to-date has been in the realm of democracy and peace. In a recent study, Taylor "concentrates on holding NEPAD's commitment to democracy and peace—signed by African elites themselves—to account" (2002:403). Using the presidential elections in Zimbabwe as a test case study, he concludes that the manner in which the controversy surrounding the elections was handled by the new generation of African heads of state "has cast serious doubts on the new partnership for Africa's development" (Taylor, 2002:403). It is believed that the failure to denounce the controversial re-election of President Robert Mugabe of Zimbabwe by President Mbeki of South Africa and other proponents of NEPAD has undercut commitment to NEPAD's principles—at least in the short-term. Although good governance and sustainable economic development are critical to NEPAD's success, its component of the Peer Review Process which is voluntary (Mayaki 2011) has not been uniformly applied. Most African countries including Uganda, "have undergone the [review] process but have not yet released the results" (Makoba, 2011:30).

In addition to serious challenges of implementation facing NEPAD and its Peer Review Mechanism, there are concerns that it will fail to achieve the objectives stated in its core principles due to lack of commitment or political will by the new generation of African leaders to act to enforce them. However, it has to be noted that the African leaders who initiated NEPAD view it as a 'road map' "representing perhaps one last hope for Africa to reverse its slide into irrelevance" (Hope, 2002:401). These new leaders share the goal of ending Africa's economic crisis and political chaos through NEPAD. As Taylor writes in his concluding remarks:

> The NEPAD presents a home-grown initiative for development based on a set of core principles that have been embraced by national, regional, and international public opinion as being pre-conditions for the renewal of the African continent. Potentially, it constitutes the most important advance in African development policy during the past four decades (2002:401).

Conclusion

It is evident that during the immediate postcolonial period virtually all African leaders stressed the dual goals of achieving economic growth and improving the well-being of the population. These leaders soon realized that political power without economic control would lead to no desired economic development. Hence these goals fueled the African states' desire (regardless of political ideology) to control economic activity in the hope of accelerating the development process. Rather than promoting economic development, policies of economic and managerial control contributed to the overextension of state resources, thereby putting a heavy burden on the state's capacity to deliver the desired economic development. Personal rule, nepotism, corruption and economic mismanagement compounded the situation, thereby contributing to both economic decline and political chaos that have characterized the African continent since the 1970s through the 1980s and 1990s to the present.

Failure to deliver sustained economic development has exposed African leaders to both internal and external pressures or demands for continued reform. While internal demands pressed for the opening up of political space in the 1990s, international financial institutions with the support of Western governments focused on the linkage between additional external funding and reforms. Given declining economies and failing states, African leaders had no choice but to yield to external demands for economic reforms starting in the 1980s and continuing to the present. As indicated, these reforms were pushed by the Bretton Woods Institutions (i.e., the IMF and World Bank). The conditionalities attached to the reforms were painful to the African leadership and to the general population, but did not deliver the anticipated economic results. This has been likened to giving a patient medicine that either exacerbates the patient's health condition or threatens to kill the patient (Arrighi, 2002).

Continued economic decline in the face of World Bank and IMF imposed economic reforms of the 1980s and 1990s has inevitably contributed to the desire by a new generation of African leaders to consider NEPAD and other regional or continental efforts aimed at reviving African economies. Such collective efforts are both refreshing and promising (Mayaki, 2011). However, they face formidable challenges. And for these efforts to succeed, they will need a committed political leadership with a vision. Whether economic development and democracy ultimately succeed or fail in Sub-Saharan Africa, "will depend ... on the choices, behavior, and decisions of political leaders and [citizen-based] groups" (Inkeles and Sasaki, 1996:404). Such a level of political commitment that was evident in the new generation of African leaders such as former South African President Thabo Mbeki is no longer as widespread on the African continent.

NOTES

1. These critics include a few African leaders such as the late President Julius Nyerere of Tanzania who initially strongly resisted the reforms (also see Haroub Othman 2000 and Bhardwaj 2002: 15), radical African intellectuals as well as the Economic Commission for Africa or ECA—a regional UN agency established in 1958 to "initiate and participate in [UN] measures for facilitating concerted action to relieve the economic and technological problems of Africa."

2. Carol Lancaster, "Economic Reform in Africa: Is It Working?," Olusegun Obasanjo and Hans d'Orville (eds.), *The Leadership Challenge of Economic Reforms in Africa,* Crane Russak, New York, 1991 contradicts this assertion by arguing instead that "the Bank increasingly appears to be taking on responsibility without power over African economic policies, while Africans retain power but diminished responsibility over these same policies" (p. 101). It is important to underscore the fact that the same author acknowledges that "officials of the IFIs, in private moments ... worry about the degree of their influence over policies in Africa" (p. 94).

3. It is important to note that since the majority of organization of African Unity (OAU, now African Union) members adopted the Abuja Treaty of June 3, 1991, there has been a proliferation of regional and continent-wide initiatives, some with the support of international organizations, especially the United Nations and its specialized agencies. These initiatives aim at fostering economic, social, cultural and political integration of the African Continent. Some of these initiatives include the joint conference of Ministers of Finance and Ministers of Planning Meeting in Algiers in May 2001 "underlined the need for a single, integrated initiative ... adopted by the OAU Summit in Lusaka in July 2001" (Mathews 2001: 125). Currently, the Presidents of South Africa, Nigeria and Algeria are "spearheading an initiative for economic and social renewal known as the Millennium Partnership for the African Recovery Program and the President of Senegal is developing the Omega Plan for Africa" (Mathews 2001: 125).

REFERENCES

Amin, A. Ajab. 2013. "Africa's Development: Institutions, Economic Reforms and Growth." *International Journal of Economics and Financial Issues*, 3, 2:324–336.

Amin, A. Ajab. 1999. "Cameroon's Export Crops and the Structural Adjustment Program." *Scandinavian Journal of Development Alternatives and Area Studies*, June and September, 18, 2 and 3:177–185.

Apter, David, and Carl G. Rosberg (Eds.). 1994. *Political Development and the New Realism in Sub-Saharan Africa*. Charlottesville: University Press of Virginia.

Arrighi, Giovanni. 2002. "The African Crisis: World Systemic and Regional Aspects." *New Left Review*, 15:5–36.

Ayittey, George B.N. 1998. *Africa in Chaos*. New York: St. Martin's Press.

Bagire, Vincent, and Juliana Mamada. 2015. "Management Theory, Research and Practice for Sustainable Development in Africa: A Commentary from a Practitioner's Perspective." *Africa Journal of Management*, 1, 1:99–108.

Bhardwaj, K.K. 2002. "Tanzania Towards Sustainable Growth and Enduring Democracy." *Africa Quarterly*, 42, 1: 12–24.

Bird, Graham. 2001. "IMF Programs: Do They Work? Can They Be Made to Work Better?" *World Development*, 29, 11: 1849–1865.

Bryceson, Deborah Fay. 2002. "The Scramble in Africa: Reorienting Rural Livelihoods." *World Development*, 30, 5: 725–739.

Bush, Rau, and Graham Harrison. 2014. "New African Development?" *Review of African Political Economy*, 41, 1–6.

Calamitsis, Evangelos A. 1999. "Adjustment and Growth in Sub-Saharan Africa: The Unfinished Agenda." *Finance and Development*, 36, 1:1–7

Callaghy, Thomas M. 1994. "State, Choice, and Context: Comparative Reflections on Reform and Interactability." In David Apter and Carl G. Rosberg (eds.). *Political Development and the New Realism in Sub-Saharan Africa*. Charlottesville: University Press of Virginia.

Decalo, Samuel. 1992. "The Process, Prospects and Constraints of Democratization in Africa." *African Affairs*, 91: 7–35.

Dicklich, Susan. 1998. "Indigenous NGOS and Political Participation." In Holdger B. Hansen and Michael Tweedle (Eds.), *Developing Uganda*. Oxford: James Currey.

Ebaidalla, Ebaidalla. 2014. "Institutions and Economic Growth in Sub-Saharan Africa: A Panel Data Analysis." *African Journal of Economic and Sustainable Development*, 3, 4: 346–362.

El Mansour Diop, Ahmed. 201. "New Partnership for Africa's Development." *Africa Quarterly*, 41, 4: 1–12.

Falton, Robert Jr. 1992. *Predatory Rule: State and Civil Society in Africa*. Boulder, CO: Lynne Rienner.

Hansen, B. Hölger, and Michael Tweedle (eds.). 1998. *Developing* Uganda. Athens: Ohio University Press.

Heidhues, Franz, and Gideon Obare. 2011. "Lessons from Structural Adjustment Programmes and Their Effects in Africa." *Quarterly Journal of International Agriculture*, 50, 1:55–64.

Honest Account 2017 Report. May 2017. "How the World Profits from Africa's Wealth." Jubilee Debt Campaign. London.

Hope, Kempe Ronald, Sr. 2002. "From Crisis to Renewal: Towards a Successful Implementation of the New Partnership for Africa's Development." *African Affairs*, 101: 387–402.

Inkeles, Alex, and Masamichi Sasaki (Eds.). 1996. *Comparing Nations and Cultures*. Englewood Cliffs, NJ: Prentice Hall.

Kasekende, Louis. 2014. "The Constraints to Structural Transformation in Africa: Suggestions for the Research Agenda." *Journal of African Development*, 16, 1: 119–128.

Kuada, John. 2016. "Culture and Leadership in Africa: A Conceptual Model and Research Agenda." *African Journal of Economic and Management Studies*, 1, 1: 9–24.

Lancaster, Carol 1991. "Economic Reform in Africa: Is It Working?" In Olusegun Obasanjo and Haus d'Orville (eds.), *The Leadership Challenge of Economic Reforms in Africa*. New York: Crane Russak.

Makoba, J. Wagona. 1998. *Government Policy and Public Enterprise Performance in Sub-Saharan Africa*. Lewiston, NY: Edwin Mellen Press.

Makoba, J. Wagona. May, 2001. "Nongovernmental Organizations (NGOS) and State Relations in Third World Countries." (unpublished paper).

Makoba, J. Wagona. 2011. *Rethinking Development Strategies in Africa*. Bern, Switzerland: Peter Lang.

Mathews, K. 2001. "The Role of the United Nations in Support of the Efforts of the African Countries to Achieve Sustainable Development." *Africa Quarterly*, 41, 3: 122–146.

Mayaki, Ibrahim. 2011. "In 10 Years, NEPAD Has Achieved a Lot." *Africa* Renewal, December 2011 (/africarenewal/taxomany/term/335).

Mbaku, John M. 1996. "Bureaucratic Corruption in Africa: The Futility of Clean Up." *The Cato Journal*, 16, 1:1–17.

Mbeki, Thabo. 2001. "Speech of Thabo Mbeki." *Africa Quarterly*, 41, 1–2: 171–178.

Mehta, S.C. 2002. "Structural Adjustment in Africa: A Review Article." *Africa Quarterly*, 42, 1: 61–70.

Mills, Greg, Jeffrey Herbst, Olusegun Obasanjo and Dickie Davis. 2017. *Making Africa Work: A Handbook*. London: Hearst and Company.

Muazu, Ibrahim, Emmanuel Kumi, and Thomas Yeboah. 2015. "Greasing or Sanding the Wheels? Effect of Corruption on Economic Growth in Sub-Saharan Africa." *African Journal of Economic and Sustainable Development*, 4. 4: 157–173.

Mubangizi, John C. 2010. "Democracy and Development in the Age of Globalization: Tensions and Contradictions in the Context of Specific African Challenges." *Law, Democracy, and Development*, 14:1–16.

Ndegwa, Stephen N. 1996. *The Two Faces of Civil Society*. West Hartford, CT.: Kumarian Press.

Nduku, Elizabeth, and John Tenamwenye (eds). 2016. *Corruption in Africa: A Threat to Justice and Sustainable Peace*. Globethics.net; www.globethics.net.

Nürnberger, Klaus. 1998. *Beyond Marx and Market*. Pietermaritzburg, South Africa: Cluster Publications.

Obasanjo, Olusegun, and Hans d'Orville (eds.) 1991. The Leadership Challenge of Economic Reforms in Africa. New York: Crane Russak.

Ogbazghi, Petros B. 2011. "Personal Rule in Africa: The Case of Eritrea." *African Studies Quarterly*, 12, 2:1–25.

Olamosu, Biodun, and Andy Wynne. 2015. "Africa Rising? The Economic History of Sub-Saharan Africa," *International Socialism*, 146:1–21.

Othman, Haroub (Ed.). 2000. *Reflections on Leadership in Africa: Forty Years After Independence*. Brussels: VUB University Press.

Otsuka, Keijiro, and Rie Muraoka. 2017. "A Green Revolution for Sub-Sharan Africa: Past Failures and Future Prospects." *Journal of African Economies*, 26, 1: 173–198.

Senbet, Lemma W., and Witness Simbanegavi. 2017. "Agriculture and Structural Transformation in Africa: An Overview," *Journal of African Economies*, 26, 1: 3–10.

Sharer, Robert L., Hema R. De Zoysa, and Calvin A. McDonald (Eds.). March, 1995. *Uganda: Adjustment with Growth, 1987-94*. Washington, D.C.: International Monetary Fund.

Stein, Howard 1992. "Deindustrialization, Adjustment, the World Bank and the IMF in Africa." *World Development*, 20, 1: 83–95.

Sundaram, Jomo K., Oliver Schwank, and Rudiger Von Arnim. 2011. "Globalization and Development in Sub-Saharan Africa." UN-DESA Working Paper, No. 102.

Tangari, Roger 1985. *Politics in Sub-Saharan Africa*. London: James Currey.

Taylor, Ian. 2002. "Commentary: The New Partnership for Africa's Development and the Zimbabwe Elections: Implications and Prospects for the Future." *African Affairs*, 101: 403–412.

Tordoff, William. 1984. *Governments and Politics in Africa*. Bloomington, Indiana: Indiana University Press.

Udogu, E. Ike. 2016. *Leadership and the Problem of Electoral Democracy in Africa*. Newcastle upon Tyne: Cambridge Scholars Publishing.

UNCTAD. 2001. "Economic Development in Africa: Performance, Prospects and Policy Issues." United Nations, New York and Geneva.

Worrell, Rodney. 2001. "Wither Global Africa? A Case for Pan-Africanism." *Africa Quarterly*, 41, 1–2: 42–60.

Yeboah, Felix K., and Thomas S. Jayne. 2017. "Africa's Evolving Employment Trends: Implications for Economic Transformation." *Africa Growth Agenda*, 14. 1: 18–22.

Microfinance and Financial Inclusion in Africa

Structures, Policy and Issues

SAMUEL WAI JOHNSON, JR.

Introduction

The significance of microfinance in economic development gained currency in the 1990s following the Microcredit Summit of 1997. At this summit world leaders and development advocates declared microfinance (then focused on microcredit) as a powerful tool in the fight against poverty and financial exclusion. This declaration came off the heels of the experiment by Grameen Bank in Bangladesh, whose results challenged earlier perceptions about the financial habits of the poor—that the poor could not save or were unable to timely repay a loan. These findings by Grameen Bank and the Bank Rakyat Indonesia (BRI) in the 1980s about the possibilities of profitable financial services to the impoverished marked the start of the evolution of the microfinance industry. As Robinson (2001:54) states, the 1990s "saw accelerated growth in the large number of microfinance institutions created [with]... increased emphasis on reaching scale."

Along with this growth in the number of microfinance institutions emerged a debate over the appropriate approach for the delivery of microfinance service—the financial system approach versus the poverty lending approach. The financial system approach emphasizes the provision of microfinance services based on the principles of commercialization—profitability and competition. Supporters of the financial system approach believe that subsidized microfinance is unsustainable. This requires charging interest rates based on the cost of microfinance service. The poverty lending approach, on the other hand, emphasizes the social mission of microfinance

–empowering the poor through the provision of subsidized financial services. While the financial system approach relies on interest rate in order to provide microfinance services, the poverty lending approach relies on donor subsidies to finance the provision of microfinance.

Microfinance is not new to Africa. Seibel (2006: 2) traces the existence of the informal microfinance institution of Rotating Savings and Credit Association (ROSCA) to the 16th Century Yorubas of Nigeria, who exported it to the Caribbean, and parts of Southeast Asia. Known across West Africa as susu, ROSCA functions as a social safety net for its members or communities in which it operates through the accumulation and reallocation of scarce resources needed to enhance the productivity of its member. Its original function was the accumulation and reallocation of non-financial resources, such as labor, in a rotating pattern among group members so that they could enhance their agriculture productivity. The non-financial ROSCA was transformed into an institution of financial intermediation with the advent of the monetary economy. Following the experiences of BRI and Grameen Bank, formal microfinance with its varied liability structures has become a fixture on the African microfinance landscape. These liability structures which govern the administration of microfinance loans are the group liability, and the individual liability. Group liability is used by microfinance institutions that do not require tangible assets as collateral in order to award loans, while individual liability is used by microfinance institutions that require tangible asset as collateral for the award of loans. Both the informal and formal microfinance institutions have continued to operate in parallel in various parts of Africa. Nonetheless, many governments across the continent have positioned microfinance, specifically formal microfinance as a primary intervention for financial inclusion.[1] This essay reviews these policies and how they have facilitated financial inclusion in Africa.

The Microfinance-Financial Inclusion Link

The term microfinance refers broadly to the supply of financial services to populations who are impoverished, economically marginalized and unable to access said services from formal financial institutions. These services include credits, savings, remittances and insurance (Ledgerwood & Gibson, 2013; Christen & Rosenberg, 2000). The populations targeted by microfinance are not only impoverished and economically marginalized but are considered high risk because they lack the required collateral and a history of creditworthiness. Microfinance provides financial services to these populations by incorporating the formal rules and arrangements that govern informal financial services in developing countries. These arrangements include the group lending technology through which loans are awarded to a group of individuals who bear the collective responsibility for the repayments by fellow group members. The default by one group member is the liability of the entire group. Through this group lending process, clients self-select themselves into groups of relatively homogenous borrowers based on their respective degrees of risk (Armendariz, & Morduch, 2010).

This minimizes the risk of default, but transfers to clients the microfinance institution's responsibility of screening, monitoring, and enforcing loan agreements with clients, imposing on them an additional cost. Peer pressure is the primary means used by loan group members to enforce the repayments by fellow group members. In some instances, however, group members are ostracized from the activities of their communities just for defaulting in the repayment of their loans. While this sanction minimizes the risk of default, it could have negative consequences for peacebuilding or reconstruction efforts in fragile regions that are recovering from conflict. In spite of this, microfinance is considered an instrument for the financial inclusion of the poor and the population that is been beyond the boundaries of formal finance. Ghosh (2013: 13) cautions however the need for regulatory safeguards to protect the poor from exploitation by profit-making microfinance institutions.

Financial inclusion involves making financial services "available, accessible and affordable to all segments of the population" (World Bank, 2014: 15; The African Development Bank, 2014: 25). Financial inclusion involves a set of initiatives aimed at addressing the factors that exclude a segment of the population from formal financial services; these factors include income level, gender, location, and economic occupation. Groups that have long history of financial exclusion, especially women, and rural dwellers, become special target in this regard. The issues of availability, accessibility, and affordability differentiate individuals who have account with a formal financial institution, such as bank or a formal nonbank financial intermediary, from those who do not. Having a bank account however does on translate into the effective utilization of financial service. The World Bank (2014:1) observes that about six million adult South Africans opened basic bank accounts in 2014, but more than half of these accounts were not used. They became dormant. While not clearly stated, the factors responsible for dormant accounts could range from the prevailing market condition to high banking costs. These factors reduce the ability of account holders to undertake gainful economic activities that would enable them to actively contribute to their economic development and respond appropriately to economic shocks. Focusing therefore only on access and availability gives no clue about the factors that drive the population's demand for or utilization of financial services. For this reason, the Alliance for Financial Inclusion (2013:5) includes "usage" as a dimension of financial inclusion. "Usage" indicates constraints on the ability of account holders to use their accounts, which also has implications for the extent to which formal finance can channel private savings into private investments, highlighting factors that could impede the construction of a financial system that is universally inclusive.

There is a growing body of evidence that suggest the significance of financial inclusion in economic development at both the micro, and macro levels, specifically through the effect of financial inclusion on poverty, income equality and economic growth. Park and Mercado (2015: 4), using a composite measure of financial inclusion, found that higher degree of financial inclusion reduced income inequality in Asia.[2] Access to credit among lower income groups increases their ability to undertake productive economic ventures. Their participation in these ventures helped them develop coping mechanisms to respond effectively to economic shocks and be gainful participants of the economy. Improving access to financial services does not only reduce poverty but inequality, and is complementary to efforts aimed at inclusive growth.

At the macro level, Sahay et al (2015:22) showed that greater access and use of financial services by households and firms have a positive effect on economic growth. This effect on growth however dissipates as the volume of financial services and the proportion of households and firms with access to financial services increase (Sahay et al, 2015:22). Sahay et al (2015: 6) also found that "greater access of firms and households to various banking services, as well as increasing women users of these services, lead to higher growth." This finding suggests that the effect of financial inclusion on economic growth is dependent on the stage of the development of a country's formal financial ecosystem. The formal financial ecosystem includes banks, stock exchanges, insurers, credit unions, and microfinance institutions. The development of a financial ecosystem determines the breadth and penetration of financial services. Financial development does not necessarily lead to financial inclusion, however. Financial sector development can lead to financial inclusion only if the approach to financial development extends the financial frontier beyond what would have been the acceptable boundaries of the financial system towards the access and efficient utilization of financial services by the marginalized and economically less endowed. Thus, as Park and Mercado (2015:17) rightly argue, financial inclusion is more than just the size of the financial sector. It is about ensuring that those left out of the mainstay of the financial ecosystem such as the women, rural and the low-income households are able to access and utilize quality and cost-effective financial services.

This requires a policy environment that positively affects both the supply and demand for financial services. Features of this environment includes macroeconomic stability, appropriate regulatory and supervision that supports the provision and use of sustainable financial services to income groups of the society (Beck, Maimbo, Faye, & Triki, 2011:115; Chibba, 2009:223). These assign a crucial role to government and financial regulatory bodies in the drive for financial inclusion.

Financial Inclusion and Economic Development in Africa

Africa's attempt at financial inclusion dates back to the 1990s when countries on the continent undertook reforms that liberalized their financial systems (Ayeetey, 2008:4). These reforms removed repressive mandatory interest-rate ceilings and other forms of credit controls that were imposed by governments in several countries. The liberalization of the financial sector led to the entry of new participants on the financial landscape across the continent. It widened the space for financial intermediation with an increase in the number of formal financial intermediaries due primarily to a surge in cross-border banking—the expansion of regional or multilateral banking across the continent. Beck (2015:134) groups the ownership of banks operating across the continent into the following categories: domestically owned, subsidiaries or branches of banks headquartered in one of the sub-regions south of the Sahara, subsidiaries of banks headquartered outside of the African continent, foreign owned banks from the emerging markets of China, India, and Malaysia, and foreign owned banks with parentage in the U.S. or Europe. Cross-border banking has changed the landscape of the financial sector across the continent since 2000, with a reduction in the share of domestically owned banks from 54 percent in 2000 to 43 percent in 2009 (Beck, 2015: 134- 135). Meanwhile, the average share of African-owned banks rose by 11 percentage points from 19 percent to 30 percent during the same period (Beck, 2015: 134- 135). Ecobank, for example has presence in 33 African countries south of the Sahara, while the United Bank of Africa (UBA) has presence in 20 countries across the continent.

Bank lending to the private sector increased over lending to the public sector. For instance, Aryeetey (2008:8) notes that the private sector in Ghana received about 62 percent lending in 1996, which was the largest volume of lending ever to the private sector at the time. Lending to the government, on the other hand, as a share of total lending dropped by 35 percentage points in 2005 from 81 percent in 1986. Despite these, the financial sector across the continent remains relatively shallow, less penetrated and vulnerable. The shallowness of a financial sector is measured by the extent to which the private sector is able to use the intermediation power of the financial system for savings and investment decisions (Nyantakyi & Sy, 2015:2; UN, 2013:14). A commonly used indicator of a financial system's shallowness is the proportion of domestic credit extended to the private sector as a percentage of Gross Domestic Product (GDP). The private sector in Sub-Sahara Africa has the lowest volume of domestic credit as a percentage of GDP. The volume of domestic credit extended to the private sector as a share of GDP is about 24 percent (Nyantakyi & Sy, 2015:3), which is nearly half the average for Latin America & Caribbean (about 45.5 percent) and less than a quarter of that for OECD countries (about 134.3 percent) (Nyantakyi & Sy, 2015:3).

Africa has the largest proportion of adults without an account at a formal financial institution, compared to other regions around the globe. As seen in the image below, a little more than a quarter of the adults on the continent had an account at a formal financial institution in 2014 (World Bank, 2014). Access to finance on the continent varies with income levels, gender, socioeconomic occupation, and geography. For instance, more than half the adult population in South Africa (68 percent) has an account at a formal financial institution compare to 3.49 percent in Niger (World Bank, 2014).

Of those with accounts at a formal financial institution, a greater proportion has occupations in the formal sector, which may be due to public sector regulations in some African countries that require public servants to have accounts at formal financial institutions in order to receive their wages. In Liberia, for instance, every employee of the government is required to

Figure 4.1: Percentage of Adults with Account at a Financial Institution by Region

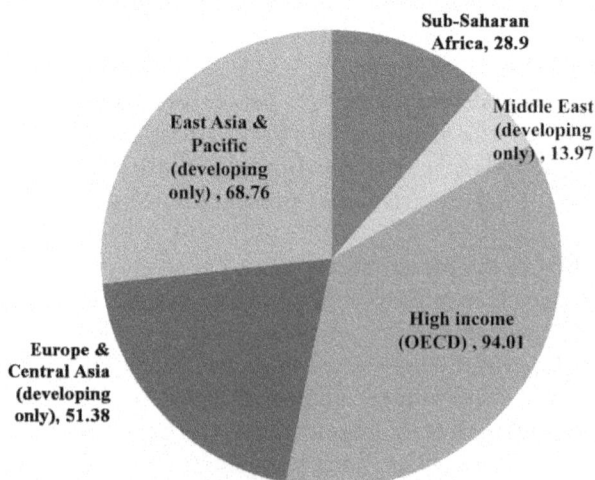

Source: The chart was constructed by the author from data collected from the World Bank, Global Findex, (Washington, D.C.: The World Bank, 2014).

have an account at a bank in order to receive the payment of his or her wages. This policy is geared towards addressing payroll padding in government.

In terms of gender, a lesser proportion of women (about 25 percent) than men (about 33 percent) have access to formal finance, a gap that is attributable to the comparatively lower levels of education and income, and formal employment opportunities among females (World Bank, 2014; Aterido, Beck, and Iacovone, 2013:104).[3]

While these factors explain the lower use of formal financial services by African women, they are beyond the contours of the financial system and speak to the degree of gender inequality in the macroeconomy of the continent. Actions aimed at addressing women's financial exclusion therefore require attention to these factors that contribute to or exacerbate this inequality. In terms of household income, about 20 percent of the poorest 40 percent of households on the continent have accounts at financial institution in contrast to about 35 percent of the richest 60 percent in 2014 (World Bank, 2014). The gap between the richest 60 percent and the poorest 40 percent doubled between 2011 and 2014.

Another factor contributing to the high rate of financial exclusion is the low level of bank penetration. Measured by bank branches per adult users, sub-Saharan Africa has about 3.54 branches per every 1,000 adults (World Bank, 2014), the lowest compared with other regions around the world. This low level of financial penetration, despite financial deepening policies reflects the imperfect nature of the financial system in much of Africa. Speaking about the financial system in developing countries, Stiglitz (1994:20) argues that "much of the rationale for liberalizing financial markets is based neither on a sound economic understanding of how these markets work nor on the potential scope for government intervention." Much of the theories upon which liberalization approaches are built assume that there is perfect information among both consumers and suppliers of financial services. Stiglitz (1994:23) shows that perfect information however does not exist in the financial market of developing countries. Information is not freely available to all. Instead the system is plagued with the challenge of asymmetric information between borrowers and lenders. Wealth holders on the continent keep a substantial fraction of their financial assets outside of the financial system, which weakens the effectiveness of interest rate as a policy instrument.

Microfinance in Africa: Policy and Structure

Microfinance has therefore become the most dominant form of financial service for a large portion of the population in Africa. The structure of the microfinance landscape in Africa is just as geographically disperse and diverse as the continent itself. Microfinance institutions on the continent include non-governmental organizations both for-profit and not-for-profit, credit unions and financial cooperatives, commercial banks, and specialized microfinance banks such as the Access Banks found in Ghana, Nigeria and Liberia. In 2009, for-profit providers accounted for over 70 percent of the total gross loan portfolio for microfinance institutions and 71 percent of total deposits on the continent (MIX & CGAP, 2011:2).

Microfinance institutions (MFIs) use a wide array of approaches including group-lending and individual lending to provide loan and savings or deposit products. The use of these approaches is based primarily on the level of outreach of the MFI, and the environment in which it operates. Microfinance provided loan service to about 9.19 million clients, and deposit-taking (i.e., savings) services to about 20.5 million clients in 2015; the industry has been projected to grow by 15–20 percent in 2016 (MIX, 2016; responsibility Investments AG, 2015:20). Deposit-taking microfinance institutions appear to be the most dominant in the industry, reaching 86 percent of all clients in Sub-Saharan Africa in 2008 (MIX and GCAP, 2010:3). This growth in deposit-making clients was due to a typical reduction in the interest rates on loans. The loan products include business enterprise, and consumption loans. Consumption loans are loans that finance goods or services not intended for use in a business, such as education and housing. More than half of the loans are consumption loans, while a little over 40 percent goes to business development. (UN, 2013:20; MIX & GCAP, 2010:7). South Africa alone accounts for almost half of the volume of consumption loan, followed by Kenya which accounts for over a quarter (MIX and GCAP, 2010:7).

International donors and investors have traditionally provided much of the external funding for microfinance in Africa, and still are for much of the younger microfinance institutions. These include bilateral and multilateral development agencies, foundations, and large non-governmental organizations (NGOs), such as the African Development Bank (AfDB) and the International Fund for Agricultural Development (IFAD). Much of this funding is directed towards specific regions on the continent. One-third of all donor funding that were committed to Africa by the end of 2008 went to Ethiopia, Ghana, Kenya, Mozambique and Uganda (UN, 2013:35). Foundations have been the relatively new entrants into the donor circle for microfinance in Africa. Between 2007 and 2008, foundations' financial commitments to microfinance grew by 53 percent, largely driven by the Bill and Melinda Gates Foundation (MIX and GCAP, 2010:13). But some microfinance institutions have been exploring other funding sources, especially international capital markets and domestic savings in the market in which they operate. By the end of 2008, about 57 percent of microfinance funding was obtained from saving deposits by clients (MIX and GCAP, 2010:13).

In various African countries microfinance has been adopted as an instrument of financial inclusion, with the development of various policy and regulatory frameworks to enhance the growth of microfinance. The Ghana Microfinance Policy (GHAMP, 2006:2), for instance, situates microfinance 'as strategy for wealth creation and poverty reduction" in the country's drive towards attaining a middle income country status, while the National Microfinance Policy of Tanzania (2000:7) aims at establishing "an efficient and effective micro financial system… that serves the low-income segment of the society and thereby contribute to the economic growth and reduction of poverty…" Liberia's sees microfinance as an instrument that facilitates the provision of "diversified and affordable financial services for all Liberians" (Central Bank of Liberia, 2009:ii). The emphasis on "all" Liberians is linked to the country's post-conflict reconstruction agenda, the Poverty Reduction Strategy which seeks to address the perennial social political and economic inequalities that gave rise to the country's unspeakable civil war in 1989–2003.

Like Liberia, Rwanda's National Microfinance Policy Implementation Strategy (NMPIS) establishes microfinance as a major cornerstone in the country's national development architecture, the Economic Development and Poverty Reduction Strategy (EDPRS II). The NMPIS aims to use microfinance to aid the country's poverty reduction through financial inclusion targeting "the formal financial inclusion of 80 percent of the population by 2020" (Rwanda Ministry of Finance and Economic Planning, 2013:9). In Nigeria, the integration of microfinance into the formal financial sector though has been considered crucial to the "provision of timely, diversified, affordable and dependable financial services to the economically active poor"… for increased household productivity and income (Central Bank of Nigeria, 2011:9).

The Journey So Far

Studies evaluating the performance of microfinance have focused mostly on the effects of microfinance on the financial outcomes of clients. These outcomes include the expenditures, and income levels of clients as well as their savings and assets. These outcomes have direct effect on the ability of clients to address their life-cycle needs; emergency needs; and needs arising from existing opportunities (Matin et al, 2002:266–267). Life-cycle needs are needs that can be anticipated and require the accumulation of large sums of money to be addressed; these needs include childbirth, children's education, home construction, funeral expenses and traditional festivals. Emergency needs arise from unanticipated circumstances and require the immediate accumulation or dispersing of cash; these needs arise from wars, a natural disaster, sickness or injury, the loss of a breadwinner, and employment, while opportunity needs arise from the need for capital to start a new business or for the acquisition of assets that enhance the productivity or economic position of the poor.

Dzisi and Obeng (2013:55) report that microfinance clients in Ghana used their loans for either their children's education, healthcare or for investment in the family's business. Dzisi and Obeng (2013:54) observed the difficulties faced by some of the clients in repaying their loans, which they attributed to the unstable flow of income from the businesses to which these loans were applied as capital. Okurut, Banga, and Mukungu (2004:13) estimate that the microfinance loans in Uganda were used for business operations, education, and healthcare. In Nigeria, microfinance provided capital for the development of microenterprises (Olu, 2014:543). According to Olu (2014:543), this role by microfinance helped to increase the flow of capital towards "indigenous entrepreneurship," reducing unemployment and poverty. In another study in Oyo State, Nigeria, Akangbe, Adeola and Ajayi (2012:138) reported however that the clients of microfinance were "not exactly the core or ultra poor."[4]

The targeting of the economically-active poor is based on the drive for financial self-sufficiency by the microfinance institutions. This drive has its basis in the financial systems approach of commercialization, profit-making, and competition, a precondition for support from microfinance funders found mostly in the global north such as private equity funds (Ghosh, 2013:7). Okurut, Banga, and Mukungu (2004:16) describe the economically-active poor as the richest of the poor." They represent a small proportion of the poor. While the average size of their incomes is small, their incomes are large enough to enable their timely loan repayments. The ultra-poor are the poorest of the poor; their income flow is irregular, and inadequate to enable them to repay loans or optimize financial services without other support services as compared to the economically-active poor. Hirschland (2005:5) therefore argues that they are better served with direct aid and not financial services like those provided by microfinance. The ultra-poor are thus largely excluded from microfinance. This strategy has also caused microfinance institution to focus on geographic areas with higher population densities and an economically viable client base. Urban centers tend to be the areas that bear these features in Africa. As a result, microfinance organizations are "less likely to extend finance to the really poor and marginalized" population who are more located in rural areas, leading to "saturation and excess competition [among microfinance institutions] in the local market in ... [urban] ... areas" (Ghosh, 2013: 1208). It is due to this profitability drive that Bateman and Chang (2012:13) have described microfinance as an extension of neoliberal orthodoxies, and a "political barrier to sustainable economic and social development, and... poverty reduction."

The poor state of physical infrastructure, especially road networks, in the rural parts of many African countries has been another factor affecting the provision of financial services. Poor road conditions render some rural areas in accessible. In Liberia, for instance, of the country's total road network of 6,162 miles, only 7.4 percent (456 miles) is paved (Government of Liberia, 2008). Most of the unpaved roads cannot be used during half of the year when there is high rainfall. This increases the cost associated with supplying financial services to the population in these areas. Populations in urban areas therefore become the most cost effective for microfinance organizations.

These constraints contribute to what Mas (2013:306) calls "access" and "usability" barriers for the ultra poor. The case of M-PESA, a mobile money technology platform service in Kenya, has demonstrated however the potential of mobile phone technology to address these barriers. M-PESA was launched in 2007 by mobile communications company, Safaricom, to provide money transfer services through the use of its mobile telephony technology with the aid of its chain of cash merchants or agents across the country. Working with the Kenyan banking sector, Safaricom has expanded its M-PESA platform to allow its customers to safely transfer money, make bills payments, purchases, and cash deposits directly into their bank accounts without the use of liquid cash (Ndirangu & Nyamongo, 2015:167).

This has made financial services, especially money transfer services, available to larger share of the Kenyan population who had been beyond the physical reach of the financial system. Financial transactions through the use of mobile money has increased significantly, doubling the share of the population accessing formal financial services from about 32 percent in 2006 to about 67 percent in 2013 (FSD Kenya, 2013). A recent study by researchers at the Massachusetts Institute of Technology (MIT) shows a reduction in poverty among the users of M-PESA. Despite these gains, the service provided through M-PESA has been mainly the provision of transactional accounts to the public that facilitates their means of bill payment and purchases. These services seem not to be linked to the financial intermediation services provided by the larger financial sector, and unable to facilitate deposits of large amounts of money for longer periods (Mas, 2013:309); Ndirangu & Nyamongo (2015:167). As a result, users of mobile money are unable to take advantage of available credit and insurance facilities that may be offer in the larger financial system.

The experience from the continent's financial liberalization process showed however that financial deepening alone does not necessarily lead to financial inclusion. While deepening may be a necessary condition for financial inclusion, it is an insufficient condition. The advent of formal microfinance has suggested that financial inclusion extends beyond liberalizing the financial system, but creating the conditions that reduce cost associated with reaching financial products that are affordable, accessible, and usable by the poor and marginalized. It is therefore no surprise that various central banks and governments across the continent have mounted a push towards the integration of microfinance into the formal financial systems of their countries as a bid to enhance financial inclusion. Many countries have established microfinance-specific laws based on universally accepted principles of microfinance, while many others including Kenya and the West African Economic and Monetary Union (UEMOA) countries have established specialized units within their central banks for the supervision of the microfinance industry and mobile money development (UN, 2013; MIX and CGAP, 2010).[5] These policies have increased the outreach of microfinance towards the continent's poor and marginalized, notwithstanding the focus more on breadth than depth of coverage.

An expanding market policy environment that is friendly towards microfinance in addition to a strong demand, increasing donors' interest, and the expanding sources of funding for microfinance in Africa have enhanced microfinance growth, and provided reasons for optimism about the prospects of microfinance supply on the continent. However, apart from the recent advances in the use of mobile money in East Africa, the drive for financial inclusion on the continent seems to be emphasizing access to financial capital as the silver-bullet to poverty reduction. This emphasis risks a neglect of the crucial structural conditions that affect the ability of the poor to efficiently access and utilize financial services to accumulate asset and graduate from poverty. While a market-friendly condition provides the incentives for the efficient supply of microfinance, and economic prosperity, the market is a function of the prevailing structural political, social, and economic conditions. These conditions include client targeting and market interference, the state of technology, infrastructure, and financial innovation, and the fragile livelihoods of (potential) clients, which, if not addressed, could make the push for greater financial inclusion elusive. For this reason, conclusion about the effect of microfinance on financial inclusion and the economic development of the continent should be done with caution.

Client Targeting
and Market Interference

The growth and effectiveness of microfinance in accomplishing its social mission on the continent is tied to the growth and structure of its client base. With a population of about 1.2 billion people (United Nations Department of Economic and Social Affairs [UNDESA], 2015:1) an overwhelming majority of the population still have no access to microfinance or other formal financial services. This acutely low enrollment of the population in microfinance service is due primarily to the focus of MFIs on the economically-active which is linked to the desire by microfinance institutions to attain financial self-sufficiency. Attaining financial self-sufficiency means microfinance operations are guided by the principles of profitability, and competition like any commercial enterprise. By these principles, the viability of a microfinance institution is reflected in its ability to earn revenues that can cover the cost of operations, and expand without subsidies. This "discriminatory" approach to outreach is seen as a means of cost minimization. Supporters of the commercialization of microfinance argue that the provision of microfinance service is cost-intensive especially the administration of smaller size loans and outreach to rural areas that have poor transport infrastructure. From a commercial standpoint, it is therefore cost-effective to concentrate on the clients seeking larger loans and in easily accessible locations than the clients in pursuit of smaller loans and in locations that are inaccessible. For this reason microfinance institutions engage in "discriminatory" outreach, emphasizing breadth of clients over depth of poverty, putting the financial mission of microfinance over the social mission. In the absence of any safety net intervention to assist the ultra-poor, this type of approach by microfinance could widen the inequality gap on the continent. In an instance where this widening inequality is perceived as the result of economic discrimination, it could have implications for political instability.

In addition to this style of client targeting, interest charges provide a significant medium for microfinance institutions to become financially self-sufficient. Interest rate is the price paid for a loan. Along with operating expense, interest earnings cover loan loss expense, and cost of funds borrowed from capital markets by microfinance institutions to supply loan facilities to clients. In order to access commercial funding, microfinance institutions are "pressed to keep costs low and generate enough revenues from interest payments on loans to cover those costs" (Armendariz and Morduch, 2010:252). Microfinance institutions in Sub-Saharan have "by far the highest expenses worldwide due to operating expenses…" (CGAP & MIX, 2011:14).

Interest rates on microfinance loans range from 42 percent in Zambia to about 23 percent in Kenya (Boyd, 2013; Ngigi, 2015). However, when compared with the global average, microfinance interest rates in Africa are significantly higher. The Zambia interest rate is about seven percentage points more than the global average of about 35 percent (Kneiding & Rosenberg, 2008). While the rate in Kenya is lower than the global average, it is about eight percentage points higher that the interest rate on loans charged by commercial banks in the country (Ngigi, 2015). Operating expense is the greatest driver of interest rates charged on loans.

There is a recognition among financial policymakers about the high interest rates on microfinance borrowing. Many African countries have therefore established interest rates ceiling to protect microfinance clients from predatory pricing on loans. About 18 of the 48 countries in Sub-Saharan Africa have established interest rate ceilings. These countries include Ghana, Guinea, Eritrea, Mauritania, Namibia, Nigeria, Sudan, South Africa, Zambia, and Zimbabwe and the member countries of the UEMOA (CGAP & MIX, 2011:7).[6] In 2013, the Central Bank of Zambia announced 42 percent as highest annual effective interest rate to be charged on loans offered by non-bank financial institutions, including microfinance institutions. While interest rate ceilings may seem beneficial for the poor, it could have distortive consequences for the microfinance market in the long-run. These include the artificial shortage of available microfinance loans, the exclusion of borrowers who are unable to acquire loans from commercial banks, and the possibility of a higher black market interest rate. Interest rate ceiling is also vulnerable to manipulation by predatory politicians seeking their own self-serving agenda. An alternative policy approach towards reducing the rates of interest could be the provision of interest rate subsidy by government to the microfinance institutions. This subsidy could be aimed at the payment of the wages or salaries of microfinance staff or the provision or the cost associated with reaching a specific clientele.

Infrastructure Constraint

In addition to high labor cost, high risk of loan default or adverse selection by clients is another driver of the high operations cost faced by microfinance institutions. Adverse selection is due to the lack of information about the credit history of clients. Credit history provides information about clients' credit behavior and the use and value of their assets as collateral. The lack of perfect information about clients' credit behavior makes them high-risk borrowers. Government can reduce this risk by improving infrastructure of information flow between clients and microfinance institutions through the establishment of credit bureaus, and public collateral registries to track the credit behavior of clients along with their assets that are used as collateral.

Clients, on the other hand, lack perfect information about the financial health of the suppliers of microfinance services. Clients need information about the financial health of microfinance institutions in order to make rational decisions about their subscription to microfinance services. Information needed to make these decisions include information about the solvency or profitability of the microfinance institution—is the microfinance institution growing profitably or headed for insolvency? The lack of information about microfinance suppliers undermines the sovereignty position of microfinance clients (Todaro & Smith, 2009:767). Governments can enhance client sovereignty by creating institutions that ensure that microfinance institutions make disclose about their solvency and profitability and strengthen the frameworks for consumer protection in their countries.

Linked to the financial infrastructure is the physical infrastructure which facilitates access to markets or areas inhabited by the population. The physical infrastructure in several parts of the continent is in a weak state, inhibiting the free movement of goods and services in addition to the provision of cost-effective financial services. Improving the physical infrastructure will reduce the high cost associated with the provision of financial services to populations in hard-to-reach regions. Foster and Briceño-Garmendia (2010: 6) estimate that the cost of addressing the physical infrastructure needs of Africa at U.S. $93 billion a year, about 15 percent of the continent's GDP. The widespread use of mobile cellular phone technology has created an opportunity for innovation to overcome this high-cost challenge in the supply of financial services to the poor. This innovation is due largely to the high penetration rate of mobile cellular phone on the continent. Africa has a 97-percent mobile phone penetration rate, a rate that is due to the rapid growth in the number of phone users on the continent (International Telecommunications Union, 2015). It has made mobile money more liquid, easily available, and convenient, removing the access barriers faced by the unbanked population in the payment of services and the transfer of cash from one point to another. While mobile cellular phone penetration remains high across the continent, the overall state of information communications technology in many countries does not seem to be fully developed to provide services beyond basic connectivity. With such state, it remains a challenge in these countries to use mobile communications as a platform that allows the population, especially the poor, to access appropriate financial intermediation services and products from the financial sector. In countries that have relatively advanced platforms, mobile money service providers still have a challenge in establishing for their clients a coincidence of time between the expected availability and usage of their money (Mas, 2013:310). Along with this is the issue of whether African financial and communications institutions have the capacity to safeguard these platforms from money laundering. Addressing this challenge, which is crucial to helping the poor build up assets through financial innovation, requires additional investment in telecommunications infrastructure.

Weak Consumer Protection

There have been concerns that the growth in microfinance creates an avenue for predatory interest rate regime by microfinance institutions. This regime has led to the over-indebtedness of clients in parts of Asia. The Client Protection Principles and Codes of Conduct were developed to address these concerns, requiring microfinance institutions to "ensure that credit is given only if borrowers demonstrated an ability to repay and loans will not put borrowers at significant risk of over-indebtedness" (UN, 2013; p. 33). Microfinance institutions are also required to ensure that their "pricing, terms and conditions are set in a way that is both affordable to clients and sustainable for financial institutions" UN, 2013; p. 33). The principles also require MFIs to establish mechanisms for the timely resolution of grievances from clients arising from their transactions with the microfinance institution.

African governments and monetary authorities have endorsed the concept of client protection. The Microfinance Information Exchange (MIX) and the Consultative Group to Assist the Poor (CGAP) reported in 2011 that there were financial consumer protection regulations in about eighty-four percent of African countries. In their evaluation, however, the two organizations described as "weak" the execution of these regulations. They argued that this weakness in the execution of these regulations is because "the institutional structures to enforce legislative requirements are very weak" on the continent (MIX & CGAP, 2011:7). Specifically, MIX and CGAP (2011:7) named the monitoring component as one of the structures that are weakening if not inhibiting the execution of the consumer protection regulations. State MIX and CGAP (2011:7): "…of the range of monitoring actions available to regulators—mystery shopping, consumer interviews, complaints statistics, complaints hotline, monitoring of Web sites/ads, and onsite inspection—onsite inspection is the only compliance monitoring mechanism that exists in a majority of countries." The enforcement arm of the structure on the other hand has been limited to "issuing warnings…[as]… the only enforcement action that is taken by regulators in more than half the countries" (MIX & CGAP, 2011:7). Other available actions such as requiring refunds of excess charges, issuing public notices of violations, withdrawing licenses to operate, withdrawing misleading ads, imposing fines/penalties, and issuing warnings to financial institutions are not taken (MIX & CGAP, 2011:7).

While about half of the countries on the continent have required the establishment of client dispute resolution mechanism by microfinance institutions, this mechanism was present in only 43 percent of the countries. These weaknesses affect the effectiveness and reliability of the regulatory agencies. In the case of monitoring, the reliance on onsite inspection alone limits the amount of information that can be available to the regulatory agency for decisions bordering on client protection against predatory practices, while issuing warnings as the only enforcement action reduces the incentive for deterrence. Cumulatively, these actions leave clients to the devices of the microfinance institutions, and limit the function of the financial protection regulation as effective tool in the fight against predatory and unfair practices.

Fragile and Economically Vulnerable Livelihoods of (Potential) Clients

The clients of microfinance come primarily from the informal sector. Petty trading, primary agriculture, or other forms of microentrepreneurship are largely the primary form of livelihood provided by this sector. Relying on data from the African Development Bank, the UN Economic Commission for Africa (2015:2) estimates that informal employment accounts for about 70 percent of employment in Sub-Saharan Africa, the largest source of employment for women, who are the largest proportion of microfinance clients. While informal sector employment provides an important form of livelihood for the bulk of the population in Africa, it does not guarantee improvement in the economic security of the population. Most of those employed in the informal sector do not have secure income, job security, or social protection. Petty-trading and primary agriculture are prone to seasonal cash flow and have little value-added with very low income, increasing the covariant risks of those employed in the sector, especially during periods of low-yields. The low income is due to diminishing marginal return to investment in the sector on account of the high number of people employed in the sector.

While the income level enables them to access and repay microfinance loans, its fluctuations severely limit their ability to seek progressively higher loans that require larger repayments, making them prone to debt recycling. This results into low saving, inhibiting the ability of clients to engage in income diversification activities, with implications for the larger economy and the pursuit of financial inclusion and inclusive growth. Financial inclusion is more than making financial services available and accessible to the population. It includes the ability of the population to utilize the available financial services to increase their productivity and earn higher income. It is through its effect on productivity and income that microfinance affects financial inclusion and economic growth. But the effect of microfinance on economic growth is dependent significantly on the inclusivity of the growth itself that is a function of the institutional functioning of the country. An economic growth that is inclusive creates equal economic opportunities for all members of the society. This equality of opportunities and economic participation are through sustainable employment or other income-generating opportunities for especially the poor and economically excluded in the wake of growth. These lead to a reduction in inequality and poverty.

This seems not to be the case with the continent, however (Onyiewu, 2015). Africa has the highest rate of inequality and poverty despite experiencing an average growth rate of five percent from 2008–2013, two percentage points above the global average of three percent (Onyiewu, 2015:1). Onyiewu

(2015:39) blames this on the "noninclusivity of economic growth" on the continent. Non-inclusive growth reduces the productivity of the population, sending them especially the impoverished and marginalized, into the informal sector in search of livelihoods. This situation begs policy actions to improve the productivity of the population of the continent, especially the economically marginalized low-income earners in order to enhance their ability to utilize microfinance services effectively for their productivity growth.

Conclusion

Financial inclusion has gained currency in the economic development agenda of sub-Saharan Africa. Governments across the continent believe that access to financial services at an affordable cost facilitates economic growth and reduces inequality and poverty. Microfinance is seen as the platform that can facilitate the supply of financial services at a reasonable cost, given its focus on the poor and economically excluded, including rural dwellers and women. This segment of the population is unable to access the services provided by the commercial banks because of the high operations cost associated with the provision of services to them. This exclusion has created the entry point for microfinance in Africa. Microfinance has continued to experience significant growth in the size of its client base, portfolio size and products, increasing the proportion of the continent's poor having access to financial services. In 2015, microfinance provided loan service to about 9.19 million clients and deposit-taking (i.e., savings) services to about 20.5 million clients in Africa. When considered in the context of a continent with a population of about 1.2 billion people (UNDESA, 2015:15), many of whom are in the informal sector, an overwhelming majority of the continent's population are still with no access to microfinance or other formal financial services. The recent advances in financial innovation in East Africa have shown that microfinance may not be the only means of reaching the poor with financial services. It is therefore important to explore other alternatives that could provide long-term financial services to the poor with appropriate technology that could include such indigenous mechanisms as ROSCAs and ASCAs.

The growth in demand or client size has attracted the attention of donors, although donors' financial commitments have been targeted at specific regions given their market niches. Apart from increased donors' interest, the demand for microfinance has also nudged microfinance institutions to explore other sources of funding; these include borrowing on the international capital markets, and deposit mobilization. While these factors enhance the growth of microfinance, there are other factors that could constrain the expansion of microfinance. These include the focus by microfinance on the economically-active poor, the weak state of the financial and physical infrastructure, the weak protection for microfinance clients, and the fragile and economically vulnerable livelihood of microfinance clients. Collectively, these factors reflect the state of economic inclusion or the inclusivity of economic growth. Economic inclusion reflects the state of equality of opportunities and economic participation within a society and affects the effect of microfinance on financial inclusion and economic development.

This equality of opportunities occurs through the creation of sustainable employment or income-generating opportunities especially for individuals in lower economic rung of society from the dividends of growth. Non-inclusive growth privileges one group of society over the other with access to the dividends of growth; economic opportunities are not equally guaranteed for all. This unequal access to the dividends of growth affects the ability of the excluded to improve their productivity and increase their chances of earning higher incomes. As a result, the informal sector, a sector with no job security, social protection or steady and higher income, becomes the option for livelihood. Bulk of the clients of microfinance has been the economically excluded. They have a relatively lower degree of economic security and are unable to seek bigger loan sizes that have larger repayment requirements. This limits their ability to attain sustenance, self-esteem or economic freedom. The action by governments to economic exclusion, inequality, and poverty through microfinance access is in the right direction. However, further actions are required to improve the productive base of these people so that they can utilize financial services effectively for their productivity growth. Improving their productivity guarantees not only an increase in their incomes but an increase in aggregate demand in the long-run, the ultimate goal for financial inclusion.

NOTES

1. For the rest of this chapter, the term microfinance is used to refer to formal microfinance.

2. The measure contained indicators of access to financial services such as the penetration of automated teller machines (ATM) per 100,000 adults, commercial bank branches per 100,000 adults, and indicators of the usage of financial services, based on the borrowers from commercial banks per 1,000 adults, depositors with commercial banks per 1,000 adults, and domestic credit to GDP ratio.

3. This gap has widened since 2011; in 2011 about 21 percent of women compared to about 26 percent of men had account at a formal financial institution (World Bank, 2014).

4. The social mission emphasizes that microfinance reach the poorest of the poor with cheap capital.

5. The countries that have established microfinance specific laws include Cameroon, Central Africa Republic, Chad, Congo, Equatorial Guinea, and Gabon, Comoros, Democratic Republic of Congo, Djibouti, Ethiopia, The Gambia, Guinea, Kenya, Madagascar, Mauritania Mozambique, Rwanda, Sudan, Uganda, and Zambia. The UEMOA countries are Benin, Burkina Faso, Cote d'Ivoire, Guinea Bissau, Mali, Niger, Senegal, and Togo.

6. These countries are Benin, Burkina Faso, Ivory Coast, Guinea-Bissau, Mali, Niger, Senegal, Togo.

REFERENCES

Akangbe, H.O., Adeola, O.O., and Ajayi A.O. 2012. "The Effectiveness of Microfinance Banks in Reducing the Poverty of Men and Women at Akinyele Local Government, Oyo State Nigeria." *Journal of Development and Agricultural Economics* 4(5), pp. 132–140.

Alliance for Financial Inclusion. 2013. "Measuring Financial Inclusion Core Set of Financial Inclusion Indicators." *Guideline Note* (4).

Armendariz, B., and Morduch, J. 2010. *The Economics of Microfinance*. 2nd Edition. Cambridge: Massachusetts Institute of Technology.

Aryeetey, E. 2008. "From Informal Finance to Formal Finance in Sub-Saharan Africa: Lessons from Linkages Efforts." A paper presented at the High-Level Seminar on Africa Finance, the IMF Institute and the Joint Africa Institute, March 4–5.

Aterido, R., Beck, T., and Iacovone, L. 2013. "Access to Finance in Sub-Saharan Africa: Is There a Gender Gap?" *World Development*. 47, pp. 102–120. https://doi.org/10.1016/j.worlddev. Accessed December 13, 2017.

Bateman, M., and Chang, H.-J. 2012. "Microfinance and the Illusion of Development: From Hubris to Nemesis in Thirty Years." *World Economic Review*, 1, pp. 13–36

Beck, T. 2015. "Cross-Border Banking and Financial Deepening: The African Experience." *Journal of African Economics*, 24 (suppl 1), pp. i32-i45.

Beck, T., Maimbo, S., Faye, I., and Triki, T. 2011. *Financing Africa Through the Crisis and Beyond*. Washington, D.C.: The World Bank.

Boyd, N. 2013. "Bank of Zambia Caps Microfinance Interest Rates at 42%." *MICROCAPITAL BRIEF*. January 18. Retrieved from http://www.microcapital.org/microcapital-brief-bank-of-zambia-caps-microfinance-interest-rates-at-42/. Accessed December 15, 2017.

Central Bank of Liberia. 2009. *The Liberian Strategy for Financial Inclusion (2009–2013)*. Monrovia: Central Bank of Liberia.

Central Bank of Nigeria. 2011. *Revised Microfinance Policy Framework for Nigeria*. Abuja: Central Bank of Nigeria.

CGAP, and MIX. 2010. Sub-Saharan Africa. *Microfinance Analysis and Benchmarking Report 2009*. Retrieved from https://www.cgap.org/sites/default/files/CGAP-MIX-Sub-Saharan-Africa-Microfinance-Analysis-and-Benchmarking-Report-2009-Apr-2010. Accessed November 28, 2017.

CGAP, and MIX. 2011. Sub-Saharan Africa. *Microfinance Analysis and Benchmarking Report 2010*. Retrieved from https://www.cgap.org/sites/default/files/CGAP-MIX-Sub-Saharan-Africa-Microfinance-Analysis-and-Benchmarking-Report-2009-Apr-2010.pdf. Accessed December 14, 2017.

Chibba, M. 2009. "Financial Inclusion, Poverty Reduction and the Millennium Development Goals." *European Journal of Development Research* 21(2), pp. 213–230.

Dzisi, S., and Obeng, F. 2013. Microfinance and the Socio-Economic Wellbeing of Women Entrepreneurs in Ghana. *International Journal of Business and Social Research* 3(11), pp. 45–62.

Foster, V. and Briceño-Garmendia, C. (Eds.). 2010. *Africa's Infrastructure: A Time for Transformation*. Washington, D.C.: World Bank.

Francis, Nathan Okurut, Banga, M., and Mukungu, A 2004. "Microfinance and Poverty Reduction in Uganda: Achievements and Challenges." *Economic Policy Research Centre Research* Series No. 41.

FSD Kenya. 2013. "FinAccess National Survey 2013: Profiling Developments in Financial Access and Usage in Kenya." *Financial Sector Deepening (FSD) Kenya*. Retrieved from http://www.fsdkenya.org/new/finacess-2013-report.html. Accessed December 2, 2017.

Ghosh, J. 2013. "Microfinance and the Challenge of Financial Inclusion for Development." *Cambridge Journal of Economics* 37, 1203–1219. Accessed July 20, 2017 at doi:10.1093/cje/bet042.

Government of Liberia. 2008. *Lift Liberia*. Government of Liberia: Monrovia, Liberia.

Hirschland, M. 2005. "Introduction." In M. Hirschland (Ed.). *Savings Services for the Poor.* Bloomfield, CT: Kumarian Press, pp. 1–11.
International Telecommunication Union .2015. *ICT Facts & Figures: The World in 2015.* Retrieved from https://www.itu.int/en/ITU-D/Statistics/Documents/facts/ICTFacts Figures2015.pdf. Accessed November 27, 2017.
Kneiding, C., and Rosenberg, R. 2008. "Variations in Microcredit Interest Ratea." *CGAP BRIEF,* July 2008. Retrieved from http://www.cgap.org/sites/default/files/CGAP-Brief-Variations-in-Microcredit-Interest-Rates-Jul-2008.pdf. Accessed December 2, 2017.
Ledgerwood, J., and Gibson, A. 2013. "The Evolving Financial Landscape." In J. Ledgerwood, J. Earne, and C. Nelson (Eds.), *The New Microfinance Handbook: A Financial Market System Perspective.* Washington, D.C.: World Bank, pp. 15–48.
Mas, I. 2013." Beyond Products: Building Integrated Customer Experiences on Mobile Phones." In J. Ledgerwood, J. Earne, and C. Nelson (Eds.), *The New Microfinance Handbook: A Financial Market System Perspective.* Washington, D.C.: World Bank, pp. 299–318.
Matin, I., Hulme, D., and Rutherford, S. 2002. "Finance for the Poor Microcredit to Micro-financial Services." *Journal of International Development,* 14, pp. 273–294
Microfinance Information Exchange (MIX). *Market Database.* http://www.themix.org/mixmarket. Accessed November 29, 2017.
Ndirangu, L., and Nyamongo, E.M. 2015. "Financial Innovations and Their Implications for Monetary Policy in Kenya." *Journal of African Economies.* 24 (suppl 1), pp. i46–i71.
Ngigi, G. 2015. "Microfinance Banks Charge High Interest Despite Taking Deposits." *Kenya Business Daily News Online, February 10.* Retrieved from http://www.businessdailyafrica.com/Microfinance-banks-charge-high-interest-despite-taking-deposits/-/539552/2619850/-/4oxgmy/-/index.html. Accessed November 24, 2017.
Nyantakyi, E.B., and Sy, M. 2015. "The Banking System in Africa: Main Facts and Challenges." *Africa Economic Brief.* 6(5), pp. 2–9.
Olu, O. 2009. "Impact of Microfinance on Entrepreneurial Development: The Case of Nigeria." A paper presented at the International Conference on Economics and Administration, Faculty of Administration and Business, University of Bucharest, Romania ICEA—FAA Bucharest, 14–15th November.
Onyiewu, S. 2015. *Merging Issues in Contemporary African Economies: Structure, policy, and Sustainability.* New York: Palgrave Macmillan.
Park, C., and Mercadio, R.V. 2015. Financial inclusion, poverty, and income inequality in developing Asia. *ADB Economics Working Paper Series 426*
responsAbility Investments AG. 2015. *Microfinance Market Outlook 2016: Developments, Forecasts, Trends.* Frankfurt, Germany: responsAbility Investments AG.
Robinson, M.S. 2001. *The Microfinance Revolution: Sustainable Finance for the Poor.* Washington, D.C.: The World Bank.
Rwanda Ministry of Finance and Economic Planning. 2013. "National Microfinance Policy Implementation Strategy 2013–2017: A Roadmap to Financial Inclusion." Kagali, Rwanda: Rwanda Ministry of Finance and Economic Planning.
Sahay, et al. 2015. "Financial Inclusion: Can It Meet Multiple Macroeconomic Goals?" *IMF Staff Discussion Note,* September 2015 SDN/15/17.
Stiglitz, J.E. 1994. "The Role of the State in Financial Markets." *Proceedings of the World Bank Annual Conference on Development Economics,* pp. 19–52.
Tanzania Ministry of Finance. 2000. *National Microfinance Policy.* Dar es Salaam, Tanzania: Government Printer.
Todaro, M.P. and Smith, S.A. 2009. *Economic Development,* 10th edition. London: Pearson.
Triki, Thouraya and Issa Faye (Eds.). 2013. "Introduction." *Financial Inclusion in Africa.* Tunis: African Development Bank.
United Nations. 2013. *Microfinance in Africa: Overview and Suggestions for Action by Stakeholders.* Retrieved from http://www.un.org/en/africa/osaa/pdf/pubs/2013microfinance inafrica.pdf. Accessed December 3, 2017.
United Nations, Department of Economic and Social Affairs, Population Division. 2015. "World Population Prospects: The 2015 Revision, Key Findings and Advance Tables." Working Paper No. ESA/P/WP.241.

World Bank. 2014. *Global Financial Development Report 2014: Financial Inclusion*. Washington, D.C.: World Bank. https://openknowledge.worldbank.org/handle/10986/16238. Accessed November 15, 2017.
World Bank. 2014. "Global Findex (Global Financial Inclusion) Database." Available online at http://databank.worldbank.org/data/reports.aspx?source=1228. Accessed December 3, 2017.

The HIV/AIDS Pandemic and Development in Africa in the Era of Neoliberal Globalization

SAMUEL ZALANGA

Introduction

This essay examines the pandemic of HIV/AIDS in Africa, particularly the Sub-Saharan region. It begins by briefly examining the controversy surrounding the origin of the HIV/AIDS virus and then proceeds to discuss two major approaches to the study of the pandemic: the biomedical / epidemiological approach and the political economy approach. The essay argues that useful as the biomedical / epidemiological approach is, it is limited in dealing with the HIV/AIDS pandemic and therefore the political economy approach needs to be used to complement it. The impact of the pandemic on Africa's development is explored. This is followed by a brief analysis of the role of the United Nations' World Health Organization (WHO) in dealing with the pandemic on a world scale. The essay also analyzes the contribution and limitations of President George W. Bush's effort to alleviate the HIV/ AIDS pandemic in Africa.

In pursuit of broader understanding, the essay elevates the analysis of the pandemic in Africa to the global level by examining the relationship between neoliberal globalization and global public health. Globalization integrates the world community into a global village but in an unequal and asymmetric manner with great unpleasant consequences for the poor. Because of the neoliberal commitment to market fundamentalism, health is increasingly becoming a commodity for sale to those that can afford to pay for it. This is best manifested in the implementation of trade-related intellectual property rights (TRIPS) as part of the World Trade Organization (WTO) charter, which affects the availability of cheap generic drugs to poor countries. The essay asserts that because globalization increases the global risks of public health while simultaneously reducing the capacity of states to deal with it directly, there is a need for a paradigm shift in how the world deals with public health. Health and wellbeing should be treated as a human rights issue and therefore be provided as public good. The essay concludes by raising one fundamental moral and ethical question for our world. Are we willing to live in a world where the rich can live while the poor die because they cannot afford to purchase what they need to maintain their wellbeing in a world that is rich?

The Controversy Over the Origin of HIV/AIDS

There is controversy over the original source of the disease. In one respect, one might argue that the important issue is not to identify the first cause of the disease but its nature and the process of spread of the pandemic and what we can do to control it. Others maintain that we cannot do much in knowing the nature of the disease and how it spreads without knowing how it started. In effect, understanding its origin is considered to be an integral part of the struggle to cure the disease. One theory which has received social support presently asserts that the virus moved from an animal primate to the body of human beings somewhere around Congo Zaire (now Democratic Republic of Congo) between the 1930s and 1950s. Mary Dobson describes this line of reasoning in the following quote:

> The current consensus as to the origin of HIV / AIDS—based on examination of accounts of unusual clinical syndromes in the mide-20th century, testing of blood stored from the 1950s, and computer-generated 'evolutionary trees' of the HIV virus—is that the human disease did probably originate in the western equatorial region of Africa, possibility between the 1930s and the 1950s. HIV-1 (the first of the human viruses to be identified) is closely related to a harmless virus (SIV or Simian Immunodeficiency Virus) of chimpanzees. HIV-2 (a less aggressive form of the human disease identified in West Africa) is more closely related to a virus found in the sooty mangabey, a monkey found in the region, and is possibly the older of the two sub-types. How, when and why either of these viruses crossed the species barrier is a mystery. It is possible that hunters slaughtering chimpanzees or monkeys may have become infected either through cuts, or by eating the meat [Dobson, 2007:196; Frontline, 2006].

It is said that there are many viruses that move from animals to human beings but fail to survive because of differences in species as Dobson highlights above. But for unknown reasons, the HIV/AIDS did find a place to thrive in human body. Once it found a place to live comfortably and thrive in human body, what remains is to explain how it spread. The exchange of germs and viruses between humans and animals is not something unique to Africa because this same kind of process occurred between humans and domestic animals in Europe, and the consequences was initially devastating on human beings (Diamond 2005; Merrill, 2016). But gradually, Europeans developed immunity to domesticated animal germs which was not the case with Native Americans. Consequently, when Europeans came in contact with Native Americans who did not develop such immune system capacity, they died in large numbers because of infectious diseases such as small pox.

Although the HIV/AIDS became part of the human species as far back as between 1930 to 1950, it did not spread very fast because in pre-colonial and early colonial Africa, the movement of people was relatively restricted, marriages were relatively more stable and sexual norms were very conservative (Barnett and Whiteside, 2002; Frontline, 2006; Bond, Kreniske, Susser, and Vincent, 1997; Abdullah and Rashid, 2017). Given that the virus uses network of human relationships and intimate contacts to spread very fast, its spread was initially very slow and negligible. But once people started moving from rural to urban centers or from one region to another as a result of the rapid process of social change unleashed by colonial rule (for example: urbanization and migrant labor system), the disease started spreading very fast. Indeed, the spread became phenomenal in the last three to four decades as Africa underwent rapid process of social and economic changes that have initiated large movements of population and undermined traditional sexual norms and stability of social institutions (Carael and Glynn 2008; Mojola 2014).

Another explanation for the origin and spread of the HIV virus was put forward by Edward Hooper in his theory of contaminated vaccine. Hooper (1999) argues that a polio vaccine that cultivated its ingredients from chimpanzee kidneys created a conducive mechanism for the virus to spread because vaccines were administered to people in rural areas during the colonial and post-colonial eras using the same needle over and over. Dobson summarizes Hoopers' argument as follows:

> In his 1999 book, *The River: A Journey Back to the Source of HIV and AIDS*, Edward Hopper shifted the blame onto Western scientists. He suggested that the origins of HIV / AIDS began in US laboratories in the late 1950s, when researchers trying to develop a polio vaccine inadvertently used infected kidney cells from chimpanzees to culture the polio virus. The vaccine was given to 1 million people in what were then the Belgian colonies of the Congo and Rwanda-Urundi between February 1957 and June 1960 [Dobson, 2007:196].

Research has proved that Hooper's argument is strong but unproven because the original vaccine that was used for polio was found and laboratory analysis did not find anything in the vaccine that is consistent with his allegation that it is the source of the HIV virus. But there are good reasons to agree with his assertion about how "the widespread use of hypodermic needles (often unsterilized and re-used time and again), both in the polio and smallpox eradication campaigns for other purposes" (Dobson, 2007:196), contributed to the spread of the virus, especially when combined with the transfusion of infected blood at a time when the HIV virus was not discovered let alone a test for identifying it. In effect, the disease could have remained restricted if it were not for the problem of using contaminated needle in many African countries (Crawford, 2015). Whatever the value of trying to identify the origin of HIV/AIDS, such an effort is not as productive as understanding approaches to the study of the pandemic, which is the subject of the next section.

Two Major Approaches to the Study of HIV/AIDS

The first dominant approach that has been used to systematically study the HIV/AIDS pandemic is the epidemiological approach (White, 1991; Webb, 2013). The approach essentially uses bio-medical strategies combined with ecological and statistical analysis to study the disease. It fundamentally stresses the scientific process which reduces a disease to the study of people's behavior and how the behavior and life style of some people predisposes them more than others to acquire a disease. In order to study the pandemic very well, the epidemiological approach relies on the strict collection and analysis of data. This is not surprising since the approach stresses strict adherence to the scientific method. But while data collection and analysis is central to any serious attempt to deal with the HIV/AIDS pandemic, in this case there are some limitations to relying solely on the epidemiological approach as an effective strategy for tackling the pandemic (Barnett and Whiteside, 2002:72; Webb, 2013).

Often when data on the pandemic is collected in Africa, there is no distinction made in many cases between HIV infection and AIDS. Yet the two are different. A person can be HIV positive and remain presumably healthy for a considerable period of time. The emergence of full-blown AIDS is an indication of the escalation of the HIV virus undermining the immune system of a person which is measured in CD4 blood cells count. When the virus undermines the immune system to a very low level, then the person develops opportunistic infection (for example: malaria, tuberculosis, skin disease, throat infection). Without any medical assistance to boost the infected person's immune system, the person develops full-blown AIDS, which culminates in death (Whiteside and Sunter, 2007; France, 2017). Unfortunately, the death certificate of many victims of the disease records the opportunistic infection as cause of death instead of HIV/AIDS (Samura: Living With AIDS).

Part of the reason for this is the denial of the reality of AIDS and the stigma attached to it. Understanding the distinction between the two and how or whether an infected person moves from one stage of the disease to another is central to how one approaches the control of the pandemic.

It is also difficult to rely on data because the data collection method and quality varies from one country to another, and within the same country it may vary from one social group to another. Indeed, the data goes through many levels of aggregation as follows: village, district, local government, state, and national levels. The qualification of people collecting and collating the data at different levels varies (Barnett and Whiteside, 2002:52–62; Jacobsen, 2016). This is particularly the case in many countries of Africa where what happens in urban centers is totally different from what the reality is in the rural interior. When data quality is poor because of the way it is collected, it affects the quality of public policy that is fundamentally informed by the epidemiological approach (Esposito 2013).

Important to note also is the fact that the data collected is socially constructed according to a variety of implicit or explicit assumptions which can be a problem because scientific assumptions and categories of reasoning may not fit very well with cultural assumptions and realities in different parts of the world (Barnett and Whiteside, 2002:72; Mertens, Cram and Chilisa, 2013). The same data might mean different things to different people. As some scholars argue, there are no facts but interpretations. Thus, sometimes even when the data is accurately collected, the interpretation of the data might vary from one scholar to the other because of the differences in paradigms that shape the scholars' reasoning. Some Western scholars because of the strong cultural influence of individualism collect and interpret data in Africa from an individualistic framework, while for many African people, life is embedded in the community and the group, with little sense of individual autonomy as is the case in the West. Finally, the data collected may be analyzed and interpreted according to biases which people harbor depending on their scholarly discipline and the human or political interest of the person collecting or interpreting the data. Furthermore, the collected data has political and social ramifications and consequences (Barnett and Whiteside, 2002:55–62; Mertens, Cram and Chilisa, 2013). Persons or social groups infected by the virus have a vested interest in whether they are identified or not because when identified they face stigmatization with serious consequences on their life chances (Epstein, 2007: 141; Liamputton, 2013). Beyond that, research indicates that the epidemiological approach works best if the disease has not reached epidemic level. At that level you can rely on behavior intervention. But once the disease has reached a pandemic level, then one needs to add to the epidemiological / behavioral approach, the political economy approach (Wermuth, 2003:45–56; Bardosh, 2016). It is because of the aforementioned limitations of the epidemiological approach that some scholars argue that a political economy approach should be used to complement the epidemiological approach (Barnett and Whiteside, 2002:80–97: Bardosh 2016).

Research indicates that the same disease can have different trajectory depending on the social and cultural context of a society, the strength of the society's institutions, and the historical forces that promote social stability or disruption (Epstein, 2007:66–95; Kimball, 2017; Abdullah, 2017). All these affect moral values and norms about human sexuality. If the moral values and norms of human sexuality are weakened at a time when there is an epidemic going on simultaneously, the epidemic will escalate into pandemic because of the rapid social changes in the society (Barnett and Whiteside, 2002:84–97; Kimball, 2017; Abdullah, 2017). Thus, the political economy approach examines the role of state institutions, social and economic changes, public policy, degree of social and gender inequality, etc., in order to see how an epidemic can have devastating consequence on a society.

An important point in understanding the HIV/AIDS pandemic from the political economy perspective is to realize that the degree of susceptibility to the disease varies with the degree to which one lives in a "risk environment." Risk environment can be explained this way: "...When a deadly disease appears and the social and economic environment is such as to facilitate rapid and or frequent partner change, then that environment may be described as a risk environment and the act of sexual intercourse becomes a risk behavior. The riskiness of the behavior is a characteristic of the environment rather than of the individuals or the particular practice" (Barnett and Whiteside, 2002:80–97).

The degree of social cohesion, which is measured by the degree of social capital in a society (Putnam, 1993; Wermuth, 2003:24–44; Kawachi, Takao and Subramanian, 2013) is central to explaining the susceptibility of infection to HIV and its spread. Societies with strong social control mechanisms, stability and social institutions that regulate behavior reduce susceptibility and infection. The degree of social inequality, as represented in the form of concentration or distribution of wealth in society is a central factor in explaining the susceptibility and spread of HIV infection. Poverty makes people to discount the future (Sauper, 2007; Human Scale Productions, 2002; Tadele and Kloos, 2013; Smith, 2014). When people are overwhelmed by how to survive today and tomorrow, they cannot easily restrain their behavior even when they know that their behavior may result in HIV infection, which would undermine their ideal future.

When we carefully examine the preceding insights we can easily conclude that the countries in Africa that have been devastated by HIV/AIDS all fit in with the preceding analysis. In South Africa, for instance, a study in

Carletonville affirms this line of argument (Gilgen, Campbell, Williams, Taljaard, and MacPhail, 2000; Aulette-Root and Boonzaier, and Aulette, 2013; Pienaar, 2016). Areas with high migration because of climate / environmental changes and economic malaise, or where war and political instability have created a socially destabilized atmosphere suffer most from the disease (Merson, Black and Mills, 2001:71–75; Muenning and Su, 2013; Semegne, 2012; Gumah 2011; Seckinelgin 2012). The Kagare and Rakai regions of Tanzania and Uganda respectively are border regions close to each other. These are the geographical locations that soldiers went through and settled when they overthrew Idi Amin and Obote (Barnett and Whiteside, 2002:126–156; Seeley, 2015). Sexual norms were highly disrupted in this area because of the destabilizing process of military occupation. The Kilimanjaro region also suffers significantly because of high out-migration owing to climatic and environmental changes that threaten traditional means of livelihood. Migration creates the tendency for multiple sex partners if it is not the whole family that has migrated. Mining regions such as the gold mines of South Africa tend to attract distant migrant labor living without their families in most cases (McDonald, 2000; Barnett and Whiteside, 2002:150–152, 333; Semegne, 2012; Gumah 2011). Consequently, prostitution business develops, which becomes an effective vehicle for the spread of HIV/AIDS. In this respect, the colonial policy of taxing the people of Africa compelled many in all regions of the continent, but particularly the Southern region, to engage in seasonal labor migration in order to earn money to pay their taxes, which is required in foreign currency (McDonald, 2000; Crowder, 1968:333–344; Gardner 2012). The preceding analysis and prognosis have serious implications for how the pandemic affects Africa's development, which is the subject matter of the next section.

The HIV/AIDS Pandemic and Africa's Development

Development at its core is about planning to change now for a better future. There are three core values of development that apply to all people everywhere even if the details or specifics of the content of the values may vary with time and society or culture. To develop is to elevate the standard of living of all the people in a society. And that elevation must be sustained, not haphazard. To be developed is to create a more humane society, a more humane social system and better life for all. There are three core values of development (Todaro and Smith, 2014). The first is: Sustenance—the ability to meet basic needs. All human beings have basic needs that need to be satisfied because they cannot do anything without satisfying those needs. The second core value of development is self-esteem to be a person. What this

means is human beings having reached a stage where they have a deep aware-
ness of being persons with a sense of self-worth, dignity and not being used
as a tool by others for their own ends. Finally, development means, freedom
from servitude, which means being in a position to choose. Freedom as a
core value of development means a state of "emancipation from alienating
material conditions of life and from social servitude to nature, ignorance,
other people, misery institutions, and dogmatic beliefs" (Todaro and Smith,
2014). Many countries seek development not just to help satisfy basic needs
and necessities but to also earn self-esteem and prestige for their countries.
The key issue of concern here is how HIV/ AIDS affect the ability of a society
to achieve the three core values of development as highlighted above.

Unfortunately, HIV/AIDS affects hope for a better future and therefore
development effort becomes extravagantly difficult to sustain under such
conditions. Without effective treatment or control of infection and spread,
HIV/AIDS would not only prevent future development but will reverse or
wipe out a sizeable portion of development achievements since independence
from colonial rule as measured by life expectancy (Garrett, 2005; Nangabo
2012; Johnston, Deane and Rizzo, 2017). While life expectancy as a measure
of development has significantly improved by controlling other infectious
diseases, HIV/AIDS has reversed much of that achievement. Given all these,
unless there is a remarkable change, one cannot seriously plan for economic
development without fundamentally addressing the pandemic.

Specifically, HIV/AIDS would highly undermine the potential for economic development owing to several reasons (Todaro and Smith, 2014). First,
if the infection and spread of HIV/AIDS is not controlled, the prevalence will
continue to be high and that means not only decline in productive human
resources but also lost of productivity and increased expenditure on HIV/AIDS
instead of the broader aspects of healthcare. Second, the more HIV/AIDS
spread, the more environment is nurtured for other killer diseases to flourish
in the form of opportunistic infection that often kill HIV/AIDS patients when
their immune system level is very low and they do not have access to anti-
retroviral therapy that can increase their immune system level (Barnett and
Whiteside, 2002:45; Nolen, 2007:180–207; Pankaj, 2013; Dutsinma, 2013). Many
of the opportunistic infections such as tuberculosis are becoming drug resistant.

Third, HIV/AIDS sicknesses not only result in the lost of the patient's
role as productive member of society, but institutional memory is impacted,
which affects continuity. Furthermore, the labor time of relatives that take
care of the sick is lost and the younger generation remains orphaned after
the death of the parents. Without the opportunity for parental care, the children cannot become productive members of society, thus affecting future
development (Epstein, 2007:228–234; Cheney, 2017). The lack of parental

care often means that the affected will grow up poor and therefore highly predisposed to the risk of being infected with the virus. If they are not infected, without good education or occupational training, even if they grow up and get married, their children will grow up with disadvantage because of their parental background. Finally, the cumulative effect of all the foregoing at the societal level will result in increased poverty and insecurity of livelihood at the community and societal level as more children become orphaned.

In this section of the essay, I want to briefly highlight the impact of HIV/AIDS specifically on some selected sectors of African society. Hopefully, this will complement the brief general discussion above about the impact of HIV/AIDS on development in Africa in the future. The sectors I will briefly highlight are government and the political process, educational demand, educational resources, health sector and for-profit enterprises, and food security.

Government and the Political Process: HIV/AIDS increases the death of the most productive people in society resulting in decisive reduction in the productivity of the society and the tax revenues that can be collected (Botswana Institute for Development Analysis, 2000; Quattek, 2000; United States Department of Agriculture, 2015). It affects the availability of leadership at all levels of society with great implications for the lost of relatively young and energetic leaders with great potential (Garrett, 2005; Joseph 2012). If many of the security forces die because of the pandemic it will affect the stability of the society when it is under emergency for security reasons. Furthermore, the failure of political elites to provide solution to the problem would promote a despondent mood among citizens towards the political system, which can have negative impact on political stability. As the public service loses many experienced elected officials, this may cause inefficiency in the political system. It is also argued that when citizens become desperate for solutions because of the social disorganization caused by the virus, this may lead them to accept any form of government that claims to have answers to their problems (Barnett and Whiteside, 2002:315; Resnick 2013). Finally, if the majority of the citizens in a society believe that they will die anyway because of the pandemic, this would affect their attitude towards citizenship roles given that their life expectancy in some cases is less than forty-years (Barrett and Whiteside, 2002:295–315; Whiteside 2017).

Educational Demand: The HIV/AIDS pandemic will affect the demand for education and given how education is central to being competitive in the global economy, this is a bleak prognosis of Africa's future if nothing changes (Garrett, 2005; Todaro and Smith, 2014; Ijumba, 2011). HIV/AIDS reduce fertility in a society and this lowers school enrollment. It increases infant mortality and the mortality of children which in turn lowers school enrollment (Barrett and Whiteside, 2002:307–312; Mojola 2017). As parents become sick, they will need the assistance of their children, which means increased demand for child labor and this normally lowers school enrollment. The pandemic also reduces family income and this affects school enrolment, especially where education is not free and so families have to pay fees. This is particularly the case when one notes that there are many children that are orphans because of the pandemic (Garrett, 2005; Cheney 2017). Normally, relatives would help them but the widespread nature of the pandemic has undermined the absorptive capacity of social networks and family support system in Africa. It is for this reason that many orphans end up dropping out of school.

Equally important is the fact that HIV/ AIDS-orphan children or children with HIV/AIDS are ostracized by their classmates and sometimes discriminated against by their teachers, which all discourage such children from going to school. It is very evident that HIV/AIDS is impacting school attendance now and will continue to do so in the future (Kauffmann, 2004; Orkin, Boyes, Cluver, and Zhang, 2014).

Educational Resources: Another way that the HIV/AIDS pandemic affects education in Africa is in the form of the impact it makes on limited educational resources to begin with. First, many school teachers are dying because of HIV/AIDS. Consequently, there are increasingly fewer experienced teachers because it takes relatively long time to train and replace teachers. Second, if the teachers are not dead, HIV/AIDS increases staff absenteeism either because the staff is sick or he or she has to take care of a sick relative or attend funeral which has become more frequent because of the pandemic. As HIV/AIDS increases the mortality rate of staff and teachers, the pension system is overwhelmed by increased pay out of benefits to relatives of the dead members of staff or teachers (Barnett and Whiteside, 2002:307–315; Azomahou, Boucekkine, and Diene, 2016).

Education also begins to receive less funding because the HIV/AIDS pandemic requires the government to increase its budgetary spending for health and human welfare and given the limited amount of resources, when health and welfare budgetary spending is increased, the expenditures in other sectors have to be reduced. As educational institutions become less funded, this will have the long term effect of fewer educated people and trained citizens in this era of globalization. All these will not augur well for the future of Africa when human capital investment is the number one factor in economic competitiveness (World Bank, 2000; Elhoweris, 2004: Ijumba 2011).

Health Sector and Programs: The HIV/AIDS pandemic affects the health sector and programs in numerous ways that have implications for Africa's development. First, it increases morbidity and mortality in the population, which has negative impact on productivity. Morbidity and mortality changes the economic resource base of the family, which can set the family in the slow but gradual process of decline. Thus HIV/AIDS affect the economic security of families by making it difficult for the sick person or those who take care of him or her to work (Barnett and Blaikie, 1992:99; Rugamela, 2000; Haacker, 2011; Azomahou, Boucekkine, and Diene, 2016). As many patients report to the hospital and stay for relatively long period of time and needing close supervision, the organizational capacity and resources of hospitals come under stress because there are fewer nurses and doctors. Many doctors and nurses have died because of the HIV/AIDS pandemic.

HIV/AIDS also increases the spread of tuberculosis in the general population given that infected persons with lower immune levels become easy targets for opportunistic infection by such infectious diseases (Barnett and Whiteside, 2002:45; Pankaj, 2013; Dutsinma, 2013). Furthermore, as the expenditure on the HIV/AIDS pandemic is increasing rapidly, other infectious diseases in the Third World that kill people receive less attention because of budgetary constraints. This means an increase in mortality from other killer diseases that have been ignored for expedient reasons. Overall, health workers become discouraged and stressed out because of the enormity of the pandemic. All these suggest the negative impact on the African health sector and programs, especially when developed countries use higher compensation to attract competent health professionals from the developing world to migrate to advanced nations.

Impact on For-Profit Enterprise: Under the hegemony of neoliberal globalization, for-profit enterprise is at the center of the great majority of efforts aimed at promoting economic development in the contemporary world. HIV/AIDS have widespread impact on this sector although for space constraint I can only highlight a few issues (Barnett and Whiteside, 2002:242–270; LUle and Haacker, 2011). For-profit enterprises will experience decline in productivity because of increased absenteeism owing to ill health, caring for the sick, and attending funerals. As many experienced business leaders die, it will be difficult to replace them. At the same time, the recruitment of new employees will cost businesses high because of increased competition. More fearsome is the fact that when for-profit businesses realize the hopelessness of the situation, investors would change their investment decisions if they see their return on investment being affected in the future. Consequently, investors may renegotiate benefits package to employees by shifting more risk to the employees. HIV/AIDS might also change the customer base of a corporation as the disposable income and purchasing power of some groups become less or diminished (Barnett and Whiteside, 2002:247–249; Tadele and Kloos, 2013). Consumption patterns might change as consumers reallocate scare resources. Some investors may introduce new product lines in response to the situation and redirect their marketing strategies to the privileged group of citizens. Finally, as a coping mechanism, some businesses may resort to the use of capital intensive methods of production, which is most likely to benefit the few skilled and highly educated workforce, thereby widening social inequality (Deutsche Securities, 2000; Mateus 2013).

Impact of HIV/AIDS on Food Security: The HIV/AIDS pandemic also affects the food security of families, communities, and societies, especially where it has had a devastating effect. The four elements of food security that HIV/AIDS pandemic impacts are: reduction in availability of food; reduction of assurance of access to sufficient food; reduction in the assurance of stability and proximity in the supply of food items; and reduction in assurance and dependability of the quality of food (Barnett and Blaikie, 1990; Abel, Bell, Blaike, and Cross, 1988; Gillespie 1989; Brenton, Mazzeo and Rodlach, 2011). The mechanisms through which HIV/AIDS impacts food security are: the diversion of productive labor from the farm to caring for the sick; funeral service cost reduces availability of cash which could be used to purchase supplies for the farm; and reduction in crop and livestock yield which affects protein sources for food. The preceding analysis obviously presents a gloomy picture for Sub-Saharan Africa if nothing changes. It is in this respect that the early effort by the United Nations, to combat the HIV/AIDS pandemic is worth examining.

World Health Organization (WHO): Global Program on AIDS (GPA): 1987 to 1995

The main thrust of the GPA's approach to HIV/AIDS was medical and epidemiological. Their focus and approach was short term. This amounts to a rushed fire-service approach. It was built on the model of past experiences with infectious diseases (Garrett, 1995; Wright 2017). The program was composed of short and medium term strategies. It was developed in Geneva and disseminated to Third World regions. Modification of the program was only allowed at the margins based on local experience. The program was developed out of deductive theoretical reasoning. The main goal was to save money for the organization, which in general is not a bad idea (Barnett and Whiteside 2002:74–75). But this is achieved at great cost.

Knowledge and Attitude Studies were conducted at local level so that the director of the program at the local level can acquire information on "local sexual culture." This was aimed at enhancing the director's ability to make implementation adjustments. Later, behavior was added to the mode of intervention which became "Knowledge, Attitude and Practice and Behavior Model" intervention (Kippax and Crawford, 1993; Campbell, 1997:274; Barnett and Whiteside, 2002:74–75; 331; Brehm, 2014). It is rooted in individualistic psychology. The Health Belief Model asserts that any behavior decision made by the individual is a product of his or her knowledge, beliefs and attitudes (Barnett and Whiteside, 2002:75; Merson, Black and Mills, 2001:64–65; Dalal, 2015). Not only does the theory assumes the individual is in full control of his or her actions, but that he or she is rational. The approach emphasizes "intention" and the rational choices made to realize chosen goals. The problem with this approach is that it abstracts human sexuality from its complex socio-cultural context. The approach is rooted in experimental psychology. It ignores the fact that human sexuality is embedded in the social and cultural context of a society (Montano, 1986; Azjen and Eishbeing, 1980; Herdt and Polen-Petit, 2013). This notwithstanding, the strength of the approach is that it has moved beyond the limited focus on body and mind. It widens the dimensions through which the epidemic could be tracked.

Although from 1987 to 1996 the WHO's Global Programs on AIDS recognized that the complexity of the HIV/AIDS pandemic was beyond the biomedical approach, the institution in practice was organizationally resistant to change its modus-operandi and mindset. Consequently, the biomedical approach persisted. The goal was to control the process of transmission of the disease by focusing on "core transmitters" or "super spreaders." But while this approach was feasible for other diseases where the social network of an infected person could be easily tracked, it was extravagantly expensive to do the same for HIV/AIDS patients. Moreover, there was no treatment for HIV/AIDS until 1987 when AZT was approved by the United States Food and Drug Administration and in 1995, the U.S. government approved the use of anti-retroviral therapy (HAART) which is considered to be the most effective drug cocktail against HIV/AIDS (Dobson, 2007:199; Fetene and Mesfin, 2013). The WHO relied on previous experience with epidemic to solve the present one, but the conditions were different. Its organizational capacity was also constrained by personality clash between the then leader of the WHO, Hiroshi Nakajima, who felt threatened by the dynamism and charisma of Jonathan Mann, who was then leading the WHO program on HIV/AIDS (Frontline 2006: The Age of AIDS).

Interestingly, there have been some resistance to the biomedical approach by some scholars that have had long working experiences in developing countries (Epstein, 2007:239–261; Bond, Kreniske, Susser, and Vincent, 1997; Patwardhan, Mutualik and Tillu, 2015). Jonathan Mann and a few of his colleagues working for the GPA and Francois-Xavier Bagnoud Center for Heath and Human Rights have asserted long ago that HIV/AIDS requires more than a biomedical approach if the pandemic is to be effectively tackled (Mann, Tarantola and Netter, 1992; Mann and Tarantola, 1996; Barnett and Whiteside, 2002: 72–78; 415–416; Herdt and Polen-Petit, 2013). This approach to the HIV/AIDS pandemic intricately connects health with human rights and it became the dominant approach at Harvard University where many scholars published works that are grounded in this perspective. It would later significantly influence the work of the United Nations on HIV/AIDS, which was established in 1996 to deal with the global HIV/AIDS pandemic. Barnett and Whiteside, however, assert the following in evaluating the work of UNAIDS vis-à-vis the attempt by the organization to transcend the biomedical approach to tackling HIV/AIDS: "Despite these efforts, until very recently the main focus of UNAIDS and all national and regional programs to do with HIV / AIDS has been on the clinical-medical and behavior levels" ((Barnett and Whiteside, 2002:73). Beyond the United Nations' effort to alleviate the HIV/AIDS pandemic, the effort of President Bush is another landmark effort in this respect. But before even reviewing President's Bush's effort, it must be asserted that the critique of the UNAIDS by Barnett and Whiteside above is also relevant for the effort by the United States to alleviate the HIV/AIDS pandemic.

President Bush and Charity: Alleviating the HIV/AIDS Pandemic in Africa

One of the remarkable positive contributions that came from President George W. Bush's administration to Africa was his decision to spend $15 billion in the form of foreign aid to alleviate poverty, the HIV/AIDS pandemic, and other related development problems in some selected countries in Africa and the Caribbean. He set up an account named "Millennium Challenge Account" under which the $15 billion would be kept for specifically these numerous purposes (Radelet, 2003; Hendrickson, 2014).

It is fair to say that President's Bush's decision to invade Iraq and the strategic failures that followed the occupation of the country would be what most people will remember him for. This notwithstanding, experts in international political economy say that smart nations and politicians always combine the use of hard and soft power (Balaam and Veseth, 2005:18; Wilson, 2008). This makes the push for the new and huge kind of foreign aid to Africa and the Caribbean after the invasion of Iraq strategically meaningful. Yet what is indeed most surprising is that during his first term's presidential campaign, President Bush asserted in answer to a question that he had no special plan for Africa because the continent did not fit the strategic interest of the United States in any way. In this case, his about-turn makes an interesting case study of public policy change within a very short time. Steven Radelet reflects on President Bush's change of heart under a subheading "From AID to AIDS" in his "Foreign Affairs" journal article titled "Bush and Foreign AID." He asserts:

> The President's HIV / AIDS proposal will provide $15 billion -$10 billion of it in new funding—over the next five years to fight the pandemic, including $5 billion to con-

tinue existing programs; $1 billion for the Global Fund to Fight AIDS, Tuberculosis, and Malaria; and $9 billion for a new program called the Emergency Plan for AIDS Relief focused on 14 countries in Africa and the Caribbean. Almost as astonishing as the level of funding was Bush's embrace of a comprehensive approach to fighting the disease, encompassing prevention, care, and treatment and including the provision of antiretroviral drugs. This was a huge step forward for an administration in which several top officials had publicly questioned whether Africans have the capacity to implement treatment programs effectively [Radelet, 2003: 112].

As Radelet indicates above, the U.S. Agency for International Development (USAID) opposed President Bush's proposal to fund the HIV/AIDS rehabilitation and treatment program in Africa. A representative of USAID, namely Andrew Natsios, testified before U.S. Congress that he opposes the program on the basis of practical concerns such as the fact that Africans cannot use triple cocktail because of cultural reasons (PBS NOW, 2005). Apart from the fact that he said Africans operate on a different time frame than Westerners, he also asserted that to implement the AIDS program, there was need for adequate doctors, nurses, good roads for communication and good refrigeration system for the safe keeping of the drugs, which presupposes the availability of electricity. It is commendable that President Bush overcame the USAID bureaucratic reluctance to support the program and the opposition of many conservative members of U.S. Congress that have pursuit the notorious vocation of indiscriminately opposing U.S. foreign Aid in general but to Africa in particular and for HIV/AIDS project in the U.S. and other parts of the world in general (Frontline, 2006).

With the help of some committed American scholars, leaders of religious NGOs such as Franklin Graham, and professionals working outside USAID, and the assistance of frontline medical professionals like Dr. Peter Mugyenyi of Uganda who has been in the forefront of treatment programs for HIV/AIDS patients in Uganda, President Bush convinced the skeptics of his party to support the program (Frontline, 2006; PBS NOW, 2005; Hendrickson, 2014). Dr. Mugyenyi was invited to the White House and he met with President Bush and White House officials who were seeking some legitimate clarifications on concrete and practical issues related to the implementation of the program. On the basis of such consultations, President Bush proposed the fifteen billion dollars as the "Millennium Challenge Account," part of which would be used for the alleviation of HIV/AIDS pandemic in Africa and the Caribbean. Out of the fifteen billion, only one billion was earmarked for the Global Fund for HIV/AIDS, which was under multi-lateral control and supervision. It was agreed that for the program to receive widespread support, it needed to be feasible, bold, and accountable.

It was recognized that the pandemic can affect economic, social development and stability. Colin Powell, the former U.S. Secretary of State once asserted that the pandemic is "a national security problem." Indeed, the national security dimension of HIV/AIDS was identified much earlier under the administration of President Clinton by the "National Intelligence Council" (Radelet, 2003:113; Salaam-Blyther and Kendall, 2012). A session of the United Nations was devoted to discuss the pandemic under U.S. initiative, when Ambassador Richard Hallbrook was the U.S. permanent representative. It was recognized that the disease was spreading to countries that have close economic, business ties, and network of human relations with the U.S. and therefore the disease can spread easily in the U.S. Given that the pandemic uses the network of human relationships to spread, it is easy to appreciate the early acknowledgment of the pandemic as a national security threat to any country in the era of globalization. The Bush program on HIV/AIDS was developed as part of a broader program called "Compact for Development" (Radelet, 2003:108), which was closely tied to U.S. participation in the United Nations' organized initiative on "International Conference on Financing Development." Radelet analyzed President Bush's Millennium Challenge Account, which funded the HIV/AIDS program among other programs (Radelet, 2003:110).

From Radelet's evaluation of the program we can deduce several factors that are considered to be positive innovation in the program, and then we can sum up this section by highlighting the limitations of the program. The selection criteria for countries that would be beneficiaries of the program were very transparent "based on 16 quantitative indicators meant to measure the extent to which countries were 'ruling justly, investing in their people, and establishing economic freedom'" (Radelet, 2003:111). The following indicators are some out of the many that were used in evaluating a country: how a country was doing with budget deficits; trading policies; the rate of immunization of children; the rate at which children completed elementary education; how corruption was tackled; the extent to which the civil liberties of citizens were affirmed, guaranteed and protected. This approach to giving foreign aid was a new phenomenon because it granted relative autonomy to the countries that benefited from it to design and administer the programs while they were held accountable for their performance in serving their citizens. The program was set up in such a way that it was less amenable to political manipulation.

In terms of the limitation of the Millennium Challenge Account, Radelet notes that one major problem among others is the multiple foreign aid programs / bureaucracies, bureaucratic rivalry, and red tape in Washington. It is not clear how all the agencies could agree and cooperate with each other. For instance, USAID's Andrew Natsios was opposed to the program to alleviate HIV/AIDS on practical grounds (PBS NOW, 2005). It was also not clear whether the huge funding of the Millennium Challenge Account would not result in starving other already existing programs such as USAID's "Child Survival and Health Program" (Radelet, 2003:114–115).

One major area of disappointment was how the Bush administration allowed the agenda of the Religious Right rather than tested public health policies to significantly influence funding and program implementation of the HIV/AIDS relief program his government sponsored (PBS NOW, 2005; Demerath, 2007). In brief, the government used acceptance of the faith values of the Religious Right by the foreign aid recipients as a condition for funding their programs. Brazil refused to accept the financial aid from the United States on grounds that their provision of public health services is not premised on the religious beliefs of recipients. To conclude this section, an assertion made by Radelet in concluding his article sums up the major limitation of this kind of charity: "…Foreign aid along will not be enough. Although most of the burden lies with the governments of developing countries to implement sound policies, Washington must rethink some of its national policies that affect these nations, especially in the area of trade" (Radelet, 2003: 115–116). Radelet prioritizes the negative impact of lack of fair trade between developed nations of the Western world and African countries, which cause more harm to the people of Africa, compared to the foreign aid that they are given.

The implication of Radelet's analysis is that the United States needs a holistic approach to dealing with foreign aid, otherwise the policies the country implements to help other countries irrespective of how well intentioned they are, can contradict each other. Some policies might undermine the feasibility of other policies as U.S. international trade policies destroy the source of economic livelihood of many poor people and therefore creating social instability (Klein, 2008; Stiglitz, 2003; Stiglitz, 2012). Interestingly, expressing their concern about charity, Barnett and Whiteside also identify several issues that they have with it. They assert that charity is often "fickle." Furthermore, it assumes the permanent dependence of the poor on the rich. It is also not about augmenting; but rather, it attempts to "substitute for concerted social, economic, and political commitment and action for common welfare" (Barnett and Whiteside 2002:348–349; Morris, 2008).

Radelet (2003), Barnett and Whiteside (2002) are not saying that charity by developed countries per se is bad but they have reservation about a global social order that focuses too much and gives more publicity to charity instead of comprehensive and fundamental changes that need to be made in the structure of the global political economy and social order in order to empower people and remove them from risk environment for HIV/AIDS, such as poverty and hopelessness. In the next section, I intend to briefly examine the relationship between globalization and public health, given the preceding critique of charity, which increasingly substitutes for justice.

Beyond HIV/AIDS Pandemic: Implications of Globalization for Public Health

Globalization surely has the potential to bring about many positive transformations in human societies but it also creates fundamental problems that are not conducive for public health. Unfortunately, much of the public discourse in the West promoting globalization is not nuanced in terms of appreciating its drawbacks, from especially the point of view of vulnerable social groups (Stiglitz, 2006; Stiglitz, 2012). We are told that there is no alternative to neoliberal globalization and the Washington Consensus. The great majority of elites in the developing world benefit from globalization. But because of their position as lackeys or relatively powerlessness in the chessboard of global politics, they often fail to articulate ways that globalization could be made better. Ultimately, the majority of Third World people lose absolutely or relatively in the globalization process (Gates, 2008; Poku and Whitman, 2017).

Globalization is an asymmetrical process of capitalist accumulation and what that means is that it has uneven consequences on different social groups and regions of the world or regions within the same country (Harvey, 2005; Harvey, 2015). It allows capital to move freely while labor is still constrained because of nationalistic immigration laws. The WTO system grants pharmaceutical corporations more power and privileges in their pursuit of profit rather than in prioritizing healthcare provision and access. Pharmaceutical corporations demand unnecessarily longer time for their patents and they file for patents on drugs in such a way that it would take forever for the patents to expire (Stiglitz, 2006:103–132; Stiglitz, 2012). They deliberately extend the life of drug patents to about twenty years thereby extravagantly frustrating efforts aimed at the production of cheap generic drugs to poor people. This is part of the "trade related intellectual property rights (TRIPS) that is part of the World Trade Organization Charter. Similarly, control over and the supply of technology is used as the new method of social control and domination, which complicates Third World development strategies. Instead of focusing on appropriate technology, Third World countries in the name of globalization are forced to embrace sophisticated technologies developed with the aim of saving labor cost in developed countries" (Todaro and Smith, 2009:266–268; Todaro and Smith, 2014). Yet most Third World countries have abundant supply of relatively cheap labor, while capital intensive technology that is not appropriate to their conditions can escalate their unemployment situation, which would in turn create risk environments for diseases by worsening their poverty situation (Anderson and Cavanagh, 2000:1–5; Ford, 2016; Brynjolfsson and McAffee, 2012).

Globalization has brought about shrinkage in time and space as distant parts of the world become closely interconnected because of more efficient means of communication technology such as electronic, digital, satellite, telephone, air and sea travel (Friedman, 2007; Baldwin, 2016). Unfortunately, the shrinkage of time and space makes it difficult to locate or assign responsibility on any specific social agent or actor as was the case during the 2008 global economic meltdown popularly known as the Great Recession. Cause and effect now become widely separated and mediated by time and space. Many nations remain nominally sovereign but in reality some Multinational Corporations (MNCs) are more powerful and richer than the nation-states that they operate within in continents such as Africa. This makes it difficult for governments of Third World countries to always formulate and implement policies that are in the interest of their citizens because neoliberal economic policies, which underpin globalization frown against the governments generating meaningful tax revenue from businesses and corporations (Piketty, 2014;Todaro and Smith, 2009:552; Terreblanche, 2002; Chitonge, 2016; Bijaoui, 2017). Such policies are considered to be a disincentive for shareholders and investors who want a higher return on their investment and lower or no taxes at all, i.e., tax holiday.

But without sufficient financial resources, even when the government of a country is committed to national development, it is constrained in terms of social spending because of the neoliberal policies it has accepted to implement in order to create a conducive business environment that will attract and keep foreign investment (Rodrik, 2012). What this means is that the state's capacity to serve its citizens is mediated by corporate policies and decisions promoted by the WTO in Geneva and the proponents of the Washington Consensus in the United States. It is well known that MNCs are not essentially committed to promoting the welfare of the citizens of the countries they operate or invest in. Milton Friedman argues for instance that the fundamental social responsibility of corporations is to protect the interest of their shareholders (Freidman, 1970; Friedman, 2016).

On the positive side, globalization has created opportunities that facilitate group social networking, and social movements operating on transnational basis (Epstein, 1996; Silva, 2015; McCallum, 2013; Edelman and Borras Jr., 2016). Many have used such social capital and transnational networks in mobilizing moral and cultural capital to challenge Third World government officials that trivialize the HIV/AIDS pandemic (for example: South Africa under President Mbeki); or pharmaceutical corporations that put their pursuit of profit over and above human health and welfare. Interestingly, while it is not deniable that maintaining healthcare and wellbeing in a globalized world requires strategic alliances, social activism, and networking on transnational scale (Brown, 1997; Cohen, 2013), it is also undeniable that not every one in the developing world has the means, wherewithal, and the technical know-how to engage in such transnational networking. This particularly explains why within the African context, the advantage that globalization provides for such transnational networking is best exemplified in the Treatment Action Campaign (TAC) in South Africa led by Zackie Achmat (Nolen, 2007:179–1987).

It is, however, common knowledge that access to the internet, financial means for distant travel and communication are extreme luxuries to many citizens of Africa who are in the category that would benefit most from such transnational networking. Even in Zackie Achmat's South Africa, which is more developed than other African countries, Black people constitute the majority of socially and economically disenfranchised people who live not only in townships but also in informal settlements that are distributed across major cities of South Africa (Terreblanche, 2002; Seekings, Nattrass, and Kasper, 2015). Thus one can conclude that the mediums that bring people together to intervene in public affairs and processes in the era of globalization are far from the reach of the urban poor and peasants.

Overall, one would conclude this section by asserting that globalization increases risks that societies and communities face in the area of health, social stability and human welfare while by the same token, drastically reducing the means and capacity of the government, communities, and people to effectively manage or control the social risks or even share it globally (Wermuth, 2003; Rodrik, 2012; Sparke, 2013).

Conclusion

Based on the analysis of the HIV/ AIDS pandemic by many scholars, there is one fundamental lesson we can draw for the 21st century with regard to public health. The lesson is that globalization as currently structured is "efficient" in providing goods and services but on a purchasing power basis. There is little emphasis in providing public goods. Indeed, every effort is being made to indiscriminately make people to be suspicious of the feasibility of the government or any other similar agency providing public goods informed by the spirit of common human welfare (Friedman and Friedman, 1980; Friedman, 2016). But if the world will not continue in this direction, then global forces will have to be restructured or reconfigured to treat health as a public good that cannot be privatized or limited to an individual's purchasing power in the market. We cannot continue with a globalization that tries to privatize everything including human health and water (CBC Radio, 2003).

Our analysis of the HIV/AIDS pandemic in the era of globalization should lead us to explore the larger question of global public health in the era of globalization. We cannot continue to promote the indiscriminate and doctrinaire privatization of all valued public goods and services because they put the socially and economically disenfranchised people in the world at risk. Yet such risks have the capacity and potential to affect all of us at a time when the world is shrinking in time and space everyday.

REFERENCES

Abdullah, Ibrahim and Rashid Ismail. 2017. *Understanding West Africa's Epidemic: Towards a Political Economy*. London: Zed Books.

Abel, N., Barnett, T., Bell, S., Blaikie, P.M., & Cross, J.S.W. 1988. "The Impact of AIDS on Food Production Systems in East and Central Africa Over the Next Ten Years: A Programmatic Paper." In A. Fleming, Carballo, M., FitzSimons, D., Bailey, M., Mann, J. (Eds.), *The Global Impact of AIDS*. New York: Alan R. Liss, pp. 145–154.

Anderson, S., & Cavanagh, J. 2000. "Top 200: The Rise of Corporate Global Power." Washington, D.C.: Institute of Policy Studies.

Auleette-Root, A., Boomzaier, F., and Aulette, J. 2013. *South African Women Living with HIV: Global Lessons from Local Voices*. Bloomington: Indiana University Press.

Azjen, I., & Fishbein, M. 1980. *Understanding Attitudes and Predicting Social Behavior*. Englewood Cliffs, NJ: Prentice Hall.

Azomahou, T., Boucekkine, R., & Diene, B. 2016. "HIV/AIDS and Development: A Reappraisal of the Productivity and Factor Accumulation Effects," *American Economic Review*. 106(5), pp. 472–477.

Balaam, D.N. &, Veseth, M. 2005. *Introduction to International Political Economy*. 3rd ed. Upper Saddle River, New Jersey: Pearson.

Baldwin, Richard. 2016. The *Great Convergence: Information Technology and the New Globalization*. Cambridge, MA: Belknap Press.

Bardosh, Kevin. 2016. *One Health: Science, Politics and Zoonotic Disease in Africa*. Abingdon-on-Thames: Routledge.

Barnett, T., & Blaikie, P. 1992. *AIDS in Africa: Its Present and Future Impact*. New York: Guilford Press.

Barnett, T., & Whiteside, A. 2002. *AIDS in the Twenty-First Century: Disease and Globalization*. New York: Palgrave Macmillan.

Bijalui, Ilan. 2017. *Multinational Interest and Development in Africa: Establishing a People's Economy*. New York: Palgrave Macmillan.

Bond, G.C., Kreniske, J., Susser, Ida, & Vincent, J. 1997. *AIDS in Africa and the Caribbean*. Boulder, CO: Westview Press.

Bond, G.C., Kreniske J., Susser, Ida, & Vincent J. 1997. "The Anthropology of AIDS in Africa and the Caribbean." In Bond, G.C., Kreniske, J., Susser, Ida, & Vincent, J. (Eds.), *AIDS in Africa and the Caribbean*. Boulder, CO: Westview Press, pp. 3–9.

Botswana Institute for Development Policy Analysis. 2000. *Macroeconomic Impact of HIV/AIDS in Botswana*. Report. (February/March). Gaborone: BIDPA.

Brehm, Barbara. 2014. *Psychology of Health and Fitness: Applications for Behavior Change*. Philadelphia, PA: F.A. Davis Company Publisher.

Brenton, Barrett P., Mazzeo, John, & Rodlach, Alexander. (eds.) 2011. *HIV/AIDS and Food Insecurity in Sub-Saharan Africa: Challenges and Solutions*. Hoboken, NJ: Willey-Blackwell.

Brown, M.P. 1997. *Replacing Citizenship: AIDS Activism & Radical Democracy*. New York: Guilford Press.

Brynjolfsson, Erik, & McAfee, Andrew. 2012. *Race Against the Machine: How the Digital Revolution is Accelerating Innovation, Driving Productivity, and Irreversibly Transforming Employment and the Economy*. Lexington, MA: Digital Frontier Press.

Campbell, C. 1997. "Migrancy, Masculine Identities and AIDS: The Psychosocial Context of HIV Transmission on the South African Gold Mines." *Social Science and Medicine*, 45 (2), pp.273–281.

Canadian Broadcasting Corporation (CBC Radio). 2003. *Water For Profit.* Compact Disc Radio Documentary.

Carael, Michel, & Glynn, Judith. 2008. *HIV, Resurgent Infections and Population Change in Africa.* New York: Springer.

Castells, M. 1996. *The Rise of the Network Society.* Hoboken, NJ: Wiley-Blackwell.

Cheney, Kristen E. 2017. *Crying for Our Elders: African Orphanhood in the Age of HIV and AIDS.* Chicago: University of Chicago Press.

Chitonge, Horman. 2016. *Economic Growth and Development in Africa: Understand Trends and Prospects.* Abingdon-on-Thames: Routledge.

Cohen, Glenn. 2013. *The Globalization of Healthcare: Legal and Ethical Issues.* New York: Oxford University Press.

Crawford, Dorothy H. 2015. *Virus Hunt: The Search for the Origin of HIV/AIDS.* Oxford: Oxford University Press.

Crowder, M. 1968. *West Africa Under Colonial Rule.* Evanston, IL: Northwestern University Press.

Dalal, Ajit K. 2015. *Health Beliefs and Coping with Chronic Diseases.* Thousand Oaks, CA: SAGE Publishers.

Demerath, N.J. 2007. "Dear President Bush: Assessing Religion and Politics During Your Administration for Posteriority," *Sociology of Religion.* 68(1), pp. 5–25.

Deutsche Securities. 2000. *ABI Limited Living With HIV/AIDS: Positioned For Growth.* November 22.

Diamond, J. 2005. *Guns, Germs and Steel.* New York: W.W. Norton & Co. Inc.

Dobson, M. 2007. *Disease: The Extraordinary Stories Behind History's Deadliest Killers.* London: Quercus.

Dutsinma, Usman Aliyu. 2013. *HIV/ AIDS Epidemiology in Kano, Nigeria: Pulmonary Opportunistic Infections, CD$ Count and Viral Loading Testing.* Scholars' Press Publishers.

Edelman, Marc, & Jr. Borras, Saturnino. 2016. *Political Dynamics of Transnational Agrarian Movements.* Black Point, Nova Scotia: Fernwood Books.

Elhowers, Hala. 2004. "Impact of HIV/AIDS on African Educational System and the Role of the American Federation of Teachers (AFT)." *Dialectical Anthropology.* 28(3/4), pp. 329–337.

Epstein, H. 2007. *The Invisible Cure: Africa, the West, and the Fight Against AIDS.* New York: Farrar, Straus and Giroux.

Epstein, S. 1996. *Impure Science: AIDS, Activism, and the Politics of Knowledge.* Oakland: University of California Press.

Esposito, Dominick. 2013. *Reliability and Validity of Data Sources for Outcomes Research and Disease and Health Management Programs.* Lawrenceville, NJ: ISPOR Publishers.

Fetene, Getnet Tizazu and Mesfin, Rachel. 2013. *Antiretroviral Treatment in Sub-Saharan Africa: Challenges and Prospects.* Nazareth, Ethiopia: OSSREA.

Ford, Martin. 2016. *Rise of the Robots: Technology and the Threat of Jobless Future.* New York: Basic Books.

France, David. 2017. *How to Survive a Plague: The Story of How Activists and Scientists Tamed Aids.* New York: Vintage Publishers.

Friedman, M. 1970. *The New York Times.* September 13.

Friedman, M., & Friedman, R. 1980. *Free to Choose: A Personal Statement.* New York: A Harvest Book.

Friedman, Milton. 2016. *Milton Friedman: The Essential Collection.* New York: Bowker Publishers.

Friedman, T. 2007. *The World is Flat 3.0: A Brief History of the Twenty-First Century.* New York: Picador Press.

Frontline. 2006. *The Age of AIDS.* DVD Documentary. Boston: Frontline, WGBH.

Gaimard, Maryse. 2014. *Population and Health in Developing Countries.* New York: Springer.

Gardner, Leigh A. 2012. *Taxing Colonial Africa: The Political Economy of British Imperialism.* Oxford: Oxford University Press.

Garrett, L. 1995. *The Coming Plague: Newly Emerging Diseases in a World out of Balance.* New York: Penguin.

Garrett, L. 2005. "The Lessons of HIV/AIDS." *Foreign Affairs*, 84(4), pp. 51–64.

Gates, B. 2008. "Making Capitalism More Creative." *Time Magazine*, July 31.

Gilgen, D., Campbell, C., Williams, B., Taljaard, D., & MacPhail, C. 2000. *The Natural History of HIV/AIDS in South Africa: A Biomedical and Social Survey in Carletonville*. Johannesburg: Council for Scientific and Industrial Research.

Gillespie, S. 1989. "Potential Impact of AIDS on Farming Systems: A Case Study From Rwanda." *Land Use Policy*. 6, pp. 301–312.

Gumah, Berard. 2011. *Political Economy of the Spread of HIV/AIDS: How Migrants Influence the Spread of HIV/AIDS in Africa*. Saarbrücken, Germany: Lambert Academic Publishing.

Haacker, Markus. 2011. "Framing Aids as Economic Development Challenge." *The Brown Journal of World Affairs*. 17(2), pp. 65–76.

Haacker, Markus, & Lule, Elizabeth. 2011. *The Fiscal Dimension of HIV/AIDS in Botswana, South Africa, Swaziland, and Uganda*. Washington, D.C.: World Bank Publications.

Harvey, David. 2005. *A Brief History of Neoliberalism*. Oxford: Oxford University Press.

Harvey, David. 2015. *Seventeen Contradictions of Capitalism*. Oxford: Oxford University Press.

Herdt, Gilbert, & Polen-Petit, Nicole. 2013. *Human Sexuality: Self, Society and Culture*. New York: McGraw-Hill Education.

Hooper, E. 1999. *The River: A Journey to the Source of HIV and AIDS*. Bel Air, CA: Back Bay Books.

Human Scale Productions. 2002. *Lifecycles: A Story of AIDS in Malawi*. A DVD Documentary.

Ijumba, Nelson. 2011. "Impact of HIV/AIDs on Education and Poverty," *United Nations Chronicle*. 48(1), pp. 18–20.

Jacobsen, Kathryn H. 2016. *Introduction to Health Research Methods*. Burlington, MA: Jones & Bartlett Learning.

Johnston, D., Deane, K., & Rizzo, M. 2017. *The Political Economy of HIV in Africa*. Abingdon-on-Thames: Routledge.

Joseph, Isiah. 2012. *The Impact of HIV/AIDS on Labor Force in Tanzania: The Case of Education Sector in Makete District*. Saarbrücken, Germany: Lambert Academic Publishing.

Kaplan, G.A., & Lynch, J. 1997. Wither Studies on Socioeconomic Foundations of Populations Health? [Editorial]. *American Journal of Public Health*, 87 (9), pp. 1409–1411.

Kauffmann, S. 2004. *Living With Slim: Kids Talk About HIV/AIDS*. Video Documentary. "WWW.nationalfilmnetwork.com/store. Accessed December 13, 2017.

Kawachi, I., Takao, S., & Subramanian, S.V. 2013. *Global Perspectives on Social Capital*. New York: Springer.

Kimball, Ann Marie. 2017. *Risky Trade: Infectious Disease in the Era of Global Trade*. Abingdon-on-Thames: Routledge.

Kippax, S., & Crawford, J. 1993. "Flaws in the Theory of Reasoned Action." In D. Terry, C. Gallois & M. McAmish (eds.), *The Theory of Reasoned Action: Its Application to AIDS-Preventive Behavior*. Oxford: Pergamon, pp. 253–269.

Klein, N. 2008. *The Shock Doctrine: The Rise of Disaster Capitalism*. New York: Picador Press.

Liamputton, Pranee. 2013. *Stigma, Discrimination and Living HIV/ AID: A Cross-Cultural Perspective*. New York: Springer.

Mann, J.M. 1999. "Human Rights and AIDS: The Future of the Pandemic." In J.M. Mann, S. Gruskin, M.A. Grodin, & G.J. Annas (eds.), *Health and Human Rights*. Abingdon-on-Thames: Routledge, pp. 217–226.

Mann, J.M., & Tarantola, D. (eds.,). 1996. *AIDS in the World II*. Oxford: Oxford University Press.

Mann, J.M., Tarantola, D., & Netter, T.W. 1992. (eds.), *AIDS in the World*. Cambridge, MA: Harvard University Press.

Mateus, Antonio. 2013. *The Socioeconomic Impact of Skills Shortage in South Africa*. Saarbrücken, Germany: Lambert Academic Publishing.

McCallum, Jamie K. 2013. *Global Unions, Local Power: The New Spirit of Transnational Labor Organizing*. Ithaca, NY: ILR Press.

McDonald, D.A. 2000. "Towards a Better Understanding of Cross-Border Migration in South

Africa." In D. McDonald (ed.), *On Borders: Perspectives on International Migration in Southern Africa*. Southern African Migration Project: St. Martin's Press, pp. 1–11.

Merrill, Ray M. 2016. 7th Edition. *Introduction to Epidemiology*. Burlington, MA: Bartlett Learning.

Merson, M.H., Black, R.E., & Mills, A.J. 2001. *International Public Health: Disease, Programs, Systems, and Policies*. Gaithersburg, Maryland: Aspen Publishers.

Mertens, Donna M., Cram, F., & Chilisa, B. 2013. *Indigenous Pathways into Social Research: Voices of a New Generation*. Abingdon-on-Thames: Routledge.

Mojola, Sanyu A. 2017. "Aids in Africa: Progress and Obstacles," *Current History*. 116(790), pp. 170–175.

Mojola, Sanyu A. 2014. *Love, Money, and HIV: Becoming a Modern African Woman in the Age of Aids*. Oakland: University of California Press.

Montano, D. 1986. "Predicting and Understanding Influenza Vaccination Behavior: Alternatives to the Health Belief Model." *Medical Care*, 5, pp. 438–453.

Morris, Andrew J.F. 2008. *The Limits of Voluntarism: Charity and Welfare from the New Deal Through the Great Society*. Cambridge: Cambridge University Press.

Muenning, Peter, & Su, Celina. 2013. *Introducing Global Health: Practice, Policy, and Solutions*. Indianapolis, IN: Jossey-Bass.

Nangabo, Simon. 2012. *The Impact of HIV / AIDS on Food Security in Rural Africa: The Impact of HIV /AIDs on Food Security in Rural Sub-Saharan Africa Since 1977: A Case Study of Zambia*. Saarbrücken, Germany: Lambert Academic Publishing.

Nolen, S. 2007. *Stories of AIDS in Africa*. London: Portobello Books.

Orkin, M., Boyers, M.E., Cluver, L., & Zhang Y. 2014. "Pathways to Poor Educational Outcomes for HIV/ AIDS-Affected Youth in South Africa," *Aids Care*. 26(3), pp. 343–350.

Pankaj, Madhu. 2013. *Spectrum of Opportunistic Infections in HIV Disease*. Saarbrücken, Germany: Lambert Academic Publishing.

Patwardhan, B., Mutualik, G., & Tillu, Tirish. 2015. *Integrative Approaches for Health: Biomedical Research, Ayurveda and Yoga*. Cambridge, MA: Academic Press.

Pienaar, K. 2016. *Politics in the Making of HIV/AIDS in South Africa*. New York: Palgrave Macmillan.

Piketty, Thomas. 2014. *Capital in the Twenty-First Century*. Cambridge, MA: Belknap Press.

Poku, Nana, & Whitman, Jim. 2017. *Africa Under Neoliberalism*. Abingdon-on-Thames: Routledge.

Public Broadcasting Corporation (PBS) NOW. 2005:11/04/05. *Global Health: Today's Challenge and America's Response*. Video Documentary.

Public Broadcasting Corporation (PBS). 2006. *Remaking American Medicine*. Video Documentary.

Putnam, R.D. 1993. *Making Democracy Work: Civic Traditions in Modern Italy*. Princeton, NJ: Princeton University Press.

Quattek, K. 2000. "The Economic Impact of AIDS in South Africa: A Dark Cloud on the Horizon." In *Konrad Adenauer Stiftung Occasional Papers, HIV/AIDS: A Threat to the African Renaissance?* Johannesburg.

Radelet, S. 2003. "On the New Foreign Aid." *Foreign Affairs*. 82(5), pp.:104–117.

Resnick, Danielle. 2013. *Urban Poverty and Party Populism in African Democracies*. New York: Cambridge University Press.

Rodrik, Dani. 2012. *The Globalization Paradox: Democracy and the Future of the World Economy*. New York: W.W. Norton & Company.

Roshen, Hendrickson. 2014. "George W. Bush and Africa in the New Millennium." In *Promoting U.S. Investment in Sub-Saharan Africa*. London: Palgrave Macmillan.

Rugamela, G.H.R. 2000. "Coping Strategies: A Global Concept for a Global Epidemic." Unpublished paper, first presented as a lecture in the series "HIV / AIDS: The First Epidemic of Globalization." University of East Anglia: Norwich: School of Development Studies (June).

Salaam-Blyther, Taji and Kendall, Alexander E. 20112. *The Global Fund to Fight Aids, Tuberculosis, and Malaria: Issues for Congress and U.S. Contributions from FY2001 to FY2013*. Washington, D.C.: Congressional Research Series.

Samura, S. nd. *Living With AIDS.* DVD Documentary on Zambia. London: Insight News.

Sauper, H. 2004. *Darwin's Nightmare.* DVD Documentary on the Lake Victoria Region, in Mwanza, Tanzania.

Seckinelgin, Hakan. 2012. *Internal Security, Conflict and Gender: HIV/AIDS is Another War.* Abingdon-on-Thames: Routledge.

Seekings, Jeremey, & Nattrass, Nicoli. 2015. *Policy, Politics and Poverty in South Africa.* New York: Palgrave Macmillan.

Seeley, Jane. 2015. *HIV and East Africa: Thirty Years in the Shadow of an Epidemic.* Abingdon-on-Thames: Routledge.

Semegne, Melesse Tamiru. 2012. *The Role of Migrants and Culture in the Spread of HIV Risk: Northwest West Ethiopia.* Saarbrücken, Germany: Lambert Academic Publishing.

Silva, Eduardo. 2015. *Transnational Activism and National Movements in Latin America: Bridging the Divide.* Abingdon-on-Thames: Routledge.

Smith, Jordan Daniel. 2014. *AIDS Doesn't Show Its Face: Inequality, Morality and Social Change in Nigeria.* Chicago: Chicago University Press.

Sparke, Mattthew. 2013. *Introducing Globalization: Ties, Tensions and Uneven Integration.* Malden, MA: Willey Blackwell.

Stiglitz, Joseph E. 2003. *Globalization and Its Contents.* New York: W.W. Norton and Company.

Stiglitz, Joseph E. 2012. *Globalization and Its Discontents.* New York: Penguin.

Stiglitz, Joseph E. 2006. *Making Globalization Work.* New York: W.W. Norton & Company.

Tadele, Getnet, & Kloos, Helmut. 2013. *Vulnerabilities, Impacts and Responses to HIV/AIDS in Sub-Saharan Africa.* New York: Palgrave Macmillan.

Terreblanche, S. 2002. *A History of Inequality in South Africa 1652–2002.* Scottsville, South Africa: University of Natal Press.

Todaro, M.P., & Smith, S.C. 2003. *Economic Development.* 8th Edition. New York: Pearson.

Todaro, M.P., & Smith, S.C. 2009. *Economic Development.* 10th Edition. New York: Pearson.

Todaro, M.P., & Smith, S.C. 2009. *Economic Development.* 12th Edition. New York: Pearson.

UNAIDS. 2000. *Report on the Global HIV/AIDS Epidemic (June).* Geneva: UNAIDS.

United States Department of Agriculture. 2015. *Resources, Policies, and Agricultural Productivity in Sub-Saharan Africa: Economic Research Report Number 145.* Amazon.Com: Create Space Independent Publication Platform.

Webb, James L.A. 2013. "Historical Epidemiology and Infectious Disease Processes in Africa." *Journal of African History,* 54(1), pp. 3–10.

Wermuth, L. 2003. *Global Inequality and Human Needs: Health and Illness in an Increasingly Uneven World.* New York: Pearson Education.

White, K.L. 1991. *Healing the Schism: Epidemiology, Medicine and the Publics Heath.* Berlin: Springer-Verlag.

Whiteside, Alan. 2017. *HIV & AIDS: A Very Short Introduction.* 2nd Edition. Oxford: Oxford University Press.

Whiteside, Alan, & Sunter, C. 2000. *AIDS: The Challenge for South Africa.* Cape Town: Human and Rousseau Tafelberg.

Wilson, Ernest J. 2008. "Hard Power, Soft Power, Smart Power." In *Annals of the American Academy of Political and Social Science,* Volume 616, Public Diplomacy in a Changing World, March: 110–124.

World Bank. 2000. *Can Africa Claim the 21st Century?* Washington, D.C.: World Bank.

Wright, Jennifer. 2017. *Get Well Soon: History's Worst Plagues and the Heroes Who Fought Them.* New York: Henry Holt and Co.

Higher Education in Africa

Challenges and Prospects

DAVID N.P. MBURU

Introduction

Higher education participation has been growing markedly around the world especially since the 1960s (Gomes 2007:3). In the era of neoliberalism and massification, the biggest challenge in higher education in Africa has been on how to balance between the tripartite of access, quality and funding of higher education. In most African countries, higher education has been traditionally the prerogative of the elite and the privileged few in society. The situation has not been made better with the International Monetary Fund (IMF) and World Bank (WB) engineered policy of cost sharing. The policy was guided by the fact that the highest beneficiaries of higher education were deemed as the individuals and their families, unlike in primary schools that were believed to have yielded higher social returns (Gomer 2007:5). Even more importantly, investments in higher education have often been considered regressive, reproducing existing social and economic inequalities (USAID 2014: iii). While enrollment has increased at the primary and secondary school levels, similar trends have not been reflected at the postsecondary institutions (UNESCO-UIS 2009). Students in these institutions have grown from five to six million, resulting in an average enrollment of 8.6 percent, with Sub-Saharan Africa recording the highest growth rate in the world (UNESCO-UIS 2009:10). But Africa contributes only 1 percent of the global knowledge, the lowest in the world (UNESCO 2015:19).

It is important that for any education equity to be achieved, the circle of opportunities should be expanded to those who are marginalized. The government should work toward reducing barriers to educational access, increasing equity and transforming the developmental prospects of individuals and nation states (Lewin 2007:6). In Africa the challenge is to increase participation for the entire age and make it possible for any student who aspires to attain higher education to do so without any inhibition. In Africa, access to higher education has been evenly distributed in relation to household wealth. In most poor countries in the world, the discrepancies in higher education relate to location, gender, and cultural affiliation, among others, and which continue to exist in society and are now becoming more conspicuous (Lewin 2007:3). In Africa the challenge is to increase participation for the entire age cohort. This is because even with the rapid growth in enrollment in higher education institutions in SSA, the gross enrollment ratio for higher education is the lowest in the world, at 7.6 percent in 2011(USAID 2014: 20). Countries in the region continue to struggle with limited capacity, overcrowding, limited infrastructure, inadequate management, poor student preparation, and high cost of instructional materials (Bloom, et al 2005:6). University massification has also seen the reinforcement of patriarchal system that favors a male patronage system that penalizes women while devaluing their work and ideas (Munene 2015:7).

Globalization has also had a major effect on education in Africa with the free flow of people, culture, ideas, values, knowledge and technology across borders. This has also created a need for strengthening quality of education and improving on certification (Knight 2006:17). Although cross-border higher education has improved access but most participants of cross-border education come from the middle and upper middle class. Most institutions were also found to be of questionable credentials and hence the importance of strengthening the accreditation process of cross border institutions.

There is also a need to improve on education financing in order to give an equal opportunity to all stakeholders in education. This comes especially in the wake of neoliberalism, of government disengagement from higher education, and healthy and service provision to a more competitive market place approach of cost sharing and cooperation with the industrial world in research (Munene 2015:1). Cost sharing is seen as the way out of preventing a development of a low cost education. The most significant challenge of higher education has been on improving relevance and quality. The quality of higher education has been severely compromised by enrollment expansion, low quality instruction and lack of financial resources (USAID 2014:21).

Overview of the Historical Background of Higher Education in Africa

The history of higher education in Africa has mostly some similar and common elements (Atuahene 2006:15). The legacy of colonialism remains a central factor in higher education in Africa and the ties with the former colonizers have remained. Colonial and postcolonial policies denied most Africans the opportunity to have higher education. The rise in population necessitated the need for creation of more secondary schools and the consequential demand for tertiary education (Atuahene 2006: 6). In East Africa after the Currie Report of 1933, the architects of higher education envisioned a system that would almost wholly be financed by the state. According to the Currie Report, there was a link between the social demand and the possibility of increased social, cultural, economic and political returns from investing in education (Musisi & Mayega 2010:195). The Channon Report recommended for the abolition of fees in the colonies and provided a cost-benefit analysis to justify the proportion of public funding which would be necessary for the provision of higher education. It was assumed that the financial responsibility for higher education in the colonies would lie with the British Government for the foreseeable future (Musisi & Mayega 2010:195). Access to higher education was to be dependent on merit and open to students from all social classes. Scholarship was to be awarded on merit to a selected few (Pillay 2010). In South Africa the colonial tertiary education funding policies mirrored the apartheid's division model. But in 1997 the government announced its intention of steering higher education towards the goals established in the National Plan for the transformation of the higher education system.

In most post-independent African countries education had become increasingly state driven (Mohadeb 2010:81). The governments extended free education for the limited student capacity available domestically to the higher education sector. In Tanzania, the government retained the free market economy it inherited from colonial rule but this radically changed in 1967 with the Arusha Declaration. The Arusha Declaration led to nationalization and the abolition of school fees and tuition in higher education. In 1974, the government abolished the bursary system and took over the responsibility of paying all the costs for higher education (Ishengoma 2010: 174). This continued until 1992 when cost sharing was reinstituted. But in the 1980s the financing of education in most African countries was greatly influenced by the World Bank and a neoliberal policy framework that led to the marginalization of many students.

Access and Equity in Higher Education

The access rate in higher education varies widely across the world with Sub-Saharan Africa having the lowest participation rate with only 5 percent of the age cohort being enrolled (Gomes 2007:1). Countries in Sub-Saharan

Africa struggle with limited capacity, overcrowding, limited infrastructure, inadequate management, poor student preparation and high cost of education (Bloom et al 2005: 6). Traditionally, higher education has been the prerogative of the privileged few, a preserve of the cultured class everywhere (Pityana (nd:2). But in spite of the massive developments over the years, there still exist accessibility and participation gap with respect to students' socioeconomic status, gender, regions of origin and the type and location of secondary school attended (Atuahene & Owusu-Ansah 2013:1). In some regions, massification started right after the second world-war, while in many other countries the university is still the privilege of a few. The expansion of education in general and of tertiary education in particular is associated with a marked social change and is a prerequisite of economic development. In most societies, higher education is seen as an important factor for upward social mobility and access has an immense power as the gatekeeper to individual promotion with very important private gains but equally relevant benefits for the whole society (Gomes 2007:1).

The importance of equal access to higher education was emphasized repeatedly in the declarations that emerged from the 1998 World Conference on Education. Inequality tends to sustain itself unless there is intervention of some kind. Article 26(1) of the Universal Declaration of Human Rights proclaims that higher education shall be accessible to all on the basis of merit (Atbach, Reisberg & Rumbley, 2009). Although much progress has been made, too many countries still enroll only a small percentage of qualified students (Atbach, 2009:37). Within most nations, access to higher education is still a preserve of a specific segment of society (Atbach, 2009).

Factors that Contribute to Inequalities in Higher Education in Africa

Access, Equity and Higher Education Admission Exam

Admission to public and private universities in most African countries is determined by the students' performance in the national high school exit examination. According to Gomes (2007: 6) disadvantaged students tend to not only perform below their potential in entrance tests, but they also find further difficulties in adapting to university academic life and need active strategies to avoid mass desertion. Yakaboski and Nolan (2011:6) observe that most education systems do not provide true universal access to primary and secondary levels, and as students move up the education ladder to the university, it becomes even more inaccessible due to limited availability of university spots. Gomes further argues that testing is normally biased towards the assessment of the information stored by the student as "intelligence" and real testing is more illusive. The performance in exams depends on how well students are prepared and students from elite schools perform better, thus reproducing social inequalities. A fair ability test to be passed by a heterogeneous population simply does not exist.

The national examination has been used in most countries to ration admission to tertiary institutions (Atbach et al 2009:43). Atbach further asserts that merit is assumed to make opportunities available equally if all aspirants are evaluated by using the same criteria. Yet because of many influential variables used, this is not the case. Traditional beliefs about meritocracy tend to reproduce privileges and exclusion in society. In a study of admission in two universities in Ghana, Addae-Mensah (2000:24) found out that the majority of the students admitted to the University of Ghana and Kwame Nkrumah University were from the country's top 50 schools, which reflected less than ten percent of the country's schools. Addae-Mensah equally observes that students from these schools also dominated in the prestigious courses like medicine and engineering, while 300 out of 504 schools in Ghana could not get a single student to the university. According to Odour (2015), in the 2015/2016 academic year, 149,717 students in Kenya scored the minimum university entrance score of C+, but the Kenya Universities and Colleges Central Placement Service (KUCCPS) could only admit 67,790 students. Most of these students were from the better equipped schools. The situation was the same in Tanzania where students from elite schools were selected to join higher education. In Nigeria, an average of 1.5 million students take the Unified Tertiary and Matriculation Examination (UTME) for entrance to tertiary institutions; and in order for one to qualify for admission, one has to score a minimum of 200 out of the total 400 points. This intake represents only 40 percent of the test takers leaving, out the sizable number of qualified students (WENR, 2011).

According to (Buchere 2009) most of the students who failed to be admitted to government sponsored courses, had to fight it out for spaces in private universities or enroll in the 'costly parallel programs. Female students were also less likely to enroll in faculties and professional programs requiring passes in science subjects because of their inadequate preparation and poor performance in university entrance exams (Eisemon & Salmi 1995:6). Those who attend the private universities; are the rich and they are also the majority in public universities, hence marginalizing the lower income segment of the society from higher education. The best public schools also charge higher tuition and they are the main avenue of gaining admission to higher education.

Gomes (2007:11) argues that the strict university entrance exams are a source of social tension and academic criticism on the grounds that they are unequal and unjust while being ineffective in selecting the best candidates. The university entrance exam is seen as the most competitive in some African countries. Students and parents invest a lot in these exams, sometimes leaving families in poverty so that their children can get the best education they can afford. According to Eisemon & Salmi (1995) access to higher education can be improved through manipulation of admission. This can be achieved through the use of affirmative action as a corrective measure of the long standing historical gender-based disparities in admission (Atuahene & Owusu-Ansah 2013:12). Uganda has three main avenues for admission which give students a wide range of avenues to university education. Students can be admitted directly after attaining two principals in Advanced Certificate of Education Examination (A-levels). They can also be admitted depending on their diploma performance or they can gain admission as adults who missed an opportunity for direct entry (Pillay 2008: 33, 35).

Regional Distribution and Access to Tertiary Institutions

Spatial or regional distribution of tertiary institutions is a major determinant of students' enrollment and participation in higher education in Africa (Atuahene & Owusu-Ansah 2013) Most students at the universities are from the best schools which happen to be located in urban centers. Virtually all rural schools are poorly equipped and they post poor results in the university entrance examination (Atuahene & Owusu-Ansah 2013:7). Equally, the rural schools are poorly equipped, lack the necessary teaching and learning resources and the necessary personnel. In almost all countries in Sub-Saharan Africa, the participation in higher education is skewed in favor of students from urban and metropolitan areas (Pillay 2008:20). Pillay further says that most students from the rural areas also happens to come from poor households and they are unable to afford the high cost of tertiary education. Rural students are also more likely to be living a long distance from the nearest high school. They also uphold the traditional values, which place little value in education, particularly in regards to girls' education (Swainson 1995:18)

To redress the challenge of spatial inequity, most countries have come up with the quota system of education where students from all corners of a country are given equal opportunity in university admission (Eisemon & Salmi 1995:1). The use of technology (ICT) can help in bridging the regional gap in tertiary education participation, but there is a major challenge in implementing such a program since most of the rural areas in Africa lack the necessary modern infrastructure and equipment needed to implement a technological program (Atbach, Reisberg & Rumbley 2009:7; Gomes 2007:3).

Most students in the rural areas also lack the necessary skills to use interactive technology in their learning and highly skilled personnel prefer to work in urban areas which are endowed with modern facilities rather than move to the marginalized areas (Atbach et al 2009). Equally, developing countries lack the resources necessary to construct new universities in remote areas. Hence, the number of students who complete high school are lower in the rural areas (Atbach et al 2009:41).

Gender Equity and Access to Tertiary Education

Access to higher education by gender remains one of the areas of concern in Africa and in other developing countries. Women encounter a number of barriers in gaining admission to tertiary education programs, which is in contrast with developed countries where female participation exceed on average that of male (Pillay 2008: 20). When female students gain admission they are mostly concentrated in degree programs with less potential which are mainly in arts and the humanities (Swainson 1995:10). According to a study by Bunting et al (2014:7) in a sample of eight sub-Saharan Africa universities, only Mauritius, Botswana and Cape Town had a female population of 50 percent or above in their undergraduate programs. The universities of Ghana, Dar es Salaam, Nairobi and Eduardo Mondlane had a female undergraduate enrollment of below 50 percent.

In the Bunting et al. (2014:7) study, it was further found that female enrollment was worse in the doctoral programs in all the eight sampled universities which was 37 percent of the enrolled students. Overall, access to higher education for female students has not seen much improvement despite the consensus about the need to correct gender-based disparity (Atuahene & Owusu-Ansah, 2013:4). The gender inequity anomaly in education has its genesis in a mostly patriarchal society in Africa. This was strengthened during the Victorian era where the male child was given priority in education. The colonial education curriculum where Africa adopted its higher education system from, women were trained on how to become good housewives and boys were given priority in higher education in order to occupy the administrative system of colonial government (Chege & Sifuna:29). Women were believed to be of low intellectual level and patriarchy was perpetuated.

Female participation in higher education can be improved through a number of affirmative actions to rectify the skewed admission towards the male students. The universities' admission boards can admit female students at a lowered cut off point in various courses like it has happened in Ghana, Zimbabwe, Kenya, Uganda and the United Republic of Tanzania (Bloom, Canning & Chan 2006:11). At the University of Dar es Salaam female candidates are admitted at 1.5 points lower than their male counterparts (UNESCO 2003:17). This is because female students face innumerable challenges in the preparation for the university entrance examination. Socioeconomically, poor parents tend to sacrifice their daughters' education in favor of boys whenever the family faces economic hardships (Atuahene & Owusu-Ansah 2013:5). Female students also spend a lot of time undertaking house chores and other domestic duties which are perceived as female domestic roles at the expense of their studies. The society also encourages most men to marry women with lower education than them. Hence, this encourages female students to acquire moderate education.

The initiatives designed to address the gender inequities can sometimes be perceived as unfair or controversial by some sectors of the society (Bloom, Canning & Chan 2005). This is because it is seen as reverse discrimination where female students gain admission at the expense of boys who might be even more qualified. This is especially where preferential treatment is deliberately designed more to penalize a particular group than to benefit it (Eisemon & Salmi 1995:5). Increasing access opportunities for girls in higher education remains a big challenge in both urban and rural areas in Africa, and the establishment of two women's universities in 2002—the African Women's University based in Harare, Zimbabwe and the Kiriri Women's University in Kenya—was a good effort in addressing this imbalance (UNESCO 2003:17).

Social Inequality and Access to Higher Education

One of the major and often-cited causes of educational inequality in developing countries is students' family background and socioeconomic status (Atuahene & Owusu-Ansah 2013: 9). According to the World Bank (2011), students' socioeconomic status affect their ability to access and to participate in all levels of education particularly at the tertiary level. In many Sub-Saharan African countries, participation in universities and other institutions of higher learning is dominated by students from the highest income quintiles (Pillay 2009: 20). The ability to pay for tuition is also determined by the location of the family's residence. Thus, the socioeconomic status of parents is a crucial factor in deciding whether a student stays in primary school or progresses to the next higher level of schooling and the opportunity to attend university (Atuahene & Owusu-Ansah 2013:9). Access to secondary schooling is strongly related to household-income in all poor countries. Urban/rural differences in access can be striking, especially where most secondary provision is urban or peri-urban (Lewin 2008:8).

Students from families with higher education also tend to perform better in higher education than students from parents with lower education. There is also a high dropout rate of students from lower end income families, while there is higher retention from families with higher income (Swainson 1994: 19). Constitutionally, pre-tiary education in Ghana is tuition free but nonetheless there remains certain incidental fees that work against students from poor socio-economic backgrounds especially, those living in the rural areas and in particular girls (Atuahene & Owusu-Ansah 2013: 9). Students from poor families have a low completion rate of university education and the government can come up with mitigating policies of alleviating poverty by giving grants to the needy students which can be repaid after a long time (Atbach et al 2009: 44).

Higher Education Access Based on Available Accommodation Places

In Africa, most universities base their admission on available bed space (Atuahene & Owusu-Ansah 2013: 2). There has been little expansion of universities, and admission based on space limits the number of students admitted. Countries like Kenya, Uganda and Ghana for a long time based their admission on available space.

The use of ICT can improve dependence on admission based on space and thus can allow a large number of students to access quality high education (Gomes, 2007:16). The use of distance education and ICT can increase enrollment since the students can take their classes outside the physical buildings. Online classes in most countries have been used to increase admission. Most students who are qualified to join universities in Kenya are left out because of lack of available places. But the universities need to have in place a program to train their skilled personnel.

Disparity in Access to Certain Professional Courses

Students' admission to professional courses has been another area of inequality in higher education. Generally, there is a huge disparity between the percentages of students enrolled in the arts and humanities related programs and Science, Technology, Engineering and Mathematics (STEM) fields (Atuahene & Owusu-Ansah 2013:10). Students from poorly equipped schools with no laboratories tend to do poorly in the STEM subjects and they are finally left out of this courses in their university admission. Students from the elite schools and by extension the middle and upper middle class dominate most of these positions. The available statistical data also shows that while women participation in higher education has increased considerably over the past few years, there remains a huge gap between male and female in STEM fields (Pillay 2009). There is also a huge gap in the universities' professional staff with female making up less than 30 percent (Bunting et al 2014:16).

Access and Cross Border in Higher Education

Cross-border education refers to the movement of people, programs, providers, knowledge, ideas, projects and services across national boundaries. This term according to Knight (2006:19) is often used interchangeably to refer to transnational and borderless education. A guideline for cross-border education and quality provision of education was developed by UNESCO and OCED (2005). This guideline was to act as a protection to students and stakeholders from low quality higher education programs, degree mills and other disreputable providers. Cross-border higher education has helped in the development of local skills and in increasing of higher education system (Garwe 2015:45). This is because developing countries cannot meet the rising world demand for tertiary education. A good example as Okoli (2013:14) observes is in Zimbabwe where although the number of universities increased from one in 1990 to 15 by 2013, the number of potential students with the requisite entry qualifications still outstripped the number of places available in local higher education institutions. This creates need for more places and hence an increase in CBHE demand. CBHE becomes a source of highly skilled labor, especially in programs that are not available in those countries. Okoli (2013:14) further observes that in Africa the U.S. is the most preferred destination for cross-border education by most countries. Sub-Saharan Africa has the highest mobility of outbound CBHE students and it stands at 5.9 percent making it almost three times greater than the global CBHE average. One out of 16 students studies abroad (UNESCO/OECD 2005:37). Students can also access CBHE without moving from their countries through opening of overseas campuses, franchises, twinning arrangements, joint or double degrees, articulation, and validation as well as through distance or eLearning (Knight 2005).

The 21st century has witnessed a rapid development in CBHE and higher education has become a real part of globalization process with cross-border meeting the demand and supply and increasing students' access to education (Okoli 2013:12). But access to CBHE has come with a lot of challenges. Students accessing CBHE are forced to pay exorbitant fees making it a preserve of the rich who can afford to study abroad. Hence, CBHE has created a new system of inequalities and inequities in that while there is general agreement on the need for greater student access in higher education, the greater concern now is that increased access will be available only to those who can afford it (Knight 2005:52). Okoli (2013:14) further observes that the other challenges that come with cross border education are on how to ensure the quality of academic programs offered and how to achieve the recognition and legitimatization of the qualifications awarded. The CBHE expansion raises the need for new initiatives to enhance quality provision at the global level. In a research carried out in Zimbabwe by Garwe (2012:45), it was found out that the changes brought about by cross-border providers include proliferation of unrecognized, fly-by-night and rogue local and cross-border providers driven by commercial interests at the expense of maintaining quality and integrity of academic programs. Stakeholders in Zimbabwe alleged that many of the foreign and new local higher education institutions provided substandard facilities, unqualified staff and lacked resources such as libraries and laboratories, and offered mainly irrelevant programs. This problem could be addressed through proper accreditation guidelines and through proper collaboration between universities and other African countries.

Financing of Higher Education in Africa

The financing of higher education in Africa has been another area of concern. There are a number of factors which affect the financing of higher education in Africa. In this section of the essay, some of the major factors will be examined.

Equity and Higher Education Financing in Africa

In most countries in Africa, there is a perception that participation in higher education is predominantly by students from wealthier backgrounds (Mohadeb 2010:93). Students participating in higher education are mostly from the best performing schools which are attended by middle and high-income populations. This has made education to remain elitist and a preserve of a few. In countries like Namibia access to education prior to independence was dictated by South Africa's colonial rules which were guided by race and ethnicity. Gross enrollment ratios for tertiary education in Namibia still lags behind that of other lower middle-income countries (Adongo 2010: 136). Johnstone and Marcucci (2007) argue that cost sharing in education can be made more or less equitable to the degree that need-based student loans or grants are provided to students from low-income families. This is based on the principle that equity is fairness and that those who benefit more and have the ability to pay should at least bear more if not all the cost of higher education. The Structural Adjustment Program had an equally major impact on access, equity and gender participation in higher education in Africa and the world at large.

Private Universities and Privatization of Public Tertiary Institutions

The WB and SAP advocated for more presence of the private sector in education. Massification had created a need for more places in higher education. In places like Kenya this brought on board the private tertiary institutions that absorbed students who had mostly missed out in the regular programs controlled by the Joint Admission Board (JAB) (Otieno 2010:33). While the public universities enrollment has continued to grow this cannot be compared with the massive numerical growth of the private universities (Otieno 2010:34). Kenya has 14 chartered universities and 12 universities with letters of Interim Authority. Namibia has more than ten private institutions. Tanzania provides loans to students attending private universities (Ishengoma 2010:183). The students in private universities pay almost two times the amount of tuition and fees paid in public institutions.

Private universities mainly depend on tuition, external donors and limited government support to run their programs. But the high fees in these institutions are at times driven by the need for profit rather than quality (Otieno 2010:44). The programs offered in these institutions are also mostly not accessible to the economically underprivileged students. A large number of these institutions had started as religious institutions but with time they diversified their courses. In order to generate more income, some public universities in Kenya and Uganda have come up with Module ll programs where students who fail to get admission in the regular intake pay higher tuition for admission. Private tertiary education is also a rapidly expanding part of higher education system in places like Ethiopia where it has increased by almost 43 percent and accounts for 23 percent of Ethiopian tertiary education enrollment (Saint 2004:90). In Uganda, privatization of public institutions like Makerere has resulted in the creation of two categories of students where one group pays full tuition and fees and the regular group chosen on merit receives full government scholarships (Pillay 2009:36). For greater achievement in access and equity in higher education, there is need to moderate the cost of private and public education.

The Impact of Structural Adjustment on Higher Education Finance in Africa

The neoliberal reform agenda fronted by the International Monetary Fund (IMF) and the World Bank (WB) prescribed to the developing countries

economic liberalization policies such as privatization, fiscal austerity, dereg-
ulation, free trade, and reductions of government spending in order to
enhance the private sector (Johnstone & Marcucci 2007:3). According to
Sanyal and Martin (1998:31), the African region was particularly hard hit by
the world economic crisis, the fall in primary commodity prices and the consequences of structural adjustment programs (SAPS) drastically reduced state
finance on higher education. This forced the African higher education to
undergo a major restructuring through a reduction in public sector expenditure by cutting down on unproductive departments, retrenchment of staff
and the privatization of some public services (Levidow 2001:7). This has also
seen the academic units in higher education that are not in line with SAP or
corporate market close down even when they have increased the number of
students in tertiary institutions. Between 1970s and 1990, the WB policy that
emphasized on the importance of basic education and higher education in
Africa was found to be incompetent, inefficient and inequitable (Samoff &
Carrol 2004:12).

The financing of higher education has seen ideological and political
changes in the last decade of the 20th and the first decade of the 21st centuries
(Johnson & Marcucci 2007:1). In the 1960s the World Bank's primary task on
higher education in Africa was to develop specific skills that African countries
needed. But within a decade of independence by most African countries that
perspective changed. The view at the time was that higher education graduates could get substantial individual returns from education particularly with
the public expenditure on student accommodation, meals, transport and
stipends. This was construed as not contributing to development but it was
seen as misdirected resources (Samoff & Carrol 2004:1). The WB priority at
the time was directed to more spending in basic education. The key message
to its staff, funding agencies, African governments and non-governmental
organizations was that higher education was too costly, too inequitable, and
marginal to the national developments goals. This policy came at the time
that higher education had experienced a rapid increase in per student cost,
tertiary level massification and the continued dependence on inadequate government revenue (Johnson & Marcucci 2007).

There has been increased austerity in the financing of higher education
that has affected the management of the tertiary institutions in Africa (Johnson & Marcucci 2007:1). The outcomes of this austerity measures have been
overcrowding of lecture theatres, dilapidated physical facilities, insufficient
and outdated library holdings, and less time for research. This has been coupled
with the loss of the most talented faculty from the African universities to
more developed countries (Johnstone & Marcucci 2007:1). In many countries
staff salaries stagnated or declined, requiring second jobs and increasing the
attraction of overseas opportunities. Book purchases, journal subscriptions,

laboratory equipment, facilities maintenance, and research support also suffered (Samoff & Carrol 2004). The deterioration of higher education in Africa like Makerere University had reached a crisis point by 1990. This situation was made worse by the perception that the university's leaders were more of a political threat to the government than a development engine. Babalola, Lungwangwa and Adeyinka (1999:1) observe that the fiscal measures that were introduced in Nigeria and Zambia during the SAP had devastating effects on the public expenditure in education, teachers purchasing power, quality of education, access to education and gender gap in the provision of higher education.

In response to these austerity measures in Sub-Saharan Africa the universities resulted to increasing class sizes and teaching loads, deferring maintenance, substituting lower cost part-time faculty for higher cost full-time faculty and dropping low priority programs. The economic solutions on increasing revenue has been instituting or increasing tuition fees, encouraging faculty philanthropy, freeze on hiring instructors and allowing and encouraging a demand absorbing private sector (Johnson & Marcucci 2007:3). According to Samoff and Carrol (2004:6), foreign aid to education in Africa was like a small animal with a loud roar. This was because in almost all the African countries the major source of higher education funding was the national governments treasury. The WB roar was on its leverage to help meet the universities deficit to respond to what the university needed to do. Otherwise, the governments met the bulk of the budget by paying of the staff, building, and maintaining the university infrastructure. Throughout Africa foreign aid has become the center of gravity for education and development initiatives (Samoff & Carrol 2004: 6).

Most of the African countries were dependent on the WB loan to finance the higher education. The largest borrowers of this fund in Sub-Saharan Africa between 1964 and 2002 were Kenya, Nigeria and Cote d' Ivoire. The conditions introduced for receiving these funds were introduction of direct charges for tuition, capping enrollments and reforming the students' loan scheme (Samoff & Carrol 2004:20; World Bank 2011:24). Ghana and Uganda, which were considered as star reformers in education by the WB, received significant support from the WB (Samoff &Carrol 2004:22). The introduction of SAPs required governments to reduce their public expenditure and increase private participation in education. Beneficiaries were expected to participate in higher education through cost sharing (Waithaka 2004:32).

The WB advocacy saw the shifting of financing of higher education from the public treasury to students and their families. The increased overreliance on fees may have brought about inequality in access to higher education as students from affluent families were in a better position to secure admission after attending well-endowed institutions which gave them an advantage when it came to the university entrance exams. These students were also in a better position to remain in school longer than the students from the low income families (Samoff & Carrol:32). SAP also saw a sharp decline in female students' participation in higher education in Zambia and Nigeria (Babalola et al 1999: 89). There was also an introduction and duplication of low cost courses in most universities (Waithaka 2004:88).

Cost Sharing and Students Loan Scheme

The term cost sharing refers to the shift of some of the higher educational cost burden from the government and by extensions the taxpayers to the students and their parents (Johnstone 2006: 17). In cost sharing the cost of higher education is shared among governments, parents, students and philanthropists. Cost sharing is mainly associated with tuition fees and other user charges like the institutionally provided room and board, registration, examination or student activity fee (Johnston 2006:17). Cost sharing policies came into effect under the SAP policy when countries were in serious economic problems and under severe budget constraints (Johnstone 2006: 53). The advocacy at the time by the WB and IMF was for more funding to be directed towards the primary level education because it had a higher social return rate. According to the World Bank (2010:56), this has seen the households contribute approximately one-fourth of national expenditure on education, with countries like Mali spending 10 percent. At least 26 countries were charging some type of tuition (World Bank 2010:59).

The forces behind cost sharing in higher education through the introduction of tuition and various charges argued that the high private benefit return rate that is both monetary and non-monetary to students and their families justify private contributions to their education (Jaramillo & Melonio 2011:44; Johnstone 2006:23). But this could have a negative effect in terms of access and equity by preventing students from disadvantaged backgrounds from participating in higher education, hence leading to social exclusion. The introduction of cost sharing required that the rise in tuition be greater than the rise in institutional cost. This was to reduce the tax payers share of offering higher education and at the same time increasing the student and their parents' share of the cost of education.

In order to cushion the students and their parents from the adverse effects of cost sharing, various student loans were introduced. In Kenya cost sharing was introduced through Sessional Paper No. 6 of 1988 and direct tuition fees was introduced in 1992 (Otieno 2010:50). The Higher Education Loans Board (HELB) was mandated to issue loans to students in collaboration with commercial banks like the National Bank of Kenya. Grants to students were channeled through the institutions. The loans are awarded to students who qualify for module 1 courses and some of those studying at private universities (Johnstone 2006:25). In Namibia, the initial students Financial Scheme was changed from a bursary scheme to a student loan. In Tanzania the Higher Education Students Loans Board (HESLB) was introduced in 1992/1993 (Ishengoma 2010:184). Tanzania had an earlier scheme introduced in the 1970s that later collapsed. HESLB was mandated to give loans to the needy students in both private and public institutions of higher learning. In Ghana, the government contracted with the Ghana Commercial Bank to provide students with loans of specific amounts (Atuehene 2006:67). Rwanda has the Higher Education Students Loans Department (HESLD) (AAHEFA 2016:1).

In Africa, there are currently 13 countries with student loan schemes to cover for higher education students' loans. Those countries are Tanzania, Kenya, Rwanda, Burkina Faso, Ghana, Ethiopia, Malawi, Zambia, Lesotho, Namibia, Swaziland, Botswana and South Africa. Most of this countries are members of Association of African Higher Education Financing Agencies (AAHEFA 2016:1) which meets to share information and experiences on how to increase students' access to higher education (AAHEFA 2016:1). However, these countries have limited students' scholarships and grants. But the general feeling is that these loans mostly go to the rich students who attend elite senior secondary schools and tend to have exemplary performance in the university entrance exam.

Financing of Tertiary Education in Africa

In most African countries the financing of higher education has been the role of the government since colonial times and African countries have made a significant investment in the development of their higher education (Atuahene 2006:1; UNESCO 2003:14). The government's role was to ensure access and equity in higher education by subsidizing the high cost of education. The governments used education as a source of socioeconomic engineering. According to UNESCO (2011), the governments worked in a complex regulated partnership with other sectors in the financing of higher education. The government funding is also complemented by funds from external partners, bilateral agreements, beneficiaries of the education system, religious organization and non-governmental organizations (Ishengoma 2009:179; UNESCO 2011:59). The World Bank estimates that around 85 percent of the operating cost in most African universities is provided by African governments. But since the implementation of SAPS in the 1980s most governments in a neoliberal environment have been trying to move away from that role

(Waithaka 2004:54). The governments also had a role in formulating various access policies applicable to the universities. The governments also controlled the source and mechanism of finance and when the universities generated their own funds, the government appropriated it. Through scholarships, students' loans and resource allocation, governments can control the size and distribution of students' intake.

Private universities have helped to deflect student demands for higher education away from the underfunded public tertiary institutions as a result of neoliberalism and SAPS' conditions. These conditions have forced governments to curtail expenditure as a means of containing deficit. For many countries in Sub-Saharan Africa, it has been difficult to raise public revenue because of macroeconomic and growth instability, high debt ratios, weak tax administration and large informal sectors (UNESCO 2011:19). Lesotho remains one of the countries in Africa with the highest expenditure on higher education relative to its GDP (UNESCO 2011:32). The presence of private universities has expanded in countries like Kenya, Ghana, Zaire, Liberia, Madagascar, Tanzania, Namibia, Rwanda and Zimbabwe (Waithaka 2004: 60, 67; Saint 1992). Although most universities are receiving taxpayer funds, they are being encouraged to be innovative and to generate their own income. This has made universities introduce a number of programs where students pay higher tuition like in Module ll programs and satellite universities which have successfully operated in Kenya and Uganda. According to Saint (1992:100), the University of Addis Ababa supplemented the public funds received from the government through its evening courses and other short courses. Addis Ababa College of Commerce produced 32 percent of its recurrent budget from fees.

Challenges of Funding Higher Education in Africa

The biggest challenge in funding higher education in Africa has been the continuous reliance on government for recurrent and capital expenditures (Atuahene 2006:6). The increased demand for higher education coupled with a high rate of population growth without any expansion and improvement of the existing physical facilities such as lecture theaters has greatly hampered the quality of higher education in Africa (Atuahene 2006:9). The situation was made worse by SAP conditions of limited government involvement in higher education. The private institutions have not improved the situation by offering high tuition and other fees that have been out of reach to low-income students. In countries like Tanzania, the government offers over subsidized loans to both the rich and the poor, which contradicts the governments' emphasis on giving loans to the poor (Ishengoma 2010:185).

Quality Assurance in Higher Education in Africa

Quality assurance refers to a planned and systematic review process of an institution or program to determine whether or not acceptable standards of education, scholarship, and infrastructure are being met, maintained, and enhanced (Materu 2007:3). Quality refers to fitness for purpose, meeting or conforming to generally accepted standards as defined by quality assurance bodies and appropriate academic and professional communities. In the diverse arena of higher education, fitness for purpose varies tremendously by field and program. Quality assurance can play a key catalytic role in revitalizing weak tertiary education systems. There is emerging consensus that traditional academic controls of quality are inadequate for today's challenges and that the more explicit assurances about quality are needed (Hayward 2006:9).

The concept of quality assurance was originally used in business but it has now been adapted in education and in other public service sector. The higher education institutions found the concept beneficial in improving the quality of educational programs by assessing their quality in the face of great competition. Quality remains the most important attribute that creates value about the product or service for the receiver (ESIB 2001:8.). Quality assurance should therefore look at a wider spectrum in higher education from teaching and academic programs to research, scholarship, staffing, students, buildings, faculties, equipment, services to the community and the academic environment and it should take the form of self–evaluation and external review (ESIB, 2001:8.; Nkinga 2013). The key challenge faced by quality assurance is lack of funding and trained staff.

Quality Assurance: A Historical Background

The concept of quality assurance emerged as a principle of business methodology in the Western world throughout the 1950's and in the early 1960's. The concept is rather elusive, because it expresses a relative, though, noticeable difference between one thing and another. Relative terms such as better, superior, acceptable are applied to judge quality. However, quality is a universally acknowledged factor in successful business. In the world of business, winning companies are those that meet quality standards and for whom customer services is an obsession in every single market in which they operate (ESIB 2001:10).

Since the 1990s, quality and quality assurance became the key themes for higher education almost everywhere. The concerns had been raised about the production or output of higher education institutions or whether societies are getting real value for their investments in higher education. Although circumstances vary from country to country, several broad trends have contributed to growing governmental interest in establishing policy mechanisms to ensure quality and accountability in higher education. Of particular significance is the trend towards mass higher education. In 2011, global enrollment in higher education was 165 million students worldwide (UIS, 2011). Within the last decade alone, many countries have seen a tremendous increase in this enrollment and in some countries it has increased more than five times. With the development of mass higher education, a greater diversity of educational offerings has emerged (ESIB 2001:9–10).

Massification and Quality Assurance

The modern universities in Africa can be traced back to between 1930 and 1960 and at the time, they were mainly places for the African western-educated elite, who saw European education as a strong tool to fight against colonialism (Assie-Lumumba 2006:5). In Kenya, education was reserved for the children of colonial chiefs and administrators. But after independence higher education started opening up to a wider segment of the population. In the late 1960s, Africa experienced a dramatic escalation in the demand for higher education (Mohamedhbai 2008:1). This demand created a rapid expansion of higher education in Africa which was felt between 1985 and 2002, where the number of tertiary education enrollment grew by 3.6 times or about 15 percent per year. According to Materu (2006:9), this increase was led by Rwanda at 55 percent, Namibia 46 percent, Uganda 36 percent, Tanzania 32 percent, Cote d'Ivoire 28 percent, Kenya 27 percent, Chad 27 percent, Botswana 22 percent and Cameroon 22 percent. The other countries that experienced massive increment of students were Angola, Ethiopia, Ghana and Nigeria. While enrollment in Nigeria represented only about 8 percent of the university population, this growth had profound negative effects on the quality of teaching and training of university students (Hayward 2006:12). The growth in enrollment was a reflection of a corresponding growth in population in the African countries (Mwesigye & Muhangi 2015:101). But in spite of the rapid growth in student population over the last two decades, Africa remains far much behind the rest of the world in terms of access and enrollment with an average enrollment of 5 percent in 2003 (Hayward 2006:12).

The massification in higher education in Africa occurred along two well-defined trajectories (Mwesigye & Muhangi 2015:101). The first one was the growth of private universities and the second one was the increasing privatization of public universities in what Levidow (2001) calls the neoliberalism in higher education. Mwesigye and Muhangi further observe that during the post-independence era in Africa, there was suspicion and even hostilities in the notion of the existence of private universities. However, there has been a paradigm shift that has seen the expansion of private universities. The emergence of private universities was in a bid to fill in the gap of the inability of the governments to cater for the big demand of higher education. A number of African countries initiated policies in the 1990's to encourage the setting up of private tertiary institutions. Kenya was among the first countries where private universities were set up followed by Senegal, Cameroon, Mozambique and Zimbabwe (Mohamedhbai 2008:19). Most of the initial private universities were under the control of religious organizations, especially Christians and Muslims, who expanded their programs to include non-religious courses.

The neoliberal trajectory was to address the dwindling state of resources allocated to universities in the face of massification. The privatization of public universities was seen as a viable option to address the twin challenges of demand and resource generation in higher education (Mwesigye & Muhangi 2015:101). The 1970s brought about economic crunch and economic years of neglect of most African universities. There was preference by the donors to fund primary education at the expense of higher education. Global policies introduced by the International Monetary Fund (IMF) gave preference to the funding of primary education (Semali, Baker & Freer 2013: 54). The golden age of African higher education had come to an end, as government subsidies were slashed. Neoliberalism was to use market-driven approach and social policy based on neoclassical theories of economics that stressed the efficiency of private enterprise, liberalized trade and a relatively open market that gave a bigger role to the private sector in the determination of the political and economic properties of the state (Semali, Baker & Free 2013:54).

The allocation given to higher education in Africa had declined from 17 percent in 1985 to only 7 percent in 1999; and many African countries started struggling to maintain even a low enrollment rate (Semali, Baker & Free 2013:55; Mohamedhbai 2008:2). The decline in funding was a big contrast to the high demand of education at the time. There was a need for personnel, construction of new facilities and infrastructure, maintenance of the existing infrastructure and libraries. Additionally, the gap left by the donors had to be filled (Fish 2009:3).

The higher education institutions in Africa responded to this situation by raising tuition and in effect passing the burden of the cost of curriculum implementation to the students, who now became consumers and debt holders. Evidence shows that in countries with inadequate public financing and resource diversification, admitting increasing numbers of students results in a deterioration in quality (World Bank 2010:22). The universities started hiring a large number of short-term, part time adjuncts who, as members of a transient and disposable workforce, are in no position to challenge the university's practices or agitate for an academy more committed to the realization of democratic rather than monetary goals (Fish 2009). Most institutions like in Kenya come up with the parallel programs where students who had missed admission in the regular programs attended the evening classes, something that was resented by students in the regular program. The regular students felt that students in the parallel program who were well-endowed were favored by the instructors at the expense of the students in the regular program (Mohamedhbai 2008).

The massiffication of the universities took a toll on professoriate standards as a big number of the academics lacked the necessary postgraduate qualifications (Baty 2009). The understaffed satellite colleges with inferior and dilapidated infrastructure sprang up in all corners where the emphasis was more on quantity than quality. Conflict between the professional bodies and universities started emerging in terms of the quality of graduates the universities were minting. In Kenya some professional bodies rejected the absorption in the job market of engineering, pharmacy, medicine and law degree students as half-baked and of very low quality (Wanzala 2005).

The private universities turned to the use of part-time or half-time teaching staff and some had little regard for scholarship (Mwesigye & Muhangi 2015:103). Some lacked the necessary infrastructure, qualified staff and standardization of their programs. Equally, massification did not favor female faculty, who continued to be marginalized.

In order to address the emerging challenges of massification there is a need to regulate the growing number of private higher educational institutions by setting up the necessary appropriate quality assurance mechanisms (Materu 2007). The public institutions should also be subjected to the same standards of quality assurance as the private institutions and their programs and infrastructures be evaluated regularly. The government should also have guidelines in place on how to upgrade the middle level technical institutions without destroying them as they play a major role in preparing mid-level technical personnel.

Accreditation and Quality Assurance

According to (Materu 2007:3), accreditation is the process of self-study and external quality review used in higher education to scrutinize an institution or its programs for quality standards and need for quality improvement. Through accreditation an institution can rationalize how it selects, validates and institutionalizes knowledge in order to meet the societal needs and what norms, procedures and standards it embraces to regulate these processes (Munene 2014:167). Hayward (2006:6) observes that accreditation usually involves self-assessment of the programs by the institution, a site visit by peer reviewers, a report of that review, and a decision to accredit, deny accreditation, or put it on probation.

Institutional accreditation is classified into three categories, namely accredited, conditional or not accredited. When an institution is accredited, its programs are seen to have satisfied the set requirements, or the institution has minor shortcomings that can be rectified without affecting its programs. When an institution is given conditional accreditation, it indicates that the institution or its programs have major shortcomings, which need to be eliminated or addressed before the institution is fully accredited. When an institution is not accredited, it means the institution, its infrastructure or its programs have serious shortcomings that affect the quality of the graduates produced by the institution (ESIB 2001:36). Accreditation is a way of providing all the stakeholders with programs that are clearly defined and appropriate for public consumption. This provides an added assurance that the programs in which the students are enrolled or are considering enrolling in are capable of achieving what it set out to do (ESIB 2001). In many countries like Cameroon and Kenya, the term accreditation is used to refer to public universities that were established by an act of parliament or statute. This is a de jure or by law kind of accreditation, and it is not done through a peer review or by site visit (Hayward 2006:5).

With the hunger for education and proliferation of private institutions, public and international satellite campuses, there is a need to reassure the public that the quality of the programs offered in those institutions meet the acceptable local and international standards. In countries like Ethiopia, Madagascar, South Africa, Ghana, the Democratic Republic of Congo and Nigeria, the public had expressed concerns about the quality of educational programs offered (Hayward 2006:7). Accreditation therefore gives assurance to the public that the quality of the programs offered are up to date. Most of the public institutions feel accreditation is meant for private and not public institutions. For quality to be attained, both public and private institutions need to be accredited by close scrutiny and evaluation of their programs.

Globalization, Access and Quality Assurance in Higher Education

As the world moves towards globalization through effecting sociopolitical and economic changes aimed at creating a single economic entity for the movement of goods, capital, skills and services, globalization in higher education has led to the widening and speeding up of interconnectedness of universities within the global world (Rooijen 2013:1). This has led to increased enrollment in higher education institutions of learning, and it has been a way of addressing the demand and access to higher education. According to Mwesigye & Muhangi (2015:101), globalization has been used to address massiffication and the problem of elitism that were associated with post-independence public African universities. This has led to increased student enrollment in higher education. But globalization has brought about the issue of quality in education as the demand for trans-border education takes effect in places like Nigeria (Nkang 2012:207).

According to Martin, Pereyra and Stella (2007:7), globalization is a phenomenon that poses immeasurable challenges to the regulation and recognition of credentials. Inadequate information systems and lack of control have resulted in new types of academic fraud such as diploma mills, the selling of credentials, and the deliberate provision of false information on the nature and validity of credentials. Globalization has also had a negative impact through commercialization of higher education where the profit motive in certain cases supersedes the need for quality provision (Mwesigye & Muhangi 2015:109). Globally, quality in education, especially university education, has become a topical issue. This can also create additional unneeded layers of status and prestige, by selling prestigious but empty credentials, and by undermining national efforts for quality. This erodes the traditional tenets of university education. Mwesigye and Muhangi (2015:109) observe that higher education in Africa operates under strong local regulation, which becomes threatened by globalization.

On the flipside, globalization brings about new standards, methodologies, teaching materials and practices, and it breaks down the artificial barriers to access higher education (Schwartzman 2003:6). It is then impossible to make higher education immune to the globalization process (Rooijen 2013:10). According to Mwesigye and Muhangi (2015:99), as globalization has increased as an organizing process in socio-economic and political reforms and relations, so too has the view that education is a significant catalyst in enabling nations to become globally competitive gained currency. This underscores the need for quality assurance at the international level (Nkang 2012: p. 207).

Conclusion

Education has massively grown in Africa in the last decade of the 20th and the first decade of the 21st century. But while this has expanded the opportunities available in higher education, students from elite and urban schools continues to have a greater advantage over the lower socioeconomic households. The higher educational growth in Africa also continues to lag behind other countries in the world with only 5 percent of the students' cohort enrolled against 54 percent in the USA. The governments need to enact selective policy, which will increase the number of students who gain admission to higher institutions, especially when it comes to the awarding of government grants and scholarships. Students from the lower income families who are disadvantaged right from birth should also be given a higher loan than middle and upper middle class students in order to reduce the inequality. They should also be given a longer grace period to repay their students loans due to the high level of unemployment in most countries in Sub-Saharan Africa. Affirmative action should also be stressed in order to have more females in higher education, as female students continue to encounter innumerable barriers in accessing higher education. Male students continue to be favored by cultural practices that give them a head start in education. The home can also become an impediment for females in accessing higher education as they are expected to take up a considerable amount of domestic work at the expense of their studies. Women also continue to be left out in science courses as they dominate in the humanities disciplines. But more should be done to create a more equal playing ground in high schools where the admission process starts.

The challenge brought in by structural adjustment programs (SAPS) in higher education in Africa still threaten equal access to education. The privatization of higher education makes it to be mostly out of reach to the lower income segment of the population. In spite of the private sector playing a major role in increasing access to education, the tuition in most of these universities is still high for the economically disadvantaged population. The government should come up with incentives for the private institutions to lower their tuition.

The government should also put in place a strong system of quality assurance to check on the massive expansion of cross-border education, and the high number of private and public university satellite colleges mushrooming in all the major towns in Africa. The public universities should also be subjected to the same quality assurance guidelines as the private ones. All the higher education institutions, both public and private, should be accredited in order to align their programs with the global market and produce high quality graduates. Certificates awarded should be acceptable globally. The ad hoc proliferation of competing satellite universities should be checked since some of their programs are substandard as they lack the necessary infrastructure and personnel to handle this courses. African universities should take advantage of globalization to increase higher education access.

The economic disparity between the rural and urban areas should be narrowed in order to attract higher education institutions in the rural areas. The private sector should also be given tax concessions in order to invest in higher education in the rural areas as the governments explore new ways of making higher education more accessible, equitable and affordable through the use of ICT and distance learning. Kenyatta University has successfully used its virtual university to reach a wider audience.

REFERENCES

AAHEFA. 2016. Promoting Access to Higher Education, *AAHEFA Newsletter*. Retrieved 16may2016 https:// www. google.com/#q= AAHEFA %2C+2016%2C+16+%2C+ Promoting +access+to+higher+education%2C+AAHEFA+Newsletter.

Addae-Mensah, I. 2000. *Education in Ghana: A Tool for Social Mobility or Social Stratification?* Paper Delivered at the J.B. Danquah, Memorial Lectures, Ghana Academy of Arts and Sciences. Accra, Ghana, April.

Adongo, J. 2010. "Kenya." In P. Phillay (ed.). *Higher Education Financing in East and Southern Africa*. South Africa: African Minds Publishers, pp. 123–151.

Assie-Lumumba, N. 2006. *Empowerment of Women in Higher Education in Africa: The Role and Mission of Research*. UNESCO Forum Occasional Paper Series Paper no. 11.

Atbach, P.G., Reisberg, L., & Rumbley, L.E. 2009: *Trends in Global Higher Education: Tracking an Academic Revolution*. A Report for the UNESCO 2009 World Conference on Higher Education. Paris.

Atuahene, F. 2006. *A Policy Analysis of the Financing of Tertiary Education Institutions in Ghana: An Assessment of the Objectives and the Impact of the Ghana Education Trust Fund*. A Ph.D. Dissertation, Ohio University.

Atuahene, F. &, Owusu-Ansah, A. 2013. "A Descriptive Assessment of Higher Education Access, Participation, Equity, and Disparity in Ghana." *Sage DOI:10.1177/21582440 13497725*. sgo.sage pub.com.

Babalola, J.B., Lungwangwa, G., & Adeyinka, A. 1999. "Education Under Structural Adjustment in Nigeria and Zambia: Report from the Field." *McGill Journal of Education*, 34(1), pp.79–98.

Baty, P. 2009. *Massification' Takes Toll on Professoriate Standards*. Retrieved on May 18, 2017, from https://www.timeshighereducation.com/news/massification-takes-toll-on-pro fessoriate-standards/407334.article. Accessed December 4, 2017.

Bloom, D.E., Canning, D., & Chan, K. 2006. *Higher Education and Economic Development in Africa*. Washington, D.C.: World Bank.

Buchere, D. 2009. *Kenya: Entry Points Lowered to Boost Access*. University World News. http:// www.universityworldnews.com/article.php?story=20090813170055514.Accessed. December 4, 2017.

Bunting, I., Cloete, N., & Van Schalkwyk, V. 2014. *An Empirical Overview of Eight Flagship Universities in Africa 2001–2011*. A Report of the Higher Education Research and Advocacy Network in Africa (HERANA). Cape Town: Center for Higher Education Transformation (CHET).

Chege, F., & Sifuna, D.N. 2006. *Girls' and Women's Education in Kenya: Gender Perspectives and Trends*. Paris: UNESCO.

Eisemon, T.O., & Salmi, J. 1995. *Increasing Equity in Higher Education: Strategies and Lessons from International Experience*. The International Institute of Educational Development.

ESIB 2001. *European Student Handbook on Quality Assurance in Higher Education*. European Commission.

Fish, S. 2009. "Neoliberalism and Higher Education." *The New York Times*. Retrieved on June 13, 2017. http://opinionator.blogs.nytimes.com/2009/03/08/neoliberalism-and-higher-education/?_r=0.

Garwe, E.C. 2015. "Managing the Quality of Cross-Border Higher Education in Zimbabwe." *Journal of Education and Training Studies*. 3(2), pp. 44–50.

Gomes, J.F. 2007. *Access and Equity in Higher Education Across the World*. Paper presented at Global Higher Education Forum. Kuala Lumpur, Malaysia, June 7.

Hayward, F.M. 2006. *Quality Assurance and Accreditation of Higher Education in Africa*. Paper prepared for presentation at the Conference on Higher Education Reform in Francophone Africa: Understanding the Keys of Success. June 13–15, 2006. Ouagadougou, Burkina Faso.

Ishengoma, J.M. 2010. "Tanzania." In P. Phillay (ed.). *Higher Education Financing in East and Southern Africa*. South Africa: African Minds Publishers, pp. 173–194.

Jaramillo, A., & Melonio, T. 2011. Breaking Even or Breaking Through: Reaching Financial Sustainability While Providing High Quality Standards in Higher Education in the Middle East and North Africa. Washington, D.C.: World Bank.

Johnstone, D.B., & Marcucci, P.N. 2006. *Financing Higher Education Worldwide: Who pays? Who Should Pay?* Netherlands: Sense.

Johnstone, D.B., & Marcucci, P.N. 2007. *Worldwide Trends in Higher Education Finance: Cost-Sharing, Student Loans, and the Support of Academic Research*. UNESCO.

Knight, J. (ed.). 2009. *Financing Access and Equity in Higher Education*. Rotterdam, Netherlands: Sense.

Knight, J. 2006. *Higher Education Crossing Borders: A Guide to the Implications of the General Agreement on Trade in Services (GATS) for Cross-Border Education*. A Report Prepared for the Commonwealth of Learning and UNESCO.

Levidow, L. 2001. "Marketizing Higher Education: Neo-Liberal Strategies and Counter Strategies." *Education and Social Justice* 3 (2), 12–24.

Lewin, K.M. 2007. *Improving Access, Equity and Transitions in Education: Creating a Research Agenda, Consortium for Research on Educational Access, Transition and Equity (Create)*. Pathways to Access Research Monograph No. 1.

Martin, M., Pereyra, J., Singh, M., & Stella, A. 2007. *External Quality Assurance of Higher Education in Anglophone Africa*. Report of an IIEP Distance Education Course. 25 September—22 December 2006, UNESCO.

Materu, P. 2007. *Higher Education Quality Assurance in Sub-Saharan Africa: Status, Challenges, Opportunities, and Promising Practices*. World Bank Working Paper No. 124, Washington, D.C.

Mohadeb, P. 2010. "Mauritius." In P. Phillay (ed.). *Higher Education Financing in East and Southern Africa*. South Africa: African Minds Publishers, pp. 81–102.

Mohamedhbai, G. 2008. *The Effects of Massification on Higher Education in Africa*. Working Group of Higher Education of the Association of the Development of Education in Africa (ADEA).

Morley, L. N.d. *Gender and Access in Commonwealth Higher Education*. Center for Higher Education Studies. Institute of Education, University of London, UK.

Munene, I.I. 2015. "Profits and Pragmatism: The Commercial Lives of Market Universities in Kenya and Uganda." *Sage Open DOI:* 10.1177/2158244015612519 sgo.sagepub.com.

Munene, I.I. 2014. *University Is ISO 9000: 2008 Certified: Neoliberal Echoes, Knowledge Production and Quality Assurance in Kenyan State Universities*. Council for the Development of Social Science Research in Africa.

Musisi, N., & Mayega, F. 2010. "Uganda." In P. Phillay (ed.). *Higher Education Financing in East and Southern Africa*. South Africa: African Minds Publishers, pp. 195–222.

Mwesigye, A., & Muhangi, G. 2015. "Globalization and Higher Education in Africa." *Journal of Modern Education Review*. 5(1), pp 97–112.

Nkang, I.E. 2012. "Challenges of Globalization and Quality Assurance in Nigerian University Education." *International Education Studies*, 6(1), pp.207–215.

Ntim, S. 2016. *Massification in Ghanaian Higher Education: Implications for Pedagogical Quality, Equity Control and Assessment International Research in Higher Education*. Online Publisher. http://dx.doi.org/10.5430/irhe.v1n1p160. Accessed December 5, 2017.

Oduor, A. 2015. "Eighty Thousand Students to Join Various Universities and Colleges." *The Standards Newspaper*. July 16. Retrieved from http://www.standardmedia.co.ke/article/2000169359/80–000-kenyan-students-to-join-varsities-colleges. Accessed December 4, 2017.

Okebukola, P. 2010. *Quality Assurance in Higher Education: The African Story of Achievements Outstanding*. Global University Network for Innovation.

Okoli, N. 2013. "Issues and Challenges in Cross-Border in Higher Education: The Sub-Saharan (SSA) Experience." *American Journal of Educational Research*. 1(1), pp. 12–16 DOI: 10.12691/education-1-1-3.

Otieno, W. 2010. "Kenya." In P. Phillay (ed.). *Higher Education Financing in East and Southern Africa*. South Africa: African Minds Publishers, pp. 29–61.

Pillay, P. 2009. "Challenges and Lessons from East and Southern Africa." In J. Knight (ed.). *Financing Access and Equity in Higher Education*. Rotterdam, Netherlands: Sense Publishers.

Phillay, P. (ed.). 2010. *Higher Education Financing in East and Southern Africa*. South Africa: African Minds Publishers.

Pityana, N.B. Nd. The Revitalization of Higher Education: Access, Equity and Quality. University of South Africa.

Rooijen, M.V. 2013. *What Does Globalization Really Mean for Higher Education?* European Association of Higher Education Blogfrom http:// www.eaie.org/blog/what-does-globalization-really-mean-for-higher-education/. Accessed on July 14, 2017.

Saint, W. 2004. "Higher Education in Ethiopia: The Vision and Its Challenges." *Journal of Higher Education* in Africa. 2(3), pp. 83–113.

Samoff, J., & Carrol, B. 2004. *Conditions, Coalitions and Influence: The Third World and Higher Education in Africa*. Paper presented at the Annual Conference of the Comparative and International Education Society. Salt Lake City, Utah, March 8–12.

Sanyal, B.C., & Martin, M. 1998. *Management of Higher Education with Special Reference to Financial Management in African Institution*. Paris: UNESCO.

Schwartzman, S. 2003. *Quality, Standards and Globalization in Higher Education*. Keynote presentation to the Biennial Conference of the International Network for Quality Assurance Agencies in Higher Education (INQAAHE). Conference Center, Dublin Castle.

Semali, L.M., Baker, R., & Freer, R. 2013. "Multi–Institutional for Higher Education in Africa: A Case Study of Assumptions of International Academic Collaboration." *International Journal of Higher Education*. 2(2), pp. 53–66.

Swainson, N. 1995. *Redressing Gender Inequalities in Education: A Review of Constraints and Priorities in Malawi, Zambia and Zimbabwe*. A report by British Overseas Development Administration.

UNESCO Institute of Statistics. 2011. *Global Education Digest 2011*. UNESCO, UIS. http:// www.uis.Unesco.org/Education/Pages/ged-2011.aspx.

United Nations Educational, Scientific and Cultural Organisation. 2015. *Continental Education Strategy for 2016–2015*. Report for Annual Continental Activities. UNESCO: Incheon Korea.

United Nations Educational, Scientific and Cultural Organisation. 2011. *Financing Education in Sub-Saharan Africa: Meeting the Challenges of Expansion, Equity and Quality*. UNESCO.

United Nations Educational, Scientific and Cultural Organisation. 2013. *Quality Assurance in Higher* Education. Educational Sector Technical Notes. June. UNESCO.

United Nations Educational, Scientific and Cultural Organisation. 2003. *Recent Developments and Future of Higher Education in Africa in the 21st Century*. UNESCO: Paris

United Nations Educational, Scientific and Cultural Organisation/Organisation for Economic Co-operation and Development. 2005. *Guidelines for Quality Provision in Cross-Border Education*. Paris. http://www.oecd.org/dataoecd/27/51/35779480.pdf. Accessed on June 16, 2017.

United States Agency for International Development. 2014. *Change for Sustainable Development: Opportunities for Transformative*. USAID.

Vossensteyn, H. 2004. "Fiscal Stress: Worldwide Trends in Higher Education Finance." *NASFAA Journal of Student Financial Aid*. 34(1), pp. 39–55.

Vukasovic, M. 2002. *European Students' Handbook on Quality Assurance in Higher Education*. The National Union of Students of Europe.

Waithaka, J.W. 2004. *Structural Adjustment Programs and Provision of Higher Education in Sub-Saharan Africa*. Unpublished master's thesis, University of Nairobi.

World Bank 2011. *Financing Higher Education in Africa*. Washington, D.C.: World Bank.

World Education News and Reviews. 2cccccc011. *Education in Nigeria*. WENR. Retrieved from http://wenr.wes.org/2011/08/wenr-julyaugust-2011-practical-information/. Accessed December 3, 2017.

Yakaboski, T., & Nolan, K. 2011. "Kenyan School Systems' Impact on Public Higher Education Access: Examination of Growth, Access, and Challenges." *Journal of International Education and Leadership,* 1(1), pp. 1–13.

Yizengaw, T. 2008. *Challenges of Higher Education in Africa and Lessons of Experience for the Africa: U.S. Higher Education Collaboration Initiative.* Washington, D.C.: National Association of State Universities and Land Grant-Colleges.

The Nexus of Food Security and Bio-Fuels in Sub-Saharan Africa

EMMANUEL O. ORITSEJAFOR

Introduction

The World Food Summit in 1996 defined food security as a condition that exists "when all people at all times have access to sufficient, safe, and nutritious food to maintain a healthy and active life" (World Health Organization, 1996). The problem of food security in developing countries is severe, particularly in Sub Saharan Africa (SSA), where 218 million people are undernourished. SSA accounts for more than 950 million people, which is about 13 percent of the global population. This translates into one quarter of the population. In sub-Saharan Africa (SSA), 30 percent of children under age five are underweight (Wiggins, 2008). Factors that have contributed to this problem include general demographic trends in third world nations that are caused by more mouths to feed, public policies that are not consistent with development realities, and crude farming methods (Oritsejafor, 2004).

The number of undernourished people as stated earlier has increased by 44 million to reach 218 million. Undernourishment has been a long-standing development challenge in SSA despite being reduced from 33 percent in 1990–1992 to 23 percent in 2014–2016. From 2014–2016, the percentage of undernourishment in SSA remains the highest among developing regions (OECD-FAO, 2016: 60).

Although, SSA countries attained slow progress towards food security between 2014–2016, food security has remained profound, despite the slow demand for food, and the decline in agricultural prices between 2014 and 2015

(FAO, 2016). Concomitantly, the increased demand for bio-fuels have brought about the need to further examine food security and its implications for developing countries and SSA in particular (Wiggins, 2008).

Examining the nexus of bio-fuels and food is important because the demand for bio-fuels as an alternative source of energy, especially in developed economies, and other issues related to the reduction of dependency on fossil fuel, is often linked to food insecurity in developing economies such as SSA.

This essay suggests that alternative sources of energy, such as bio-fuels, are needed to decrease the dependency on petroleum. Developing economies, particularly those in SSA, are most likely to be affected by the use of fuel crops such as wheat, maize, and sugarcane to support bio-fuels industries. Therefore, economies in SSA, should implement socio-economic measures such as school feeding, comprehensive education programs, and food subsidies in order to better address food security problems in a region that is already vulnerable to poverty. The next section provides a review of the dominant development orientations. It provides the context through which an alternative approach for sustainable agricultural development could be advanced.

Development Orientations

There are four dominant orientations often used by development agencies, policy makers, and some social scientists for addressing food security in Africa: Dualism, Agro-Technological, Socio-Anthropological, and the Development orientation. The theoretical works on economic development by the Keynesian school of thought provides some of the dominant orientations in the effort to explain the problem of economic decline in developing countries. However, this school of thought appears to have had an enormous influence on contemporary neoclassical theoretical models used for explaining agricultural development in developing regions. Examples of such models are the Bohemian notions of static dualism, and the Higginian dynamic dualism.

The first neo-classical orientation, dualism, uses the growth model as the point of departure for its own model of economic development. Hayami and Ruttan in their essay on agricultural development, define dualism as: The attempt to understand the relationship or the lack of a relationship between a lagging traditional sector and a growing modern sector within non-western societies affected by the economic and military institutions of western colonialism (Hayami and Ruttan, 1971). Later studies by scholars such as Naude (2013 and Currie-Alder (2016) interrogated the nature and dynamics of the modern sector in the economies of developing countries. Similarly, Rizek (2015) and Clement ((2015) examined the nature and operation of the informal sector in the economies of developing states. Specifically, Ruzek (2015) argues that the informal sector, which does not usually get the desired attention both in scholarly and policy discourses, is critical to the socio-economic development of developing countries.

Within this orientation, dualism can be seen as either static or dynamic, that is, from a sociological and technological perspective (Vollrath, 2009; Lombardo, 2012; Clement, 2015; Stiglitz, 2016). However, static dualism is concerned with the description of the two sectors of the economy, showing the static nature of the traditional sector while concurrently recommending that such sectors are best left alone (Hayami and Ruttan, 1971). Boeke (1953) in his study of Dutch colonialism in Indonesia provides this thesis on dualism: the traditional sector, he claimed, could never be transformed by outside resources and materials. Thus, any attempt to transform this sector would only result in the continuance of its inherent problems. The general outcome of this recommendation by Boeke (1953) has further encouraged the emergence of the enclave model of growth within which has emerged the perspective that a high productivity sector producing for export must co-exist with a low productivity sector producing for domestic consumption.

Winger (1976) on the other hand, elaborates on "enclave dualism." He views dualism on the basis of the technological differences between the modern and the traditional sectors. The modern sector is concentrating on the primary production of commodities in mining and plantation through its importation of technology from outside while the traditional sector is characterized by wide substitution possibilities between capital and labor and the use of labor-intensive production methods.

Lewis' (1954) study on developing countries has likewise made an equal contribution to the understanding of the neo-classical orientation of dualism. Lewis' analysis is mainly concerned with exploring the relationship between the modern and the traditional sectors. His analysis views developing countries as characterized by an unlimited labor supply in the rural sector, but if this supply is carefully utilized, it can lead to needed economic development in both the traditional and modern sectors. This model has failed to produce the desired results in most developing countries because policy makers and development agencies have not been able to strengthen the relationship between the traditional and modern sectors of their economies

The second orientation that has been utilized in explaining the reason for rural agricultural decline in Africa is the agro-technological orientation. This orientation seems to have the greatest impact on the development strategies that are designed to help ameliorate productivity problems in the agricultural sector. The most important model within this orientation is the diffusionist model. This model is premised on the belief that new farming methods that have been discovered in developed nations would inevitably lead to high agricultural productivity when transferred to developing countries (Schultz, 1964).

The third neo-classical orientation frequently used in explaining the problem of agricultural productivity in developing economies is the socio-anthropological approach. This approach is concerned with the question of why traditional farmers in developing economies seem to have a negative perception of programs directed at transforming their development. Thus, proponents of this approach suggest that developing agencies cannot become successful in transforming traditional societies until they take into account the values and social orientations of these societies because they are conditioned by long periods of traditionalism. Thus, change in these societies will occur slowly or, in some cases, never occur (Foster, 1967).

However, scholars such as Mouzeli (1980), Amin (1976), and Brett (1973), rejected the growth criteria of the neoclassical orientations, where quantitative increases in such indexes as Gross Domestic Product (GDP) and per capita income are yardsticks for measuring development. Instead, they argue that development should be examined through a country's actual economic, political, cultural structure, and their historical development within the context of the world economy. In this regard, Amin contends that underdeveloped countries have certain characteristics that oblige us not to confuse them with the now advanced countries. These characteristics are as follow:

1. The extreme inequality that is typical of the distribution of productivities in the periphery and in the system of prices transmitted to it from the center,

2. The disarticulation due to the adjustment of the orientation of production in the periphery to the needs of the center, which prevents the transmission of the benefits of economic progress from the poles of development to the economy as a whole, and

3. Economic domination by the center, which is expressed in the forms of international specialization and in the dependence of the structures whereby growth in the periphery is financed (Amin, 1976).

However, given the challenges of sustainable agriculture development in sub-Saharan Africa, the primary use of modern agricultural practices such as biotechnology has not been sustainable. Instead, alternative agricultural development approaches, such as the use of traditional farming methods with other forms of modern agricultural practices, must be examined (Oritsejafor, 2004). In this regard, Gana (2003) focused on the use of natural plant materials such as agro-chemicals among small-scale farmers in three villages in Niger State, in Northern Nigeria. The study revealed that these farmers were able to reduce and control the population of cowpea pests in the field, and parasitic nematodes found in the soil with the use of botanic chemicals as alternatives to the use of toxic-synthetic agro-chemicals.

In another study, Ajibade and Shokemi (2003) found that Indigenous Knowledge (IK) was used effectively by 95 percent of 200 farmers to identify five weather systems such as rainfall, harmattan, thunderstorm, windstorm, and sunshine. The study suggests that if IK is integrated with a western-based weather forecast system, it could prove to be an essential element of the development process for farm communities in Nigeria.

Similarly, in other developing countries such as Bangladesh, farmers are noted to have used the store of knowledge they have built over time to enhance food production. For example, in the absence of sufficient natural forests in Bangladesh, more than 50 percent of timber, 85 percent of fuel-wood, and 90 percent of bamboo used are derived from trees and shrubs grown by people on their homesteads (Qudus, 2000). In this case, IK is integrated with modern technology to address farm forestry challenges that were caused by over-exploitation of homesteads for food crops and medicinal resources.

Food Versus Oil: Competing Interests?

Around 2008–2010, the developing economies faced significant challenges in achieving basic food security, because of increasing demand for fuel-crops such as wheat, maize, sugarcane, and oilseeds for the production of bio-fuels, bio-electricity, and bio-heat in oil importing developed economies such as the United States (Schmitz and Kavallari). The ethanol industry statistics forecasts from 2008 through 2012 showed that world ethanol production would exceed 20 billion gallons by 2012. The projections for world ethanol production in the next four years (2013–2017) underscored the increasing importance of bio-fuels as an alternative to fossil fuels.

The demand for alternative energy stems from the need to reduce greenhouse gas emissions and the dependency on petroleum based oil with its attendant unpredictable market-driven price (Bala and Havva, 2009).

To promote the production of alternative energy, such as ethanol for transportation, the United States' national policies, such as the Energy Policy Act of 2005, targeted the consumption of 28.4 billion liters of bio-ethanol by 2012. The Act provided and extended the bio-diesel fuel excise tax credit through 2008 and provided a $0.03 per liter income tax credit to small bio-diesel producers in the United States (Bale and Hava, 2009). Despite these measures and incentives to support bio-fuels, the price of fossil-fuels continued to surge over $0.79 per liter in the spring of 2007, and remained constant during the summer, except for a slight retreat, but returned to the same price at the beginning of 2008 (Bala and Havva, 2009).

Nonetheless, the rising demand for fuel-crops such as wheat, sugar cane, and maize is bound to have a mixed and profound effect on most sub-Saharan African countries. On the one hand, the use of bio-fuels as alternative sources of energy in sub-Saharan Africa is likely to reduce the dependency on petroleum oil. This could be the case given that 39 countries in Africa are net importers of petroleum oil and about 39 percent of the total energy consumed in sub–Saharan Africa is imported against the world average of 19 percent (Mulugetta, 2009).

On the other hand, the reliance on bio-fuels in sub-Saharan Africa would most likely reduce greenhouse effects and reduce the emissions of carbon monoxide (CO) and carbon dioxide (CO_2). This is especially significant for sub–Saharan Africa economically and environmentally because it could reduce the cost of road transportation. Road transportation is the primary method of moving goods and services in the region. This commercial area accounts for about 85 percent of the total fossil fuel used in the transportation sector. Diesel fuel accounts for over 55 percent of the fuel consumption in this sector (Mulugetta, 2009).

The demand for bio-fuels in developed and developing economies also presents major challenges for food security. This demand will potentially lead to increased pressure to clear land for farming in order to increase the production of fuel crops such as sugarcane for ethanol, and palm oil plantations for bio-diesel. The clearing of mass areas of land for farming presents major threats to animal and plant diversity (Mulugetta, 2009). However, recent world food production trends suggest that increased demand to clear land is precipitated by the need to address food security which would invariably impact the demand for biofuels (HLPE 5 Report, 2013:80).

Though oil prices have dropped sharply since mid 2014, driven by slow demand and record increases in supplies, particularly shale oil from North America, as well as the policy decision by the Organization of Petroleum Exporting Countries (OPEC) to leave its production unchanged. Nonetheless, demand for biofuels has continued to be highly influenced by domestic policies in conjunction with sustained fuel demand globally (Xu and Bell, 2015)

Investments in fuel crops production and the attendant competition for land is likely to lead to increased pressure on farm based economies to produce alternative food crops (Mulugetta, 2009). This was the case in Latin America and the Horn of Africa when farmers switched from growing traditional food crops and coffee to coca and quat production as a response to diminishing returns in the food commodities sector. The demand for fuel crops emerged at a time when the world food stocks were at their lowest level in about 40 years. With 76 million more people to feed each year, this presented enormous social and economic challenges for sub-Saharan Africa, especially with the extensive number of "food deficits in the region" (Mulugetta, 2009).

The next section of this essay examines the social and economic implications of the food and fuel nexus followed by policy recommendations and conclusions.

Social and Economic Effects of the Food Insecurity

The surge in food prices was driven by the combination of the rising fuel costs, the demand for fuel-crops for bio-fuel production, and trade restrictions that led to upward price pressures. The World Bank projected that the price of grains and other major food crops would double their 2004 levels through 2015. This trend is being experienced in developing economies where the rising global price of major food crops has affected domestic prices. For example, median inflation in non–Organization for Economic Cooperation Development (OECD) countries peaked from 5 percent in 2006 to 8.1 percent in 2008, and inflation increased by more than 5 percentage points in 21 countries. In the case of sub-Saharan Africa, price inflation was higher than the 2005–2007 average at about or, in some cases, above 14 percent. The rise in food prices has also led to an increase in the number of poor people. The overall estimate of the global increase in the number of poor people as a result of the food crisis averages between 3–5 percentage points in global poverty rates, which is equivalent to around 100 million people (World Bank, 2008). This number is profound in developing regions such as sub-Saharan Africa, where millions live on less than a dollar a day and the rate of unemployment and income inequality is among the highest in the world (Guseh and Oritsejafor, 2009). Recent estimates have also shown that poverty is deepening among those that are already poor. For instance, poor households in developing countries that typically spend between 60–80 percent of their income on food have found out it almost impossible to meet other needs such as shelter, clothing and medicine when food prices rise (World Food Program, 2012).

In addition, the surging food prices have also led to some households eating less in developing economies. Thus, poor households have begun to switch from nutritious sources of food, such as fish, meat, and eggs, to less nutritious cereals. It is in this regard that Sheeran suggests that:

> People living on less than a US $2 a day have cut out health and education and sold or eaten their livestock. Those living on less than US $1 a day have cut protein and vegetables from their diet [Sheeran, 2007–2008].

The implications of such a nutritional switch are micro-nutrient deficiencies in iron, iodine, and vitamins. Consequently, this will lead to weight loss and acute malnutrition among poor households (World Bank, 2008). However, despite halving the percentage of malnutriton by 23 percent in 2015, SSA region has continued to be challenged by population growth which consequently will affect access to food and supply. The population has grown from 507 million in 1990 to 936 million in 2013 (FAO, Regional Overview of Food Security, 2015)

Nonetheless, women and young girls in sub-Saharan Africa appear to be profoundly affected by these social crises. Albeit, women are responsible for 60 to 80 percent of the agricultural labor supplied in the market place, and form the majority of the labor in the commercial sectors in many African cities and towns. However, they are inhibited by the lack of formal economic support and educational opportunities (Gappah, 2011). Thus, their recognized economic role in most African countries has remained challenged by the direct and indirect social cost of the limited access to resources such as land, affordable health care, and educational opportunities.

Accordingly, social indicators for education suggests that the number of girls per 100 boys in tertiary education dropped from 67 to 63 between 1999 and 2009; the numbers also dropped in secondary education from 82 to 79, but rose in primary education from 85 to 92(Gappah, 2011).

Evidence from developing countries in other parts of the world such as Brazil, Peru, and Bangladesh underscores the relationship between loss of income and schooling and the current surge in food prices (World Bank, 2008). For instance, a longitudinal study in Brazil showed that sudden loss of primary household income could lead to 50 percent higher probability of a female youth leaving school to seek employment, while evidence from Peru suggests that economic factors affect the quality of education a child receives as a result of reduced private spending on education (World Bank, 2008).

The next section examines policy options and provides an assessment of best practices in developing countries that could be implemented in sub-Saharan Africa to address the social and economic effects of the surge in food prices.

Policy Options And Recommendations

Given the social and economic implications of the current food crisis, policy makers and development agencies would need to provide safety nets for poor households in developing regions. The ability to address the adverse effects of high food prices would require policy options and an assessment of best practices in sub-Saharan Africa and other developing regions. Thus, the following recommendations are proffered:

1. Food and transport vouchers: Programs that have used food vouchers have been known to be successful in some developing countries, though there is less experience with transport vouchers. The challenge of distributing near cash instruments, such as vouchers, is that benefits are amenable to diversion when compared to cash transfers. For example, Indonesia has been successful in the implementation of a time-limited cash transfer program to about one-third of its population in order to absorb the shocks of food and oil prices (World Bank, 2008);

2. Inclusion of Women in agri-business: In line with the African Union (AU) Declaration and Agenda for 2063, women who have typically been at the forefront of agricultural development in SSA should be provided the financial support they need to be competitive in agri-business (FAO, Africa Regional Overview, 2016:11);

3. School feeding: School feeding programs are increasingly popular in developing countries, particularly in sub-Saharan Africa. Countries such as Ghana, Benin, Burundi, Liberia, Lesotho, Sierra Leone, Senegal, Mauritania, and Mozambique have all implemented school feeding programs. However, the benefits of school feeding could be enhanced through increasing funding (World Bank, 2008);

4. Cash Transfer Programs: Government initiated unconditional cash transfer programs can be employed to assist households that are facing social and economic hardships. For instance, in Ghana caretakers of orphans and vulnerable children (OVC) receive cash transfer to register their children and ensure that they are enrolled in school (Daidone, Daris, Handa, & Winters, 2017)

5. Comprehensive education: To alleviate the present social and economic impact of high food prices on poor households, social protection should be implemented to reduce the pressures of children being pulled out of school. For example, in Ghana, primary school enrollments peaked by 14 percent after user- fees were abolished in 2005 (World Bank, 2008);

6. Nutrition and health options: Eating less and switching from expensive sources of protein such as fish, meat, and eggs to cheaper cereal will invariably have long term health consequences for poor households. Younger children and pregnant women are more susceptible to weight loss and malnutrition. Therefore, national governments and multilateral institutions must collaboratively intervene to address food and health-care shortages during crisis periods to the poor households (World Bank, 2008);

7. Food taxes and subsidies: Several countries have implemented programs to reduce food taxes and increase subsidies. For example, in North Africa, Egypt has increased the ration of food subsidies and in Latin

America, Brazil has increased the benefits of the Bolas Familia conditional cash transfer (World Bank, 2008);

8. Alternative bio-fuels production site: The increased global demand for bio-fuels whereby, production increased from 20 billion liters in 2001 to 100 billion liters in 2011, has drawn development expert's attention to alternative production process. In this vain, it would bode well to address food security in SSA by producing bio-fuels in areas that are socially and economically viable.

9. Alternative sources of energy: Given the pressure to seek alternative sources of energy partly because of the costs and partly because of the declining production of fossil-fuels, scientists have begun to seek alternative sources of energy such as solar energy and bio-fuels. However, this study suggests that in light of some of the environmental advantages of bio-fuels, its advantages may not augur well for poor farmers and food security. For instance, the use of palm oil, an edible for bio-fuels, has been promoted by some scientists in Malaysia. However, the concern is that the conversion of food crops such as palm nut for bio-diesel would consequently lead to undernourishment among millions in developing countries that depend on palm oil for their daily nutrition (KeeLam et al., 2009). Moreover, the use of bio-fuels such as bio-diesel, as an alternative source of transportation energy is mired with production costs because the price and availability of the main by-product, glycerin, presents economic and environmental issues (Bezergianni and Kalogianni 2009). It is against this backdrop that alternative sources of energy, such as used cooking oil, should be explored as a feedstock for biodiesel production.

In addition to the recommendations provided to address the adverse social and economic effects of high food prices in sub-Saharan Africa, this study offers an alternative approach for addressing food security. The next section examines how "Traditional Management Regimes" could enhance food security in sub-Saharan Africa.

Traditional Management Regimes and Food Security

"Traditional Management Regimes" refer to the processes and products of agricultural diversification. It includes the ways in which farmers use the natural diversity of the environment for production, and the management of water and land (Gyasi et al., 2004).

Given the challenge of food security in sub-Saharan Africa, it is instructive that policy makers and development agencies should continue to embrace and encourage agro-diversity and traditional farming practices. The use of indigenous methods for managing the land, water, and biota for crop and livestock production is not only a practical approach for addressing food security, it is also less capital intensive and sustainable. The table below provides examples of traditional food management regimes in southern Ghana and their advantages.

Traditional Agricultural Practices in Southern Ghana

Practices/Regimes	*Major advantages*
Minimal tillage and controlled use of fire for vegetation clearance, mixed cropping, crop rotation, and mixed farming	Minimal disturbance of soil and biota. Maximize soil nutrient usage.
Traditional agro-forestry: cultivating crops among trees left in situ	Conserves trees; regenerates soil fertility through biomass litter. Some trees add to productive capacity of soil by nitrogen fixation.
Bush fallow with land rotation	A means of regenerating soil fertility and conserving plants in the wild.
Usage of household refuse and manure in home gardens and compound farms.	Sustains soil productivity.

Source: Compiled by the Author from A. Gyasi, Edwin Gordana Kranjac-Berisavljevic, Essie T. Blay, and William Oduro. Managing Agro Diversity the Traditional Way: Lessons from West Africa in Sustainable Use of Biodiversity and Related Natural Resources (New York: United Nations University Press, 2004).

Traditional food management regimes have also been successfully adopted in other developing regions such as southwest Asia. For example, Bangladesh has developed an array of sophisticated farm practices to sustain their agricultural needs. For instance, Neem leaves are dried to protect stored grains from insect infestation (Qudus, 2000).

Conclusion

The surge in food prices was driven by the combination of rising fuel costs, the demand for fuel crops for bio-fuel production, and trade restrictions that led to upward price pressures. It was projected by the World Bank that the price of grains and other major food crops will double their 2004 levels through 2015 (World Bank, 2008). Not only was the projection confirmed in 2015, but the challenge of higher prices for grain and other food products has continued since then. Consequently, there is the increasing incidence of food insecurity in Africa, because amid mass poverty people cannot afford to buy grains and other food products. As we approach the end of the second decade of the 21st century, food insecurity in Africa has become a major national security issue.

This global trend is profound in developing economies, where the rising global prices of major food crops have affected domestic prices. For example, median inflation in non–Organization for Economic Cooperation Development (OECD) countries peaked from 5 percent in 2006 to 8.1 percent in 2008, and inflation increased by more than 5 percentage points in 21 countries. Over the past eight years (2009–2017), inflation has remained a major challenge. In the case of sub-Saharan Africa, price inflation was higher than the 2005–2007 average at about or, in some cases, above 14 percent. Since then (over the last decade—2007–2017), the situation has not improved.

Given the challenges that the recent rise in food prices presents to developing economies, farmers in these countries must be empowered socially and economically. This is particularly the case in Sub-Saharan Africa where about 70 percent of the population live in rural areas and depend mainly on agriculture. African countries also represent about 50 percent of the top 20 countries in terms of total agriculture exported merchandise in the world, and women are responsible for about 80 percent of the total food production.

Despite the pivotal role of women in the food production process, women continue to face several social and economic constraints. Thus, in order to empower farming communities in sub-Saharan Africa and address food security, one has to examine the implications of such intervention for women farmers. The following are examples of some of the social and economic constraints that rural women farmers face in sub-Saharan Africa:

1. Less access to land than men. The land tenure systems in most sub-Saharan African countries seem to be porous and are typically gender bias. Even in cases that women farmers own land, the land is often located in marginal areas;

2. Women farmers have less access to credit which often limits their ability to purchase seeds and fertilizers and other farm inputs;

3. The role of rural women farmers as mothers, and in some cases bread winners is vital to household food security. However, they are further challenged by the lack of access to adequate healthcare facilities; and

4. Women farmers are also challenged by lack of educational facilities. Most rural educational infrastructures are weak and in most cases, do not address the socio-economic realities of rural communities.

To address these challenges, countries such as Malawi, Uganda, Tanzania, and Ethiopia have established partnerships with local and international Non-Governmental Organizations (NGOs) such as the Canadian Physician for Aid and Relief (CPAR) to develop intervention programs focusing on food security for rural women farmers in sub-Saharan Africa. One of such programs is the *Farmers First Program*. The program identified the following interventions for addressing food security for women:

1. Entrepreneurship training for women and training women in the use of fuel efficiency stoves for cooking in order to limit the time they spend in collecting wood for cooking;

2. Health education sessions on family planning and HIV prevention;

3. In Tanzania CPAR has developed a training program in soil conservation, and provides labor saving devices such as ploughs and wheel barrels for local farmers; and

4. Training programs have been developed in Malawi, Tanzania, Uganda, and Ethiopia for equipping women farmers on food processing, budgeting, management of household consumption, and production for better nutritional outcomes.

Training is provided to improve crop storage facilities and other farm based asset needs such as support to construct vitamin rich food gardens, and to keep specific livestock types.

Overall, the rise in food prices has led to an increase in the poverty rate. This rate is profound in developing regions such as sub-Saharan Africa, where millions already live on less than a dollar a day, and the rate of unemployment and income inequality are among the highest in the world. Therefore, policy makers and development agencies must continue to provide social and economic safety nets such as nutritional programs, credit facilities, and universal free education for farming communities in order to better address the adverse effects of high food prices and to attain food security in sub-Saharan Africa.

REFERENCES

Ajibade, I., and Shokemi, O. 2003. Indigenous Approach to Weather Forecasting in ASA Local Government, Kwara State, Nigeria. *Indinlinga: African Journal of Indigenous Knowledge Systems*, 2, pp. 37–46.

Amin, S. 1976. *Development: An Essay on the Social Formation of Peripheral Capitalism*. New York: Monthly Review Press, pp. 9–23, pp. 201–202.

Bala, M., and Havva, B. 2009. "Recent Trends in Global Production and Utilization of Bioethanol Fuel." *Applied Energy*, 86, pp. 2273–2282.

Bezergianni, S., and Kalogianni, A. 2009. "Hydrocracking of Used Cooking Oil for Biofuels Production." *Bio-Resource Technology*, 100, pp. 3927–3932.

Boeke, J. 1953. *Economics and Economic Policy of Dual Societies as Exemplified by Indonesia*. New York: Institute of Pacific Relations.

Brett, E. 1973. *Colonialism and Underdevelopment in East Africa: The Politics of Economic Change 1919–1939*. New York: Nok Publishers.

Clement, Claristine. 2015. *The Formal-Informal Economy Dualism in a Retrospective of Economic Thought Since the 1940s*. Working paper no. 43/2015. Globalization and Employment Program, University of Oldenburg, Germany.

Currie-Alder, Bruce. 2016. "The State of Development Studies: Origins, Evolution and Prospects." *Canadian Journal of Development Studies*. 37(1), pp. 5–26.

Daidone, S., Daris, B.; Handa, S., and Winters, P. 2017. The Household and Individual Level Economic Impacts of Cash Transfer Programs in Sub-Saharan Africa. *OECD-FAO Agricultural Outlook 2016–2025.*

Food and Agriculture Organization of the United Nations, Food and Agriculture Organization of the UN OECD/FAO. 2016. [online] Paris: OECD Publishing. http://www.fao.org/3/a-i5778e.pdf.

Food and Agriculture Organization of the United Nations. 2017. "Africa: Regional Overview of Food Security and Nutrition." http://www.fao.org/3/a-i6813e.pdf. Retrieved October 6, 2017.

Food and Agriculture Organization of the United Nations. 2013. "Bio-Fuels and Food Security: A Report by the High Level Panel of Experts on Food Security and Nutrition." http://www.fao.org/3/a-i2952e.pdf.

Food and Agriculture Organization of the United Nations. 2015. "Regional Overview of Food Insecurity: Africa." http://www.fao.org/3/a-i4635e.pdf. Retrieved October 6, 2017.

Foster, G. 1967. *Tzintunzan: Mexican Peasants in a Changing World.* Boston: Little, Brown.

Gana, F. 2003. "The Usage of Indigenous Plant Materials Among Small-Scale Farmers in Niger State Agricultural Development Project." *Indilinga: African Journal of Indigenous Knowledge Systems*, 2, pp. 53–64.

Gapped, P. 2011. "Women Are Our Best Hope for the Continent." *The African Report.* August-September, pp. 24–25.

Guseh, J., and Oritsejafor, E. 2009. "The African Growth and Opportunity Act and Economic Growth in Sub-Saharan Africa." *The Whitehead Journal of Diplomacy and International Relations* 10 (1), pp. 123–140.

Gyasi, E., et al. 2004. *Managing Agro Diversity the Traditional Way: Lessons from West Africa in Sustainable Use of Biodiversity and Related Natural Resources.* New York: United Nations University Press.

Hayami, U., and Ruttan, V. 1971. *Agricultural Development: An International Perspective.* Baltimore: Johns Hopkins University Press.

KeeLam, M., Kok, T., Teong, L., and Rahman, M. 2009. "Malaysian Palm Oil: Surviving the Food Versus Fuel Dispute for a Sustainable Future." *Renewable and Sustainable Energy Reviews*, 13, pp. 1456–1464.

Lewis, A. 1954. "Economic Development with Unlimited Supplies of Labor." *Manchester School of Economics and Social Studies*, May 22, pp. 139–191.

Lombardo, Vinceno. 2012. *Modern Foundaitons of Dual Economy Models.* CRISEI Discussion Paper Series No. 8. Department of Economics, Universite deglistudi di Napli-Parthenope.

Mouzeli, N. 1990. "Modernization, Underdevelopment, Uneven Development: Prospects for Theory of Third World Formations." *Journal of Peasant Studies*, 1, pp. 13–15.

Mulugetta, Y. 2009. "Evaluating the Economics of Biodiesel in Africa." *Renewable and Sustainable Energy Reviews*, 13, pp. 1592–1598.

OECD—FAO. 2016. Agricultural Outlook 2016–2025. Paris: OECD Publishing.

Oritsejafor, E. 2004. "Food Security in Africa: The Case of Biotechnology and Environmental Conservation in Nigeria." *Journal of African Policy Studies*, 10(2 and 3), pp. 1–22.

Qudus, M., and Stillitoe, P. (ed.). 2000. *Use of Indigenous Knowledge in the Sustainable Development of Bangladesh Farm Forestry in Indigenous Knowledge Development in Bangladesh: Present and Future.* London: Intermediate Technology Publications.

Renewable Fuel Association, Ethanol Industry Statistics. [online] Available at http://www.ethanolrefa.org/industry/statistics. Accessed June 15, 2017.

Schmitz, P.M., and A. Kavallari. 2000. A. "Crop Plants Versus Energy Plants on the International Food Crisis." *Biorganic and Medicinal Chemistry.* 17(12), pp. 4020–4021.

Schultz, T. 1964. *Transforming Traditional Agriculture.* New Haven: Yale University Press.

Sheeran, J. 2007–2008. "High Global Food: The Challenges and Opportunities." *International Food Policy Research Institute (IFPRI) Annual Report Essays*, 12.

Stiglitz, Joseph. 2016. "The State, the Market and Development." WIDER Working Paper 2016/1. World Institute for Development Economics Research, United Nations University.

Vollrath, Dietrich. 2009. "The Dual Economy in Long-Run Development." *Journal of Popular Economics*, 14(4), pp. 287–312.

World Bank. 2008. "Rising Food and Fuel Prices: Addressing the Risks to Future Generations." World Health Organization Food Security. http://wwww.who.intl/trade/glossary. Accessed June 18, 2017.

World Food Program. 2012. How High Food Prices Affects the World Poor. https://www.wfp.org/stories/how-high-food-prices-affect-worlds-poor. Retrieved October 6, 2017.

World Health Organization. 1996. World Food Summit. Geneva, Switzerland: WHO.

Xu, C., and Bell, L. 2017. "Near-Term Oil Market Outlook Remains Complicated." http://www.ogj.com/articles/print/volume-115/issue-7/special-report-midyear-forecast/near-term-oil-market-outlook-remains-complicated.html. Retrieved October 6, 2017.

Political Instability
and Development in Africa

GEORGE KLAY KIEH, JR.

Introduction

The discourse on political instability in Africa—both in the scholarly literature and in the corridors of policy-making in the metropolis—tends to treat the phenomenon as an idiosyncrasy of African polities. In other words, the impression is conveyed that African societies are intrinsically unstable. To the contrary, the repository of empirical evidence clearly demonstrates that political instability is neither unique to Africa nor any other region of the world. Neither is the phenomenon new. Instead, it has been a major enduring feature of the state-building project even prior to the advent of the Westphalian International System in 1648: Various states in Africa, Asia, Europe and the Americas were plagued by political instability and its attendant adverse consequences.

This trend has continued over the last three centuries and half. For example, in the 1960s, the United States was rocked by various political instability events—riots, demonstrations, etc.—as manifestations of the pantomimes of the American "apartheid system" (Gibson, 1979; Archer, 1974; Rubenstein, 1970; Demaris, 1970). From 1971–2000, there were 20 coups d'état, 451 political assassinations, 217 riots, and 113 crises that threatened to bring down the sitting government (Blanco and Grier: 2007:1). In Europe, for example, the Balkans imploded in the 1990s, as evidenced by, inter alia, the genocidal civil war in the Bosnia-Herzegovina (Phillips, 2004; Greskovits, 1998). In Asia, especially its central region, the vagaries of political instability have jolted various states (Lal, 2006). The continent's Middle Eastern section continues to experience political instability (Long and Reich, 2002; Berboroglu, 1999). In the case of Africa, it has, and continues to experience political instability.

Against this background, using Africa as a case study, this essay seeks to address four major interrelated questions. First, what is the state of political instability in Africa? Second, what are the major causes of political instability in Africa? Third, what are the consequences or the costs of the phenomenon for development? Fourth, how can Africa address the phenomenon and its adverse effects?

Conceptualizing Political Instability

The study employs Gyimah-Brempong and Traynor's (1999:54) conceptualization of political instability: "A situation, activity or pattern of behavior that threatens to change or actually changes the political system of a country in a non-constitutional way."

Explaining Political Instability: A Review of the Literature

What are the causes and manifestations of political instability—the taproots and events? Several theoretical frameworks have been developed in an effort to address this critical question. However, it is not possible to explore all of these constructs. Hence, I will map out the major contours of three of the major theories: cold war, ethnic and rent seeking.

The Cold War Theory

The Cold War theory is anchored on several major tenets. At the core is the argument that the Cold War was an intense competition between the United States and the Soviet Union, the two global superpowers that emerged at the end of World War II. As Oyebade and Alao (1998:2–3) note, "...the Cold War became the primary force governing East-West relations."

Fundamentally, the Cold War was designed to serve the multifaceted interests of the two superpowers. Hence, it was not intended to promote the development of other states, especially client states. For example, according to Lawson (2007:1), "During the Cold War, United States foreign policy toward Sub-Saharan Africa had little to do with Africa. As with other developing regions, African countries were first and foremost pawns in the global chess game."

Another pillar of the theory is that the two superpowers used an assortment of methods to promote their respective interests. And these methods induced instability in their various client and non-client states. For example, in their client states, the two superpowers sided with particular political factions against others. The resultant polarization, among other things, led to violent conflicts. As Emeh (2004:1) observes in the case of Africa, "The Cold War inspired brutal armed conflicts in Southern Africa (Mozambique and Angola) and the Horn of Africa (between Ethiopia and Somalia)." In the non-client states, the efforts by both superpowers to dislodge various regimes from power and to replace them with client ones made these states politically unstable.

The Ethnic Theory

The ethnic theory has, and continues to be the dominant framework for problematizing political instability in Africa and elsewhere in the Third World. The theory is hoisted on several pillars. First, it is argued that ethnic pluralism is promotive of rivalries that are destabilizing. As Osinubi and Osinubi, 2006:101), argue, "Ethnic diversity may lead to increased political strife."

Second and related, these inter-ethnic rivalries are linked to the competition for state resources, and tend to spillover into other areas, especially in divided societies. Given what Horowitz (2000:8) calls the "permeative propensities of ethnic affiliations in divided societies," ethnicity finds its way into a myriad of issues: development plans, educational controversies, trade union affairs, land policy, business policy, tax policy." Importantly, these ethnically-based competitions often produce "winners and losers" within a "zero sum" framework." These outcomes reinforce ethnic rivalries as privileged and marginalized ethnic groups engaged in on going "tugs and pulls" with their attendant destabilizing effects.

Third, the fact that the government is often aligned with a privileged ethnic group coupled with the lack or inadequacy of institutional mechanisms to mediate ethnic conflicts nurture the seeds of instability. Over time, instability becomes a permanent fixture of the political landscape. In turn, this sets the stage for the occurrence of instability events such as strikes, demonstrations, riots, coups and civil wars.

The Rent-Seeking Theory

At the vortex of the rent-seeking theory is the proposition that individuals engage in instability events such as demonstrations, riots, coups and civil wars based on self-interests. That is, the participants in these events make rational calculations based on "costs and benefits." Thus, if they determine that their engagement in a particular instability event would advance their personal interests, then they participate. Conversely, if based on their calculations, the personal dividends to be accrued are comparatively smaller than the transaction costs, they would not participate.

Another tenet is that the government apparatus is employed to create and extract rents (Mbaku and Paul, 1989: 64). In this context, the ruling elites exclude groups from getting their share of the rent. Such an approach to resource allocation adversely affects the well-being of marginalized or excluded groups, thereby exacerbating the undercurrents of instability.

Hence, blocked from competing for gains in government controlled markets and from competing for rents by exclusion from institutionalized political process, members of excluded groups attempt to capture control of government by extra-constitutional or violent political means (Mbaku and Paul, 1989: 64). The resultant instability activities such as coups and civil wars are reflections of the underlying state of instability that is anchored on the "politics of exclusion." However, the desired outcomes are driven by the desires for personal gains than a commitment by the participants to redesign the allocative process by making it more equitable.

An Alternative Theoretical Framework

The Cold War, ethnic and rent-seeking theories explain various dimensions of the non-hegemonic and dependent complexion of the peripheral capitalist state in Africa and the resultant crises of underdevelopment that are consequences of the nature and dynamics of this construct. In other words, each of the theories emphasizes "specific species of trees" (aspects of the crisis of the state) without examining the "broader forest in which these species of trees" exist (the state itself). The Cold War, ethnic rivalries and rent-seeking behavior are manifestations of the imperial global order and its internal peripheral capitalist political economies in African states.

Against this background, I employ the peripheral capitalist state theory as the framework for this study. The theory is premised on several postulations. First, the "Berlinist state" (Kieh, 2007:3) that was bequeathed to Africa at independence is a product of the imperial global capitalist order. Hence, even in its so-called post-colonial variation, it is a weak, non-hegemonic and dependent construct that is designed to serve the interests of the ruling classes and their dominant states both during the Cold War, and currently in the post–Cold War era. Thus, the post-colonial state in Africa is a peripheral capitalist formation that plays a marginal role in the international capitalist system and its "balance of power."

Second, the domestic political economies are based on the peripheral capitalist mode of production in which the major means of production (especially capital and technology) are owned and controlled by various members of metropolitan-based ruling classes in the United States and Europe. The central function of the peripheral capitalist economies is the production of raw materials—agricultural products, minerals and oil—to feed the industrial-manufacturing machines of the advanced capitalist states, and to provide investment havens in which the multinational corporations from the developed capitalist states can accrue huge profits. Significantly, these peripheral capitalist states are operated by non-hegemonic or what Cabral (1970) calls "pseudo bourgeoisies." Their major function is to ensure that the peripheral capitalist state serves the interests of the ruling classes in the metropolis and their dominant states. In order to perform this function, the various factions and fractions of the local compradorial classes in the peripheral states compete for the control of state power.

Third, based on the logic of the power relationships that underpin the peripheral capitalist political economy, the compradorial fraction or faction that has control of state power at any given time excludes other fractions and factions of the compradorial classes, ethnic groups and other identities from the political process, especially from the benefits of the state. In so doing, the ruling local compradorial fraction or faction uses an assortment of means, including repression and violence. In turn, a climate of tension and conflict is created, and instability then ensues. In essence, political instability is the by product of the dialectical tensions between the anti-people, anti-development and anti-democracy policies of the peripheral capitalist state, on the one hand, and subaltern classes and other groups, on the other.

The Peripheral Capitalist State: The Taproot of Political Instability In Africa

The precondition for understanding the roots of political instability in Africa is based on the examination of the historical development and dynamics of the peripheral capitalist state in Africa. The peripheral capitalist state in Africa has its roots in the colonial or the "Berlinist state" (Kieh, 2007:3) that was designed by the European imperialists at the notorious Berlin Conference of 1884–1885. The conference was designed to parcel out African territories to the various imperialist powers—Belgium, Britain, France, Germany, Italy, Portugal and Spain—in an "orderly manner." That is, realizing that the "rat race" for the plundering and pillaging of African territories could have led to chaos and conflict between and among the predatory imperialist powers, the colonialists therefore decided to establish a framework in which, based on the dynamics of the global "balance of power," hitherto sovereign African states could be conquered through the use of brute force. According, the resultant "partition plan" ended the state-building projects in the various indigenous African polities. As Oliver and Atmore (1994:100) aptly observe, "The European powers partitioned Africa among themselves with such haste, like players in a rough game, that the process has been called the "scramble for Africa." Thereafter, the imperialists "sent armies to Africa in order to turn the boundaries on their maps into frontiers on the ground. Owners of the land who resisted the arrival of the self-styled forces of 'civilization' were to be 'pacified' by conquest" (Birmingham, 1995:3).

By 1914, the lives of all Africans were being affected by the changes brought about by the foreign rulers (Oliver and Atmore, 1994). The most transcendent change was the establishment of the colonial state and its political economy. Given Europe's role as the center of global capitalism, the imperialists were able to establish their dominance by incorporating Africa into the world-system (Quijano,2000:5) as "hewers of developmental wood and fetchers of growth water" (Garuba, 1998:4). The emergent peripheral capitalist political economy developed as a consequence of Western capitalism's quest for markets, raw materials and profits (Kaya, 2008:303).

Conditioned by the exigencies of imperialism and global capitalism, the colonial state in Africa had a distinctive portrait. Its nature reflected the historical, cultural, economic, political and social imperatives of the imperialist powers. In other words, the vision that was deposited in the colonial state reflected the interests of the dominant classes in the various imperialist states. Hence, the operation of the colonial state demonstrated its intrinsic class bias.

The major mission of the colonial state was two fold. First, it created the conditions that were favorable to the accumulation of capital by the members of the capitalist classes from the imperialist powers, who were either resident in the metropolis or the colonies. This clearly demonstrated the centrality of economics as the motor force for colonialism and imperialism. Through this framework, wealth was transferred from Africa to countries overseas (Davidson, 1994:19). Second and related, in order to create the conditions that were propitious to the profit-making agenda of the dominant classes, the colonial state developed a full battery of repressive tools that sought to cow colonized Africans into submission.

The character of the colonial state was multidimensional. Edie (2003:48) provides an excellent summation of the absolutist core of the "multi-headed hydra":

> All colonial states in Africa had certain characteristics: they were conceived in violence and issued from conquest; they established imperial sovereignty on the conquered territories; they were all centralized and coercive; they all created a bureaucratic elite; they dominated economic activities; they employed racist ideologies; they all sought to integrate the economy of the colony into the imperial economy.

One or more tendencies of the colonial state's character were ascendant at particular historical moments (Agbese, 2007). Some of the dimensions of the state's character included repression, violence, negligence, exploitation and exclusionary. The repressive dimension of the colonial state's character was reflected in its total disregard for the cultural, economic, political and social rights of Africans. As a violent construct, the colonial state primarily relied on the use of brute force as the dominant mode for the conduct of state-society relations. As Crowder (1987:11) notes, "[The colonial state engaged] in burning of villages, destruction of crops, killing of women and children, and the execution of leaders." The colonial state was also negligent. That is, it deliberately refused to provide the basic human needs of the African peoples—jobs, housing, education and health care. However, the colonial state forced Africans to pay taxes and to provide sundry services to the state, including the construction of buildings and roads. As an exploitative formation, the state facilitated the transfer of Africa's resources to the metropolis through plunder and pillage. The exclusionary tendency of the colonial state was reflected in the fact that it divided the colonial society into classes, races and ethnicities. In class terms, there were the ruling classes consisting of the owners of capital, and the state managers, who were White Europeans. The petit bourgeois class consisted of malleable and subservient Africans who were skilled in various areas. These individuals, who were drawn disproportionately from the colonially designated "dominant indigenous ethnic groups," served as junior managers of the colonial bureaucracy. The lowest tier or the subaltern classes consisted of the African working and peasant classes. These socio-economic identities were mutually re-enforcing. Accordingly, an individual's or group's access to state resources was dependent upon its station in the colonial socio-economic order. For example, the members of the dominant capitalist classes and race enjoyed disproportionate shares of the state's resources, and dominated the political economy through the marginalization of the subaltern classes and the various indigenous African ethnic groups.

During the independence era, the imperialists transferred the colonial state to the first generation of African rulers. Unfortunately, these members of the emergent African local ruling classes, with few exceptions, maintained the portrait of the colonial state. In other words, the post-colonial state in Africa was simply the continuation of the colonial state, but with new state managers—indigenous Africans. The first and subsequent generations of African leaders failed to deconstruct, rethink and democratically reconstitute the colonial state.

Against this background, the post-colonial African state retained the basic portrait of its colonial progenitor, For example, the nature of the post-colonial state is foreign in origin. Its basic complexion is peripheral capitalist. Like the colonial state, the peripheral capitalist state is at the margins of the global capitalist system. Its basic role is to serve as a plantation for supplying the raw materials—agricultural products, minerals and oil—that are required for the continual development of the major Western Powers. The major resultant effect was the continuation of the same dialectical process in which the major Western Powers continued to develop, while African states are underdeveloping (Rodney, 1984). In terms of character, the peripheral capitalist state retained the multifaceted tendencies of its colonial predecessor—repressive, violent, negligent, exploitative and exclusionary, among others. Similarly, like its colonial parent, the values, structures, rules, processes and policies of the peripheral capitalist state are designed to promote the interests of the dominant capitalist classes based in the metropolis and their states.

The portrait of the peripheral capitalist state is clearly expressed in the operation of the peripheral capitalist political economy. Among others, the peripheral capitalist political economy is anchored on the asymmetrical distribution of power between and among the various classes—ruling, petit bourgeois, working, peasant and lumpen. Overall, the ruling or the bourgeois class, which comprises a dominant external wing consisting of metropolitan-based capitalists, and an internal or local wing embodying the state managers and indigenous entrepreneurs, controls the state, and has a disproportionate share of economic and political power.

The State of Political Instability in Africa (The Fragile States Index), 2017

Very High Level of State Fragility Category

Country Score

1. South Sudan 113.9
2. Somalia 113.4
3. Central African Republic 112.6
4. Sudan 110.6
5. Democratic Republic of Congo 110.0

High Level of State Fragility Category

1. Chad 109.4
2. Guinea 102.4
3. Nigeria 101.6
4. Zimbabwe 101.6
5. Ethiopia 101.1
6. Guinea-Bissau 99.5
7. Burundi 98.9
8. Eritrea 98.1
9. Niger 97.4
10. Côte d'Ivoire 96.5
11. Kenya 96.4
12. Libya 96.3
13. Uganda 96.0
14. Cameroon 95.6
15. Liberia 93.8
16. Mauritania 93.7
17. Republic of Congo 93.4
18. Mali 92.9
19. Angola 91.1
20. Rwanda 90.8

Medium Level of State Fragility Category

1. Egypt 89.8
2. Gambia 89.4
3. Sierra Leone 89.3
4. Mozambique 89.0
5. Djibouti 88.9
6. Swaziland 88.0

 7. Burkina Faso 88.0
 8. Zambia 87.8
 9. Equatorial Guinea 85.0
10. Comoros 84.8

11. Madagascar 84.0
12. Togo 83.9
13. Senegal 82.3
14. Lesotho 81.7

Low Level of State Fragility Category

1. Tanzania 80.3
2. Benin 77.6
3. Algeria 76.8
4. Morocco 74.9
5. Tunisia 74.2
6. Gabon 73.8
7. South Africa 72.3

 8. São Tomé and Principe 72.1
 9. Namibia 70.4
10. Cape Verde 70.1
11. Ghana 69.7
12. Botswana 63.8
13. Seychelles 59.4

The Stable State Category

1. Mauritius 41.7

Note: The state fragility (political instability) score is the sum of 12 indicators, and is based on a scale of 0–120: 0 represents the most stable, and 120 the least stable.

Source: Compiled from The Fund for Peace, Fragile States Index, 2017 (Washington, D.C.: The Fund for Peace, 2017).

The State of Political Instability in Africa

In 2017, South Sudan was ranked the most unstable state in Africa. The major source of the country's instability is the ongoing civil war that commenced not too long after the gaining of independence in 2011. The civil war pits two factions of the emergent local ruling class against one another: one faction is led by President Salvia Kiir Mayardiit, and the other by the ousted Vice President Reik Mechar (BBC News, 2015). The crux of the war is the competition for power by these two factions of the local ruling class (Koos and Gutscheke, 2014). At stake is the fact that the control of political power would ensure the control of the country's oil resource, and the resulting revenues that are generated from it (Koos and Gutscheke, 2014). Characteristically, both factions have, and are using ethnicity instrumentally: President Kiir Mayardiit has mobilized the members of his Dinka ethnic group, and the former Vice President Mechar, his Neur kin (Raghavan, 2013; Rolandsen, 2015). In other words, since both factions lack broad national appeal, they have made the determination to use the perennial "ethnic card" as an instrument for the mobilization of support (Raghavan, 2013; Rolandsen, 2015).

However, the reality is that the war is class-based rather than ethnic-based. That is, the two dominant factions of the South Sudanese emergent ruling class are competing for political power cum the control over the oil resource. Hence, ethnicity is simply being used as a vehicle for mobilization by the two factions.

In addition, Somalia, the Central African Republic, Sudan and Democratic Republic of Congo are also classified as very highly unstable. In the case of Somalia, since the collapse of the Barre regime in 1989, the country has descended into a seemingly endless civil war among various factions. The various internationally-driven efforts to end the war have proven futile, as one transitional government after another has been unable to shepherd the process of national reconciliation and post-conflict peace building (Soomaalyeed, 2015; Menkhaus, 2016). To make matters worse, Somalia is the base for Al-Shabaab, an emergent regional terrorist group, that has carried out various gruesome attacks in Kenya, for example, as well as against the African Union peacekeeping force, and international aid agencies (Reuters, 2014; Mullen and Shaal, 2015). As for the Central African Republic, it has been embroiled in a civil war since 2012. In the case of the Sudan, the major source of its political instability is the genocidal war that the Bashir regime has been conducting against in the country's Darfur region since 2003. In fact, in 2009, the International Criminal Court (ICC) issued an arrest warrant for President Bashir for the commission of war crimes and crimes against humanity in the conduct of the state-led war in the country's Darfur region (Barnes, 2011).

In the highly unstable category, there are 21 states headlined by Chad, which has been plagued with political instability for most of its post-independence years, including a civil war, the centerpiece of its political instability is the campaign of destabilization that has been waged by various armed militias (Hansen, 2013). Also, included in the top tier of this category are Guinea, Nigeria, Zimbabwe, and Guinea-Bissau. In Guinea, the major source of political instability is the military: some factions have attempted to oust the incumbent regime from power (Bah, 2015). As for Nigeria, the whirlwind of terror that was unleashed by Boko Haram, a budding regional terrorist group, in 2009, is the major source of instability in the country (Akpan et al, 2014). In the case of Zimbabwe, the excesses of the Mugabe authoritarian regime coupled with the poor socio-economic conditions are at the core of political instability in the country. As for Guinea-Bissau, there are two major drivers of political instability. A key one is the failure of various elected governments to provide the leadership for building a democratic and prosperous country, and the pretext this has provided for coup making. The other driver is the country's role as a major transshipment point for illegal drugs (Loewenstein, 2016).

Egypt, the Gambia, Sierra Leone, Mozambique and Djibouti occupy the top tier of the states with medium level of political instability. Thirteen states, including Tanzania, Benin, Algeria, Morocco, and Tunisia are in the low level of political instability category. With a political instability index of 41.7, Mauritius was rated the most stable country on the African Continent.

Finally, what factors explain the variability in political instability among African states? There are several major factors that account for this. But, for the purpose of this essay, some of them will be examined. A key one is the level of political democracy. This includes the state of the respect for political rights and civil liberties, the nature and functioning of public institutions, including "checks and balances" and the resulting "horizontal accountability," the quality of elections, the state of the rule of law and the independence of the judiciary, and the nature and functioning of civil society. In addition, the availability and functioning of both legal and non-legal channels through which grievances can be channeled and addressed are also critical determinants of political stability.

Another major set of factors concern human material well-being. Specifically, the core issues include the standard of living, the cost of living, the rates of poverty, unemployment, underemployment, vulnerable employment, corruption and the mismanagement of public resources, and particularly the ways a government deals with these issues. Essentially, African states that address the welfare of their citizens better as measured, for example, by the human development index, tend to be comparatively more stable than the ones that do not. This is because human issues and the resulting tugs and pulls are at the heart of state fragility and political stability.

Also, major cultural factors such as the level of integration and inclusion, and the resulting peaceful co-existence of various identity groups are quite important for political stability as well. For example, if an identity group believes that it is marginalized, especially economically, politically and socially, then it is highly likely that it would engage in actions that could contribute to political instability. This is made worse by the absence of fair conflict mitigation and resolution mechanisms.

As well, some states like Gabon have developed inhibitors to political instability. These include political repression and suppression, and the resulting instilling of fear in the minds of citizens, patronage, clientelism, the cooptation of major identity groups and leaders, and the provision of minimum basic human needs that keep people afloat. Operationally, political suppression and repression are often mixed with one or more of the other inhibitors

The Derivatives and Events of Political Instability in Africa

The Derivatives

BACKGROUND

As the overarching tapestry, the peripheral capitalist state has generated various causes of political instability in Africa. However, it will not be possible to examine all of these derivatives. Hence, the focus will be on some of the major ones.

INTERNAL DERIVATIVES

At the domestic level, there are three major causes of political instability in Africa: compradorial political factionalism, ethnic polarization and regime performance. This section of the essay will examine the nature and dynamics of each of these factors.

COMPRADORIAL POLITICAL FACTIONALISM

Compradorial political factionalism is one of the intrinsic features of the peripheral capitalist state in Africa. At the foundation of this phenomenon is the central issue of the genealogy of the peripheral capitalist state in Africa and its consequent role in the international "division of labor." As has been discussed, the peripheral capitalist African state is a creation of the international capitalist system. The principal role of the peripheral capitalist African state is to superintend the processes of the supply of raw materials to the metropolis and the accumulation of capital by the metropolitan-based bourgeoisies. Accordingly, the resultant portrait of the peripheral capitalist African state is embodied in a non-hegemonic, weak and dependent cocoon.

Against this background, the various factions and fractions of the local wing of the African ruling classes are locked in on going epic battles for the managerial control of the peripheral capitalist state. The faction or fraction that "wins" control of the managerial responsibilities of the state becomes the functionary of the global capitalist system and its dominant ruling classes and states. That is, the incumbent ruling faction or fraction assumes the principal responsibility for ensuring that the peripheral capitalist state plays its subservient role in serving the interests of the metropolitan-based bourgeois classes. In return, as compensation, the incumbent ruling faction or fraction has carte blanche power to loot the resources of the state for the benefits of its members and their relations. In other words, the state is akin to a "buffet service" in which the ruling faction or fraction of the local ruling class and their surrogates can "eat all they can eat" (Kieh, 2009:10).

Significantly, the competition between and among the various factions and fractions of the local wings of the African ruling classes for the position of handmaid of the metropolitan-based external wings of the ruling classes is a "life and death struggle." Given the high stakes, the struggle is conducted in a "zero sum" framework in which a "win" for one faction or fraction simultaneously results in a "loss" for the others. Importantly, this phenomenon underscores the fusion between state power and factional or fractional power (Fatton, 1988). Consistent with the intrinsic nature of the peripheral capitalist economy, the "winning faction or fraction" then takes various steps, including the use of repression, ostensibly designed to exclude the "defeated factions or fractions" from participation in the conduct of the affairs of the state, especially the process of using the state as an instrument for the private accumulation of capital. This is because state power, in fact, is the key to the appropriation and sale on the international market of both national assets and resources (land, gold, diamonds, oil timber), or assets possessed by rival or weaker groups (Federici, 2005 1).

Clearly, these dynamics preclude the development of the political space required for the crystallization of compromises between and among the various sectors of the compradorial classes in Africa (Fatton, 1988: 257). Consequently, inter-factional and inter-fractional relations generate tension, suspicions, mistrust and conflicts. In turn, these adversely affect the stability of the polity as the various compradorial factions and fractions jockeyed for position and power.

ETHNIC POLARIZATION

Another major cause of political instability is ethnic polarization between and among various groups within an African polity. This problem is the by product of both legitimate ethnic claims and the manipulative designs of ethnic entrepreneurs or those Osaghae (2006:5) refers to as "ethnic gladiators." As have been argued, one of the fundamental tenets of the character of the peripheral capitalist African state is the exclusion of other groups—classes, ethnic groups, etc.—from the conduct of the affairs of the polity. Consequently, as part of the contours of the peripheral capitalist political economy, the excluded or marginalized groups receive little benefits from the allocation of state resources compare to the dominant group. In the case of ethnic relations, it is quite common for one ethnic group to capture control of the state (Marshall, 2005). That is, the state becomes what Mengisteab (2007:108) calls an "ethnic state" that privileges one ethnic group at the expense of the others in a polity. The capture of the state by a dominant ethnic group is a reflection of the fact that the peripheral capitalist political economy militates against the construction of multi-ethnic societies that are anchored on equal access to state resources. Thus, based on the capitalist logic of exploitation and marginalization, the dominant ethnic group uses its relationship to the state managers to command a disproportionate share of national resources. For example, in Ethiopia, the Amharic ethnic group is using its privileged position in order to receive a disproportionate share of public resources at the expense of the Oromo and other marginalized ethnic groups.

Over time, ethnic privileging sows and nurtures the seed of ethnic polarization between dominant and subaltern groups. Convinced that the state is not a neutral arbiter but an instrument of ethnic hegemony, the marginalized ethnic groups then engage in what Osaghae (2006: 4–5) refers to as "counter-mobilization and counter-nationalism." The ultimate objective might either be to remain in the state and bargain for increased allocation of public resources or exit the state and organize a new polity. In the case of the former, the marginalized ethnic groups try to position themselves strategically so as to force the state managers to negotiate with them. Depending on the perceived strength of the marginalized ethnic groups as determined by the state managers, the state may then respond to these legitimate ethnic claims in various ways: the making of concessions, including increases in the ethnic groups' shares of the national resources, the co-optation of their leaders as a way of silencing the ethnic groups, the refusal by the state to make concessions, and at the extreme, the use of repressive means to cow the marginalized ethnic groups into submission. Ultimately, the state's response to these legitimate ethnic claims would determine the implications for political stability. In contradistinction, the latter case involves the decisions of marginalized ethnic groups to secede from the state and establish their own polities. One of the major examples was the "war of secession" waged by Biafra, an amalgam of the Igbos and other marginalized ethnic groups based in the eastern region, against the Nigerian state from 1967 to 1970. The "war of secession" reflected the belief of the Igbos and the other marginalized ethnic groups that the Nigerian state had privileged the Hausa and Yoruba ethnic groups at their expense. Moreover, these marginalized ethnic groups were convinced that even the making of concessions by the state managers would not have been enough to address their claims. Hence, secession was the best resolution. In response, the state managers made the determination that they could not allow these marginalized ethnic groups to exit the state. The resultant situation led to tension, crises and eventually war and their associated adverse effects on political stability in Nigeria.

Also, ethnic polarization may result from the manipulative antics—what Landsdale (1994) calls "political tribalism—"of various leaders, factions and fractions of the local African ruling classes Lacking the ability to garner broad-based national support that transcends social identities, compradors and compradorial factions and fractions use their ethnic groups as instruments to serve their particularistic agenda and interests. In other words, inter-compradorial rivalries are cleverly masked as ethnic ones. Importantly, the instrumental use of ethnicity is successful because it goes hand in hand with a strong cultural identification with ethnic groups on the part of followers—"moral ethnicity" (Rawlinson, 2003: 2).

The resultant "ethnic struggles" negatively affect political stability. A notable case was the way in which Master-Sergeant Samuel Doe, the former Head of State and subsequently President of Liberia, adroitly camouflaged the rivalry between him and General Thomas Quiwonkpa as an "ethnic conflict" between the Krahn (Doe's) and the Gio and Mano (Quiwonkpa's) ethnic groups. The reality was that both President Doe and General Quiwonkpa were closed allies and leaders of the 1980 military coup in Liberia. However, by 1983, Sergeant Doe became concerned that General Quiwonkpa was becoming "too popular" with Liberia's subaltern classes. Hence, Head of State Doe decided to "clip General Quiwonkpa's wings" by removing him from the powerful position of Commanding General of the Armed Forces of Liberia and the number four leader of the People's Redemption Council, the ruling military junta. Consequently, General Quiwonkpa was assigned the position of Secretary-General of the military council, a ceremonial position. Interestingly, General Quiwonkpa refused to accept the demotion. Characteristically, tension ensued; and the two members of the local wing of the Liberian ruling class quickly mobilized their respective ethnic groups. The resultant effect was the needless development of animosity between the Krahn ethnic group, on the one hand, and the Gio and Mano ethnic groups, on the other hand. This situation led to an increasing state of instability in Liberia, as the expectations developed that a violent confrontation between the two ethnic blocs was inevitable. However, it was not until 1985 that the two ethnic blocks became locked in a bloody conflict that left the state teetering on disintegration. The trigger was an abortive coup that was led by General Quiwonkpa against the Doe regime. As expected Sergeant Doe blamed the Gio and Mano ethnic groups for the coup, and using the full battery of the state's repressive arsenal, undertook a "scorched the earth" campaign targeted at the members of the Gio and Mano ethnic groups. This led to the murder of thousands of members of the Gio and Mano ethnic groups.

REGIME PERFORMANCE

By and large, both civilian and military regimes in Africa have, and continue to perform very poorly. Mbaku (2000:1) captures the enormity of the sordid performance of the continent's various state managers:

> During the last forty years, most governments in Africa have either been unwilling or unable to perform their traditional duties—providing public goods and maintaining a framework of security. In fact, in some regions of the continent, governments have become irrelevant to the lives of the people.

Several indicators can be used to evaluate regime performance on the continent. However, three indicators will be used: the state of basic human needs, the respect for political rights and civil liberties and political governance. First, in terms of basic human needs—food, education, healthcare, the means of minimal decent survival and housing—, the state of the continent's subaltern classes hangs perilously in the balance. For example, in 2016, about 383 million people lived in extreme poverty on the African Continent (people living on less than $1.90 per day), the highest in the world (Action Against Hunger, Global Poverty and Hunger, 2016). The situation was made worse by the twin problems of unemployment and under-employment: About 55 percent of the continent's population experienced a combination of unemployment and underemployment (United Nations Economic Commission for Africa, 2016). The latter consisted of those who were nominally employed because they did not earn enough salaries to adequately meet their basic needs. 1).

In terms of access to clean drinking water, in 2005, about 54 percent of the total population lacked such amenity (United Nations Development Program, 2006). Similarly, 52 percent of the population did not have access to acceptable level of sanitation. However, the situation improved in 2017, with rate dropping to a little over 33 percent (about 320 million people)(Mail and Guardian, 2017). In the area of sanitation, during the same period, about 60 percent of the people had access to adequate sanitation (Water and Sanitation Program, 2017).

As for food security, in 2005, about 186 million Africans did not have access to food products (Food and Agricultural Organization, 2005). Moreover, even among those who had access to food, 33 percent of them were malnourished (International Food Policy Institute, 2005:1). By 2015, about 254 million people in Africa were food insecure (Rosen et al, 2015:v).

Another dimension of the human insecurity conundrum on the continent is the lack of adequate housing, especially in the urban cities. One of the major consequences is the prevalence of slums in most of the large cities such as Lagos in Nigeria and Nairobi in Kenya. In 2003, for example, between 40–70 percent of the urban dwellers on the continent live in slums (Mutume, 2004: 19). By 2014, the housing problem had not improved, as about 200 million Africans lacked habitable houses (United Nations Habitat Program, 2014). Cumulatively, the basic human needs deficit that is prevalent on the continent has myriad ramifications for well-being. For example, the continent's subalterns are vulnerable to various diseases. In fact, thousands of them die each year from curable diseases. Furthermore, the overall impact could be gauged by the aggregate continental-wide life expectancy of 52 years (Mwanika, 2007: 1; World Health Organization, 2014). In short, to use Hobbesian parlance, life for the members of Africa's subaltern classes is "short, brutish and nasty" (Hobbes, 1998).

Second, although some progress has been made in terms of the respect for the political rights and civil liberties of individuals by the state and its managers, there is still a lot of work to be done. This is because the majority of the states on the continent are what Freedom House (2017) terms "partially free" and "not free." This means that the political human rights of Africans in most of the continent's states are still being violated by state functionaries. For example, the freedoms of speech, thought, association, the press, assembly and movement are still being violated.

Third and related, while appreciable amount of progress has been made in the area of political governance, there are still major challenges that need to be addressed. One of the major lacunas is the "presidential third term phenomenon." This involves the emergent practice wherein incumbent African presidents either successfully or unsuccessfully orchestrate changes in their countries' constitutions so that they can serve beyond their prescribed two successive terms of office. Some of the notable cases of successful "third term" constitutional manipulation are Sam Njoma in Namibia, Yoweri Museveni of Uganda, Pierre Nkurunziza of Burundi, and Paul Kigame of Rwanda (Roth and Sawyer, 2015; Zounmenou, 2015; Spooner, 2016). In the case of President Museveni, who has ruled Uganda since 1986, he abolished presidential term limit in 2005, thereby enabling him to have unlimited terms (Green, 2015). As for President Nkurunziza, his third term bid plunged the country into violence in 2015. For example, there were mass demonstrations by pro-democracy forces (IWACU, 2015). Also, there was an abortive military coup (Karimi and Kriel, 2015). In the case of President Kigame, he orchestrated a constitutional amendment that cleared the way for him to run for a third term in 2017(Dixon, 2016). On the other hand, the most widely known unsuccessfully bid was made by then President Olusegun Obasanjo of Nigeria. However, he successfully installed Omari Yar'Adua, his handpicked successor through one of the most fraudulent elections ever conducted on the continent. Clearly, the "third term bid" undermines political democratization, constitutionalism and the "rule of law." Another challenge is the scourge of what Schedler (2007:2) calls" electoral authoritarianism." This is a situation in which some incumbent governments on the continent have manipulated one or more aspects of the electoral process for the purpose of ensuring that the ruling party wins either the presidential and/or legislative elections through a plethora of fraudulent practices ranging from corrupting the voters' registration rolls to the manipulation of the counting of the ballots. Two cases are instructive. During the 2007 elections in Nigeria, incumbent President Olusegun Obasanjo used the electoral commission to ensure that his ruling People's Democratic Party (PDP) won the presidential election, as well as the majority of the seats in the National Assembly and the governorships. In order to ensure the desired outcomes, the electoral commission employed an assortment of fraudulent tactics to ensure that the ruling PDP, especially the "Obasanjo fraction," remained the dominant sector of the Nigerian compradorial class. In the same vein, the Kenyan elections commission acting under the influence of incumbent President Mwai Kibaki used fraudulent means in the counting of the ballots for the presidential election. To the chagrin of the majority of the Kenyan voters and the international observers, President Kibaki was declared the winner of the election.

Cumulatively, the overall general sordid performance of regimes in Africa, especially in terms of human security—especially the economic, political and social dimensions—has led to political instability. Several cases are noteworthy. In Nigeria, the failure of the bureaucratic wing (state managers) of the compradorial class to use the huge financial "windfall" from the country's oil resource to improve the material conditions of the members of the subaltern classes has made political instability a major item on the political menu. For instance in the Niger Delta where most of the oil resource is located, the members of the subordinate classes in the region are suffering from, among other things, abject poverty, unemployment, inadequate healthcare and education and sundry other dimensions of social and economic malaise. In turn, this has led to the development of tension between the people of the region on the one hand, and the Nigerian government, on the other. Particularly, the chronic failure of the Nigerian state to improve the basic needs of the people in the region, and the resultant disillusionment of the latter have sowed and nurtured the seeds of instability. Overtime, the seeds of instability have blossomed into instability events such as economic sabotage against the oil companies, riots and small-scaled armed violence. In Kenya, the efforts by the Kibaki regime to retain power through the 2007 fraud-plagued presidential election led to the outbreak of violence and its adverse consequences. In 2008, there were widespread demonstrations in Cameroon against the failure of the Biya regime to meet the basic human needs of the people.

External Derivatives

At the external level, there are various causes of political instability on the continent. However, only two of these causes—clientelism and neo-liberal reforms—will be discussed. The focus will be on the nature, and the forces and factors that condition each of the external derivatives of political instability on the continent.

Clientelism

Clientelism has, and remains one of the major mainstays of neo-colonialism in Africa. The phenomenon has several dimensions. But, the focus will be on three: imperialist intrusion into the domestic politics of African states for the ostensible purpose of bringing their lackeys to power; imperialist provision of support for client regimes; and the imperialists' use of client regimes as handmaids in the execution of the former's foreign policy agendas. Cases abound regarding the imperialist states' interference in the internal affairs of African states for the purpose of installing client regimes. For example, during the Cold War, Belgium and the United States played pivotal roles in the overthrow of the regime of Patrice Lumumba, the prime minister of the Congo (now the Democratic Republic of the Congo)(Ray et al., 1979; Blum, 1995; De Witte, 2003), and his subsequent replacement by the imperialist client Mobutu Sese Seko. In the case of Ghana, Britain and the United States engineered the removal of Kwame Nkrumah from power by the military (Ray et al., 1979; Justice Africa, 2007). In Ethiopia, the Soviet Union aided Mengistu Hailemariam in his ascendancy to power (Harbeson, 1988). In Liberia, the United States orchestrated the removal of the Tolbert regime from power in 1980 (Dunn and Tarr, 1988; Tolbert, 1996), and its replacement by a regime of military subalterns led by Master-Sergeant Samuel Doe. Given the dynamics of the post–Cold War international system in which military coups have become aberrations, the imperialist powers have determined to use the electoral process as a way of supporting either their incumbent client regimes or bringing their clients to power. In the case of incumbent client regimes, the United States, for example, despite its pro-democracy rhetoric, supported fraudulent elections in Egypt in 2005, Uganda in 2006, and Kenya in 2007. In terms of bringing client regimes to power, a notable case was the United States' support for the "Obasanjo coup" that masterminded the conduct of the fraud-plagued presidential, legislative and gubernatorial elections in Nigeria in 2007. At the end of the presidential race, Obasanjo's handpicked successor, Musa Yar'Adua, became the new President of Nigeria. Characteristically, the United States recognized the regime, despite President Yar'Adua's own admission that the election was fraudulent: "The April elections were so heavily marred by vote-rigging ... they fell far below basic international standards and were not credible" (Adewole, 2007: 1).

Another major manifestation of clientelism is the support that the various imperialist powers have, and continue to provide for their client regimes on the continent. For example, during the Cold War, the United States provided economic and military aid to various dictatorial regimes, including Mobutu in Zaire (now Democratic Republic of the Congo), Barre in Somalia, Mubarak in Egypt and Doe in Liberia. Similarly, the Soviet Union provided economic and military assistance to the Hailemariam authoritarian regime in Ethiopia. Not to be outdone, France provided the political, economic and military-security "oxygen" that kept the autocratic regime of Houphet Boigny "alive" for over three decades. During the current post–Cold War order, the United States, for example, contrary to its professed claim of promoting democracy in Africa and elsewhere, provided economic, political and military support for several authoritarian regimes, including the then Mubarak in Egypt, the then Kibaki in Kenya, Museveni in Uganda, Kigame in Rwanda, and the regime of the late Meles Zenawi in Ethiopia.

Also, client regimes in Africa have, and continue to serve as "foot soldiers" in the execution of the foreign policy agendas of their respective patrons. For example, during the Cold War, Zaire under the Mobutu regime served as the principal conduit for the funneling of money and military equipment from the United States to the National Union for the Total Liberation of Angola (UNITA) led by the notorious Jonas Savimbi, and the Front for the Liberation of Angola (FNLA) headed by Holden Roberto. During the emergent post–Cold War era, several American client regimes are serving as handmaids in the U.S. "'War on Terror." For example, the Zenawi regime in Ethiopia was used by the United States to invade neighboring Somalia in 2007 to drive out the members of the Union of Islamic Courts, an amalgam of Islamic groups that the Bush administration charged are agents of terrorism (Soomaalyeed, 2015). The United States has supplemented the Ethiopian invasion with periodic bombing raids in various parts of Somalia. Clearly, the Ethiopian-American actions are contributing to the creation of a permanent state of instability in Somalia, as well as increasing tensions in the Horn of Africa.

Additionally, the United States has developed other military frameworks that are serving as vehicles through which it is using some of its client regimes in Africa to serve as the "frontlines." These military frameworks include: the East Africa Counter-Terrorism Initiative and the Trans-Sahel Counterterrorism Initiative. Under these military arrangements, the United States is providing training and equipment to the armed forces of various countries in East Africa and the Sahel region of the continent. Clearly, these American military initiatives draw these African states into the conflict with those Islamic groups that the United States has classified as terroristic because they have joined the fight against these groups. In addition, these African states' territories have been transformed into "battlegrounds" with these groups. This is because since Muslims within these African countries have been made the focus of the American-led "war on terror," there is the emergence of suspicion and mistrust and resultant conflicts between these American client regimes, on the one hand, and the Islamic populations in these countries, on the other.

Neo-Liberal Reforms

In 1986, most African states were enveloped in economic crisis as reflected, inter alia, in precipitous declines in growth rates and productive capacity. In turn, these occasioned burgeoning rates of unemployment and poverty, and the overall deterioration of the standard of living of the members of the subaltern classes. Overall, the worsening of the material well-being of the preponderant majority of Africans underscored the broader crisis of the peripheral capitalist African state and its political economy that has been gathering since the post-colonial era.

Characteristically, the local wings of the African ruling classes demonstrated their bankruptcy by failing to formulate and implement policies that would address the economic crisis. Instead, they turned to their metropolitan patrons, including the United States and Britain, and their international financial institutions—International Monetary Fund and the World Bank—for solutions. With the emergence of neo-liberalism as the dominant development ideology of international capitalism as a consequence of the influence of United States President Ronald Reagan and British Prime Minister Margaret Thatcher, the crisis plagued African states were instructed to uncritically accept the new dogma. However, the metropolitan powers and their international financial institutions' decision was not driven by concerns about the material well-being of impoverished Africans, but by the fear that the affected African states would not have the capacity to service the enormous odious debts they owed metropolitan commercial banks, metropolitan powers and the metropolitan-led international financial institutions.

Against this background, the neo-liberal dogma was packaged into the notorious "structural adjustment programs" (SAPs) by the International Monetary Fund (IMF) and the World Bank. Among other, the program required African states seeking loans from these metropolitan-led global financial institutions to remove all of the barriers to trade and foreign investment; to devalue their currencies; to lay off workers in the public sector; to freeze employment; to keep wages in the public sector stagnant; to raise interest rate; and to dismantle their "social safety nets." Shortly thereafter, it became abundantly clear that the structural adjustment programs were worsening the economic and social conditions of the African states that adopted them, especially the overwhelming majority of their citizens. Consequently, tension ensued between the government and various sectors of the society—workers, farmers, students, youth, etc. Over time, the tension generated the tremors of political instability. For example, violent conflicts exploded in some of the affected African states (Federici, 2005).

The Events

BACKGROUND

Political instability in Africa has, and continues to be reflected in various events—demonstrations, strikes, riots, insurrection, coups and civil wars. These events represent the physical manifestation of the seeds of political instability planted and nurtured by the crises of underdevelopment generated by the operation of the peripheral capitalist state in Africa and its political economy. In this part of the essay, two of these events—coups d'état and civil wars—will be examined.

COUPS D'ÉTAT

Since the post-independence era in Africa, coups d'état have been dominant events of political instability. By and large, coups have involved the usurpation of political power by segments of the militaries—commissioned or senior officers and what Kandeh (2004) calls "the lumpens or subalterns"— through the threat of, and the use of military force. The phenomenon became an integral part of the governance architecture in Africa beginning with the 1952 coup in Egypt led by Gamal Abdul Nassar and the "Free Officers." Then like a pandemic, the "coup virus" infected various African states in the regions of the continent. By the end of the 20th century, there were a total of 85 successful coups in Africa (Kieh, 2004: 44). 58 of these coups were staged against incumbent civilian regimes, and 27 against military regimes (Kieh, 2004: 45). Put in the regional context, Central Africa experienced 20 coups, East Africa 15, North Africa 4, Southern Africa 4, and West Africa, the most coup-prone, 42 (Kieh, 2004: 44–45).

Generally, the causes of coups in Africa have been twofold: societal and corporate. The societal causes have revolved around the poor performance of incumbent civilian and military regimes. In other words, the coupists have used the crises of underdevelopment as justifications for staging military takeovers. However, it is important to note that by and large this has not meant that putschists have had interest in the plight of continent's peoples. Instead, citizen grievances against incumbent regimes have simply provided excellent pretexts for coup-makers to hijack democratic struggles across the affected states. Another set of causes has related to the corporate interests of the military as an institution. Some of the coups on the continent like the ones in the Gambia in 1991, and Sierra Leone in 1992 were caused by grievances the military had about the irregular payment of salaries, poor living conditions and the lack of materiel and equipment.

Generally, military regimes have performed poorly even worse than their civilian predecessors. This has been reflected in, among other things, the continuation of political repression, social malaise and economic hardship for the preponderant majority of the citizens of the affected states. In fact, military regimes like Idi Amin's in Uganda gained international notoriety for brutality and the mass murder of thousands of citizens, who were both real and imagined opponents.

Civil Wars

Civil wars have, and continue to represent the most violent manifestations of political instability in Africa. The stage was set with the implosion of the Sudan in 1956, barely few months after it gained independence. Thereafter, various African states were infected by the "civil war virus." By the time the first decade of independence ended on the continent, civil wars were raging in four countries. From then until the end of the 20th century, the continent experienced 26 civil wars. Since the emergence of the new millennium,

Africa has experienced four new civil wars, including the genocidal civil wars in Rwanda, Liberia, Sierra Leone and the Democratic Republic of the Congo.

The civil wars that have, and are occurring on the continent can be classified thus: secessionist, struggles over state power, ethnic, and mixed. Secessionist civil wars such as the ones in Nigeria (1967–1970), and Senegal (1982–2004) pitted the state against regional groups—Nigeria against ethnic groups in its eastern region (Biafra), and Senegal against its Casamance region. In Angola (1975–2002) and Mozambique (1975–1992), the civil wars were over the struggles for state power—the three sided competition among the Popular Movement for the Liberation of Angola (MPLA), the Union for the Total Liberation of Angola (UNITA) and the Front for the Liberation of Angola (FNLA) in Angola, and the bitter struggle between Front for the Liberation of Mozambique (FRELIMO) and Mozambican Resistance (RENAMO) in Mozambique. Ethnic conflicts have involved the state and the dominant ethnic group, on the one hand, and marginalized ethnic group or groups, on the other. For example, in Djibouti, the one-year-old civil war (1991–1992) was between the Afar minority ethnic group and the Isaa majority. The crux of the war was the grievance that Afar ethnic group had regarding its marginalization in the political and economic realms. Most of the civil wars on the continent have been of the mixed variety with several factors derived from the crisis of the neo-colonial state at the base. The cases include the Sudan, Somalia, Liberia, Sierra Leone and Democratic Republic of the Congo.

Clearly with the exceptions of the Angolan and Mozambican civil wars (these two countries were plunged into civil wars from the onset of the post-independence era), civil wars in Africa have reflected the inability of the managers of the affected peripheral capitalist African states to effectively manage the crises generated by the vagaries of the political economy. These multidimensional crises have included political repression, abject poverty, the inadequacy of health care and educational opportunities and ethnic disagreements both real and manufactured. One or more of these crises has generated and nurtured the seeds of conflict that eventually degenerated into armed violence.

The Consequences of Political Instability and Its Events for Development in Africa

The consequences of political instability and its events for development are legion. Hence, it is not possible to cover all of them. Instead, the focus will be on some of the effects. For example, coups have affected African states in, among others, human and economic terms. Violent coups have led to the death of government officials. In the case of the 1980 Liberian coup, President

Tolbert and several government officials were killed, including the public execution of thirteen officials. In Ghana, in 1979, the military regime of Flight Lieutenant Jerry Rawlings executed several former state officials, including former military heads of state Generals Fred Akuffo and Ignatius Acheampong. Economically, coups have led to capital flight, as foreign investors tried to take out their capital. Also, coups have served as obstacles to the influx of foreign investment. This is because investors were fearful that an unstable political climate would adversely affect the business environment, especially the capacity to accumulate profit.

Civil wars have had similar adverse effects on the affected countries in various ways. For instance, in human terms, from 1975–1989, the total deaths from Africa's various civil wars stood at an alarming 750, 000(Toole and Waldman, 1997:284). Also, since 1997, more than 4 million people have died in Democratic Republic of Congo's seemingly unending civil wars (Scaruffi, 2016). In addition, between 2013 and 2015, more than 10,000 people have died in the South Sudanese civil war (Scaruffi, 2016). In terms of refugees, there were 5.2 million in 2006 (United Nations High Commission for Refugees, 2006:1). During the same period, there were 13 million internally displaced persons, as consequences of armed violence (United Nations High Commission for Refugees, 2006:1). Further, in 2015, there were about 15 million refugees in Africa (United Nations High Commissioner for Refugees, 2015:1). During the same period, there were over 14 million internally displaced persons (Internal Displacement Monitoring Center, 2015). Economically, armed conflicts in Africa cost around $18 billion per year, seriously derailing development (International Action Network on Small Arms, Oxfam International and Safeworld, 2007:1). For example, from 1990–2005, the total "economic price tag" for civil wars on the continent was about $300 billion (Oxfam International, 2007:1).

Overall, the costs of political instability and its events have been both enormous and expansive in human, economic, social, environmental, security and political terms. In other words, political instability is antithetical to human security (the broad range of human-related issues). Simply put, the tremors of political instability undermine human progress to the extent of making live perilous for millions of people from across the class, ethnic, regional, religious, gender and age divide.

Addressing the Political Instability Conundrum in Africa: Some Suggestions

So, how can Africa address the vexing issue of political instability that has bedeviled the region since the post-colonial era? The central issue that needs to be addressed is the democratic reconstitution of the peripheral capitalist state. This is a process that involves various phases and dimensions. First, the peripheral capitalist African state needs to be deconstructed. This would involve purging the state of its anti-people, anti-democracy and anti-development core. In other words, the peripheral capitalist African state was not designed to promote development and democracy with human development as its centerpiece. Hence, the process of rethinking the African state must involve the reconfiguration of the essence of the construct.

Second, the state must be rethought. That is, an alternative state form must be designed. Irrespective of the specific name of the form, it is critical that the new construct has human centered-development and democracy as its core.

Third, the democratic reconstitution phase would entail redesigning the nature, mission, character, values, institutions, rules, processes and policies of the new construct so that they promote the cultural, ecological, economic, political, religious, security and social rights and freedoms of all citizens, regardless of ethnicity, race, region, class, gender and age. In other words, the emphasis will be on substantive or deep democracy as the overarching architecture with empowerment, social justice and multi-layered equality as the foundational pillars. In turn, this guides the process of reconstructing the domestic political economy in ways that make the state autonomous, and thus free from the control of the various factions and fractions of the ruling class. Thus, the state would serve the general interests of all citizens.

Overall, given its constitutive elements, the democratically reconstituted African state would manage conflicts in ways in which they do not generate instability and instability events. For example, with the realization that they are empowered, their well-being is at the center of state policies, and they have available to them avenues that would fairly adjudicate their grievances, citizens would not engage in activities that would make the polity unstable. This is because they would realize that instability and its events would not be in their best interests as individuals and groups.

Clearly, a democratically reconstituted African state would be in an advantageous position to confront the inequities and injustices that are the hallmarks of the global capitalist political economy. For example, with the support of citizens, the reconstituted African state would be well positioned to combat the venalities of the imperialist policies of the metropolitan ruling classes and their dominant states. Also, the reconstituted state would be able complement its national strategy of combating imperialism with a partnership with a league of democratically reconstituted states in the Third World. Such a solidarity would strengthen the bargaining positions in dealing with such issues as the unfair and unjust "international division of labor" that has assigned African and other Third World states the role of producing raw materials and purchasing manufactured goods from the metropolitan states; the unjust "system of exchange" in global trade that dictates that African and other Third World states pay more for manufactured goods, but receive less for their primary products; and the odious debts and their strangulating effects.

Conclusion

The essay has attempted to examine the undercurrents of political instability in Africa. The central thesis is that the phenomenon is the consequence of the multifaceted crises of underdevelopment generated by the peripheral capitalist state that was designed and bequeathed to Africa at the dawn of the independence era. Unfortunately, beginning with the first generation of African leaders, the succeeding ones have failed to democratically reconstitute the state. Thus, since the 1960s, the crises of underdevelopment engendered by the peripheral capitalist state has sown and nurtured the seeds of political instability. In several African states, the nurtured seeds of instability have led to events such as coups and civil wars. And these events have adversely affected the African states concerned in various ways, ranging from the human to the social costs.

Thus, the best way to address political instability and its events is to democratically reconstitute the peripheral capitalist state. This is a multidimensional process that entails deconstruction, rethinking and reconstitution. The end product is to establish substantive or deep democracy with human development and well-being as the fulcrums. In turn, this would make citizens to have vested interests in the stability of the reconstituted state, since such a condition would be indispensable to their own well-being. Hence, ways would be found to express, demonstrate and manage conflicts in ways in which they do not lead to instability and instability events that could plunge the polity into chaos and disorder.

Finally, the essay took cognizance of the constraints that are imposed by the unjust and unfair global capitalist political economy and their attendant contribution to instability. The essay suggested that the best approach is for the reconstituted African state to use mass support and the development of a partnership with a league of democratically reconstituted African and other Third World states as the defense against the deleterious effects of the imperialist policies of the metropolitan ruling classes, their dominant states, and their handmaids such as the International Monetary Fund, the World Bank and the World Trade Organization.

REFERENCES

Action Against Hunger. "Global Poverty and Hunger: Take Action!" 2016. www.actionagainsthunger.org. Accessed November 5, 2017.
Adewole, Lanre. 2007. "April Polls Massively Rigged—Yar'Ardua Admits," *Tribune*. August 29, p.1.

Agbese, Pita Ogaba. 2007. "The Political Economy of the African State." In George Klay Kieh, Jr. (ed.). *Beyond State Failure and Collapse: Making the State Relevant in Africa*. Lanham, MD: Lexington Books, pp. 33–50.

Akpan, Felix et al. 2014. "Boko Haram Insurgency and Counter-Terrorism Policy in Nigeria." *Canadian Social Science*. 10(2), pp. 151–155.

Archer, Jules. 1974. *Riot: A History of Mob Action in the United States*. New York: Hawthorn Books.

Bah, Mamadou Diouma. "The Military and Politics in Guinea." *Armed Forces and Society*. 41(1), pp. 69–95.

Barnes, Gwen. 2011. "International Criminal Courts Ineffective Enforcement Mechanisms: The Indictment of President Omar Al Bashir." *Fordham International Law Journal*. 34(6), pp. 1584–1619.

BBC News. 2015. "South Sudan: Country Profile." December 7, p.1.

Berborogh, Berch. 1999. *Turmoil in the Middle East: Imperialism, War and Political Instability*. Albany, NY: State University of New York Press.

Birmingham, David. 1995. *The Decolonization of Africa*. London: University College of London Press.

Blanco, Luisa, and Robin Grier. 2007. *Long Live Democracy: The Determinants of Political Instability in Latin America*. Research Paper. Malibu, CA: Pepperdine University, and Norman, OK: University of Oklahoma.

Blum, William. 1995. *Killing Hope: U.S. Military and CIA Interventions Since World War II*. Monroe, ME: Common Courage Press.

Chitiga, Margaret, et al. 2016. "Income Inequality and Limitations of the Gini Index: The Case of South Africa." *HSRC Review*, pp. 1–2.

Crowder, Michael. 1987. "Whose Dream Was It Anyway? Twenty-Five Years of African Independence. *African Studies Review*. 86(342), pp. 7–24.

Davidson, Basil. 1994. *Modern Africa: A Social and Political History*. Harlow: Longmans.

Demaris, Ovid. 1970. *America the Violent*. New York: Cowles Book Company.

De Witte. 2003. *The Assassination of Lumumba*. New York: Verso.

Dixon, Robyn. 2016. "Rwanda President Becomes Africa's Latest to Seek Extended Time in Power." *Los Angeles Times*. January 1, p.1.

Edie, Carlene. 2003. *Politics in Africa: A New Beginning?* Belmont, CA: Wadsworth.

Emeh, Okechukwu. 2004. "Africa and the Crisis of Instability." *Vanguard*. March 20, 1–4.

Federici, Silvia. 2005. "On the Roots of War: These on the War in Iraq." *ACAS Bulletin*. 70, pp. 1–3.

Food and Agricultural Organization. 2005. *The State of Food Insecurity in the World*. Rome: FAO.

Fund for Peace. *Fragile States Index, 2015*. Washington, D.C.: The Fund for Peace, 2015.

Garuba, Chris. 1998. "Crisis in Africa and the Challenge of Capacity Building." In Chris Garuba (ed.). *Capacity Building for Crisis Management in Africa*. Lagos: Gabumo, pp. 96–112.

Gibson, Robert. 1979. *The Negro Holocaust: Lynching and Race Riots in the United States, 1880–1950*. New Haven, CT: Yale University Press.

Green, Andrew. 2015. "Uganda Museveni Succeeds Where Others Failed in Eluding Term Limits." *World Political Review*. June 23, pp. 1–2.

Greskovits, Bela. 1998. *The Political Economy of Protest and Patience*. Budapest: Budapest Central European University Press.

Gyimah-Brempong, Kwabena, and Thomas L. Traynor. 1999. "Political Instability, Investments and Economic Growth in Sub-Saharan Africa." *Journal of African Economies*. 8(1), pp. 52–86.

Hansen, Ketil Fred. 2013. "A Democratic Dictator's Success: How Chad's President Deby Defeated the Military Opposition in Three Years (2008–2011)." *Journal of Contemporary African Studies*. 31(4), pp. 583–599.

Harbeson, John. 1988. *The Ethiopian Transformation: The Quest for the Post-Imperial State*. Boulder, CO: Westview Press.

Hobbes, Thomas. 1998. *The Leviathan*. Oxford: Oxford University Press.

Horowitz, Donald. 2000. *Ethnic Groups in Conflict*. Oakland: University of California Press.

Internal Displacement Monitoring Center. 2015. *Africa*. Geneva: Imprimerie Harder.

International Labor Organization. 2014. *Global Employment Trends, 2014*. Geneva: ILO.

International Labor Organization. 2016. *World Employment Social Outlook Trends, 2016*.

IWACU. "Burundi: Controversy Over Third Term for Nkurunziza." *allAfrica*. March 20, p.1.

Justice Africa. 2007. "Ghana at Fifty." March 1, pp. 1–2.

Kandeh, Jimmy. 2004. *Coups From Below: Armed Subalterns and State Power in West Africa*. New York: Palgrave-Macmillan.

Karimi, Faith, and Robyn Kriel. 2015. "Burundi: Leaders of Attempted Coup Arrested After President's Return." *CNN*. May 19, p.1.

Kaya, Hassan Omari. 2008. "The Salient Features of the Political Economy of Africa and Continental Challenges in the New Millennium." *Coleccion Edicion Especial*, pp. 301–330.

Kieh, George Klay. 2009. "The State and Political Instability in Africa." *Journal of Developing Societies*. 25(1), p. 1–25.

Kieh, George Klay. 2007. "Introduction: The Terminally Ill Berlinist State." In George Klay Kieh, Jr. (ed.). *Beyond State Failure and Collapse: Making the State Relevant in Africa*. Lanham, MD: Lexington Books, pp. 3–21.

Kieh, George Klay. 2004. "Military Engagement in African Politics." In George Klay Kieh, Jr., and Pita Ogaba Agbese (eds.). *The Military and Politics in Africa: From Engagement to Constitutional and Democratic Control*. Aldershot, UK: Ashgate Publishing, pp.

Koos, Carlo and Thea Gutscheke. 2014. "South Sudan's Newest War: When Two Old Men Divide a Nation." *IGA Focus*. No. 2, p.1.

Lal, Rollie. 2006. *Central Asia and Its Neighbors*. Santa Monica, CA: Rand Corporation.

Lansdale, John. 1994. "Moral Ethnicity and Political Tribalism." In P. Kaarsholm and J. Hultin (eds.). *Inventions and Boundaries: Historical and Anthropological Approaches to the Study of Ethnicity and Nationalism*. Roskilde, Netherlands: Institute for Development Studies, Roskilde University, pp. 131–150.

Lawson, Letitia. 2007. "U.S. Policy Since the Cold War." *Strategic Insights*. 6(1), pp. 1–14.

Loewenstein, Anthony. 2016. "How Not to Fix an African Narco-State. *Foreign Policy*. January 6, pp. 1–4.

Long, David, and Bernard Reich. 2002. *The Government and Politics of the Middle East and North Africa*. Boulder, CO: Westview Press.

Mail and Guardian, 2017. "Water at Heart of Africa's Growth and Survival." January 27, p.1.

Marshall, Monty. 2005. *Conflict Trends in Africa, 1946–2004: A Comparative Macro-Comparative Perspective*. Arlington, VA: Center for Global Policy, George Mason University.

Mbaku, John Mukum. 2000. "Governance, Wealth Creation and Development in Africa: The Challenges and Prospects." *African Studies Quarterly*. 4(2). www.africa.uf/edu.

Mbaku, John Mukum, and Chris Paul. 1989. "Political Instability in Africa A Rent Seeking Approach." *Public Choice*. 63(4), pp. 63–72.

Mengisteab, Kidane. 2007. "State-Building in Ethiopia." In George Klay Kieh, Jr. (ed.). *Beyond State Failure and Collapse: Making the State Relevant in Africa*. Lanham, MD: Lexington Books, pp. 99–114.

Menkhaus, Ken. 2015. "Diplomacy in a Failed State: International Mediation in Somalia." *Accord* No. 21, pp. 16–19.

Mullen, Jethro, and Khushbushal. 2015. "UN Aid Workers Among Six Killed in Al Shabaab Attack in Somalia." *CNN*. April 20, p.1.

Mutume, Gumisai. 2004. "Water, Sanitation and Housing Among Africa's Environmental Priorities." *Africa Renewal*. 18(2), pp. 19–20.

Oliver, Roland, and Anthony Atmore. 1994. *Africa Since 1800*. Cambridge: Cambridge University Press.

Osaghae, Eghosa. 2006. *The Ethnicity and the State in Africa*. Working paper series no. 7. Afraasian Center for Peace and Development Studies.

Osinubi, Tokunbo Simbowale, and Oladipupo Sunday Osinubi. 2006. "Ethnic Conflicts in Contemporary Africa: The Nigerian Experience." *Journal of Social Science*. 12(2), pp. 101–114.

Oyebade, Adebayo, and Abiodun Alao (eds.).1998. "Introduction: Redefining African Security." In Adebayo Oyebade and Abiodun Alao (eds.). *Africa After the Cold War: The Changing Perspectives on Security.* Trenton, NJ: Africa World Press, pp.
Phillips, John. 2004. *Macedonia: Warlords and Rebels in the Balkans.* New Haven, CT: Yale University Press.
Quijano, Anibal. 2000. "Coloniality of Power, Eurocentrism, and Latin America." *Nepantla: Views from the South.* 1(3), pp. 533–580.
Raghavan, Surdasan. 2013. "South Sudan's Growing Conflict Reflects Rivalry Between President and His Former Deputy." *The Washington Post.* December 23, pp. 1–2.
Rawlinson, Alexis. 2003. "The Political Manipulation of Ethnicity in Africa." Insolars. January, 1–7.
Ray, E., et al. 1979. *Dirty Work 2: The CIA in Africa.* Secaucus, NJ: Lyle Stuart.
Reuters. 2014. "Al Shabaab Claims Responsibility for Attack on AU Base in Mogadishu." Newsweek. December 25, p.1.
Rodney, Walter. 1984. *How Europe Underdeveloped Africa.* Washington, D.C.: Howard University Press.
Rolandsen, Oystein. 2015. "A Year of South Sudan's Third Civil War." *International Area Studies Review.* 18(1), pp. 87–104.
Roth, Keith, and Ida Sawyer. 2015. "Congo-Kinshasa: Joseph Kabila Forever." *allAfrica.* July 29, p.1.
Rubenstein, Richard. 1970. *Rebels in Eden: Mass Political Violence in the United States.* Boston: Little, Brown.
Scaruffi, Piero. 2016. *Wars and Casualties of the 20th and 21st Century.* Piero Scaruffi.
Soomaalyeed, Jamhuriyada. 2015. "Somalia Republic." In Tom Lansford (ed.). *Political Handbook of the World, 2015.* Thousand Oaks, CA: Sage, pp. 1323–1329.
Spooner, Samantha. 2015. "Rogue View: Africa's Pole of Inaccessibility and How It Contributes to the Central Region's Third Term Disease." *Mail & Guardian.* November 3, p.1.
Tolbert, Victoria. 1996. *Lifted Up.* St. Paul, MN: Macalester Park.
United Nations Economic Commission for Africa. 2015. *Economic Report on Africa 2015.* UNECA.
United Nations Habitat. 2014. *UN Habitat and AFDB in Joint Efforts to Address Africa's Housing Challenges.* March 4, p. 1.
United Nations High Commissioner for Refugees. 2015. *2015 UNHCR Regional Operations Profile—Africa.*
Water and Sanitation Program. 2017. *Africa.* www.wsp.org. Accessed October 14, 2017.
World Health Organization. 2014. *Global Health Observatory Data Repository.* Geneva: WHO, p.1.
World Hunger Education Service. 2017. "Africa Hunger Facts." *Hunger Notes.*
Zounmenou, David. 2015. "AU Must Prevent Third Term Bids from Destabilizing Africa." *ISS Africa.* June 11, p. 1.

Rethinking Development in Africa

The Lessons

GEORGE KLAY KIEH, JR.

Introduction

There is no doubt that African states have made some progress, since the dawn of the post-independence era, especially since the "third wave of democratization" that swept across the continent beginning in the 1990s. For example, in the political sphere, progress has been made to end authoritarian rule on the continent (Freedom House, 2017). Prior to the commencement of the "third wave of democratization," there were two democratic states—Botswana and Mauritius—on the continent (Freedom House, 2017). However, by 2016, the number rose to ten (10) (Freedom House, 2017).

Notwithstanding the progress that has been made, much work remains to be done on the continent. In the political sphere, for example, public institutions such as the parliament and courts need to be strengthened, and the "hegemonic presidency" and its strangulating hold on power need to be caged (Prempeh, 2008; Kieh, 2012a). Also, the continuing scourge of authoritarianism needs to be addressed: In spite of the progress that has been made in terms of political democratization, the majority of the states—43—on the continent are still undemocratic (Freedom House, 2016b).

Similarly, concerted and sustained efforts are required to address the sordid state of human needs and material well-being. For example, according to the United Nations Development Program's annual Human Development Report for 2016, in 2015, 36 African states (67 percent) were ranked in the lowest stratum (United Nations Development Program, 2016). This means that the overwhelming majority of Africans are living perilously in terms of their material well-being. Even some of the continent's democratic states like Benin, Lesotho and Senegal are ranked in this category (United Nations Development Program, 2016; Freedom House, 2017). Clearly, this reflects the fact that real development on the continent requires continual progress in all spheres—economic, political, etc. Olukoshi (2005:187) provides an excellent summation of the imperative for the continuing quest for real development in Africa:

> Overall, the transitional process has registered important new shifts in African politics which ought to be acknowledged for the significance in Africa's post-independence history. Of these shifts, perhaps the most important are the embrace by the key players of a multi-party liberal constitutional framework for managing political competition, the expansion of the pluralization of the public space.... But, these changes have also been tempered by the deepening socio-economic inequalities occurring in most countries ... and the continuing incapacitation of the state as a public institution... [as well as] democratic reform failing to yield some of the economic dividends that could have been expected.

This essay's central argument is that the *sine qua non* for achieving human-centered real development in Africa is anchored on two major pivots. First, the neo-colonial African state must be deconstructed, rethought and democratically reconstituted (Mbaku,1999; Kieh, 2009a). Second, the current dominant neo-liberal development strategy that serves as the pathway to development on the continent must be jettisoned, and replaced by the democratic developmental state model. In short, development must be rethought.

The Travails of Neo-Liberal Development in Africa

The Origins

The end of colonialism in Africa was greeted with exuberance throughout the continent. This was because Africans believed that with the end of colonialism and its deleterious effects on human material well-being, among others, indigenous governments would set the various states on the pathway to human-centered democracy and development. As Ramsay (1993:3) notes, "the times were electric. In country after country, the flag s of Britain, Belgium and France were replaced by the banners of the new states, where leaders offered idealistic promises to remake the continent and the world."

However, the requiem for the end of colonialism had barley ended, when the subalterns came to the realization that the post-colonial era would be an epic struggle for survival (Ramsay, 1993). For example, the first generation of African leaders, with few exceptions (e.g., Kwame Nkrumah (Ghana)) retained the colonial state and its anti-subaltern classes social and economic policies. Similarly, succeeding generations of leaders continued the policies that essentially made the state analogous to "a buffet service in which the members of the ruling class and their relations eat all they can eat" (Kieh, 2009b:10), while the subalterns were, and still are enveloped in mass abject poverty and deprivation and social malaise. Further, the state managers engaged in unbridled corruption as the *terra firma* for the private accumulation of capital. In addition, there was the mismanagement of resources.

Amid the sordid performances of most of the governments of African states, two major global developments occurred in the early 1970s that had profound ramifications for African states. First, the increase in the price of oil imposed major strains on the economies of the overwhelming majority of African states. This was because these oil-dependent countries had to spent more money to purchase oil to satisfy needs in various areas of their economies and societies. Second, there was a global recession. The resulting adverse effect for African states was the precipitous decline in the prices of their primary products—e.g., agricultural products such as coffee, and cocoa. This led to a major decrease in their export earnings, due to the vulnerability of their economies to the vicissitudes in the prices of their primary products, their major export earners. To make matter worse, the core states like the United States, Britain and France reduced their foreign aid to various African states.

By 1980, most African states were experiencing major economic and social problems such as unemployment, declining standard of living, and crumbling public education and public health systems due to the lack of state investments in these basic human needs. The severity of the continent's economic and social crises led to the 1980s being declared "the lost decade" (Meredith, 2011). Interestingly, African leaders had two major policy choices. One was the opportunity to formulate and implement homegrown policies with the ostensible goal of improving the materials conditions of the subaltern. The other was to characteristically look to the core states and the international economic institutions—the International Monetary Fund (IMF) and the World Bank—that they dominate for the panacea. Disappointingly, most crisis-plagued African states chose the second option. In response, the core states and the Bretton Woods Institutions—the IMF and the World Bank— imposed on the African states the neo-liberal development model that had gained global ascendance due to the election of Ronald Reagan as President of the United States, and Margaret Thatcher as the Prime Minister of the United Kingdom. As Monbiot (2016:1) observes, "Neo-liberalism arose as a conscious attempt to reshape human life and shift the locus of power."

The Axles

The neo-liberal development strategy is based on several major axles. A core one is the suzerainty of the "market"—what Amable (2011:3) calls "market fundamentalism." That is, "markets for neoliberals and the rules for exchange are sacrosanct to the functioning of the economy and, by implication, to the existence of capitalism; they exist as the only alternative to some form of rational organization of economic life" (Turner, 2008:115). For example, neoliberals insist that "the market ensures that everyone gets what they deserve" (Monbiot, 2016:1). However, this portrays a "false sense of egalitarianism of the market" (Monibot, 2016:1). This is because the "private goods and services," which are available in the "market," can only be gotten by those who have the money to purchase them. This means that the impoverished citizens cannot benefit from the "market." Instead, they exit on the periphery of the "market."

Another major tenet is that "citizens, as consumers democratic choices are best exercised by buying and selling, a process that rewards merit and punishes inefficiency" (Monibot, 2016:1). In other words, the "market" is an open arena that is accessible to all citizens, irrespective of their economic station in a society. Citizens therefore can participate in the "market" either as buyers or sellers. Whatever status a citizen uses to participate in the "market" is freely chosen.

Similarly, neoliberalism is anchored on the argument that "human well-being can be best achieved through liberating individual entrepreneurial freedoms and skills within an institutional framework characterized by strong private property rights, market regulations, and free trade" (Amahazion, 2015:1). In other words, entrepreneurship can only thrive in a capitalist economic system in which people have the right to own property; the regulations do not adversely affect the capacity of businesses to make profit; and there is the unhindered flow of goods and services. Ultimately, neoliberals argue, among other things, this will lift people out of poverty through the so-called "trickle-down effect."

Further, there is the assertion that the state is an anathema to development—what Herrera (2006:41) refers to as "an anti-state strategy." Hence, neoliberalism prescribes a "minimalist state" that is confine to the role of providing security, enforcing contracts, and formulating and implementing regulations that do not adversely affect profit-making. In other words, neoliberalism calls for the "rolling back of the state" and the simultaneous ascendancy of the "market" as the precondition for promoting socio-economic development.

Moreover, with the "caging of the state," public services such as sanitation would then be privatized. The rationale is that the "market" is more efficient than the state in the provision of services. In other words, the state is inefficient, as evidenced by waste. Hence, it cannot be tasked to serve as the "engine of development."

Finally, neoliberalism stresses the importance of limited government spending. In other words, the government's financial resources should be focused on activities that help provide physical security and enforce contracts.

Then, with the creation of such an enabling environment, businesses will thrive. Importantly, the resulting wealth that is accrued would then be shared by all through the dynamics of trickle-down."

The Major Policy Pillars

THE STRUCTURAL ADJUSTMENT PROGRAMS (SAPs)

The Structural Adjustment Programs (SAPs) were designed by the

Bretton Woods Institutions—IMF and World Bank—professedly as the panacea to the crises of socio-economic underdevelopment that African states were experiencing beginning in the mid–1970s. Every crisis-plagued African state that sought loans from the IMF and the World Bank was compelled to accept SAP, as the sine qua non. SAP was anchored on several major contours. At the vortex was the assertion that "an unregulated free market and private sector are the engines of unrestricted growth, the benefits of which will trickle down from the owners of capital to the entire population [Welch and Oringer, 1998:1].

Another tenet was the imperative of reducing government spending (Welch and Oringer, 1998). Two major ways of doing this were the downsizing of the public sector by retrenching employees, not filling vacancies, and keeping wages stagnant. A related requirement was the privatization of state-owned enterprises. Also, loan-seeking African states were ordered to remove all barriers to trade, create propitious conditions for foreign investment, devalue their currencies, and increase interest rates.

Significantly, SAPs had several major effects on the African states that implemented them. A major one was SAPs' failure to establish a foundation for sustained socio-economic development (Welch and Oringer, 1998). Instead, SAPs created the conditions for African states to service their loans to the "Bretton Woods Institutions," the core states, and their commercial banks. Hence, the financial resources that the crisis-ridden African states needed to revive their economies, and address the labyrinthine of human material well-being issues was siphoned off through debt-servicing. For example, by 1999, indebted African states were spending about $14 billion per year on debt servicing (Panapress, 2016:1).

Another deleterious effect of SAPs was the destruction of the "social safety net" of various African states. The requirement that African states should remove subsidies from such major human needs areas as education and health care undermined the efforts to develop human capital that is exigent for development, and contributed to the decimation of the public health system and the resulting increased vulnerability to diseases (Cheru, 2002).

Also, the downsizing of the public sector led to an increase in unemployment. This is because the state is the largest employer in the majority of the African states. Therefore, the reduction in the labor force in the public sector sent millions to the unemployment line. To make matters worse, even vacant positions were not filled

Further, SAP undermined local businesses by privileging foreign-owned multinational corporations and other outfits (Welch, 2005). This was done by requiring loan-seeking African states to create a favorable climate for foreign investors, including the offering of tax breaks and duty free privileges. However, these privileges were not extended to local businesses. Thus, these local businesses had to compete on a "playing field" to give an undue advantage to well-resourced foreign-owned businesses. One of the major consequences was the undercutting of domestic entrepreneurship, as evidenced by the folding of several local businesses that were forced out of the market by foreign firms (Welch, 2005).

The undermining of the autonomy of the state was one of the major adverse effects of SAP (Krasner, 2009). This was done by the "Bretton Woods Institutions" imposing their suzerainty over the levers of economic governance. For example, so-called experts from the IMF and the World Bank dictated policies dealing with budgets and public projects, among others. Essentially, these IMF and World Bank officials had "veto power" over economic decision-making. Interestingly, the economic decisions that these "experts" made were not designed to improve the material conditions of the subaltern classes through state investment in such critical areas as education, health care and food security. On the contrary, the various austerity measures that were imposed by SAP contributed to mass abject poverty (Munever and Toussaint, 2013). By weakening the state and making it incapable and unable to deliver "public goods," SAP also contributed to the erosion of state legitimacy, as the subalterns viewed the state as an irrelevant construct (Agbese and Kieh, 2007; Kieh, 2008a, 2008b, 2012a, 2012b, 2015).

THE HEAVILY INDEBTED POOR COUNTIES INITIATIVE (HIPCI)

The failure of SAPs to improve the material conditions of the subaltern classes in Africa led the suzerains of the global political economy—the United States, the United Kingdom, and the other advanced capitalist developed states and the "Bretton Woods institutions"—to rethink their externally-designed and imposed development models on African states. Without abandoning their hegemonic control over the political economies of African states, the major players in the international political economy made the decision that "debt forgiveness" was a panacea to African states' socio-economic lacunae. According to the rationale, if the advanced capitalist states and the "Bretton Woods" institutions were to "forgive" the debt of African states, then the latter would spend the money saved from debt servicing on human needs.

Against this backdrop, the Heavily Indebted Poor Countries Initiative (HIPCI) was developed in 1996. However, because of its narrow contours, the model was enhanced in 1997. Under the model, indebted African states have to meet a set of criteria in order to qualify for "debt forgiveness": 1). They must be heavily indebted; 2) they must be poor; 3) they must recommit to capitalism as their economic system; and 4) they must adopt liberal democracy as their governance tapestry. Thereafter, the qualified African states have to go through various stages before their debts are forgiven. As of 2015, 30 African states have completed the process (International Monetary Fund, 2016a). Hence, they are eligible for "debt forgiveness" by the developed states and the IMF and the World Bank.

Importantly, the core limitation of HIPCI is that debt forgiveness is occurring in the context of a state construct that has not been democratically reconstituted. That is, the "third wave of democratization" has essentially led to the sanitization of the "political space," rather than a fundamentally restructuring of the political economies of African states. In other words, debt forgiveness would only make the desired impact within the context of a restructured state.

THE POVERTY REDUCTION STRATEGY

The poverty reduction strategy (PRS) emerged in the late 1990s, as a centerpiece of the Enhanced Heavily Indebted Poor Countries Initiative. The reason for the IMF and World Bank formulating the PRS was based on the grudging realization that the major neo-liberal development strategies—from SAPs to HIPCI—have failed to address the crises of socio-economic under-development in Africa, especially the vexatious issue of abject mass poverty. Hence, the PRS represents the latest effort by the United States, the IMF, the World Bank and the other dominant forces in the global political economy to sanitize the adverse effects of the neo-liberal development model, which they imposed on African states.

At the core of the PRS is the initial requirement that African states that are seeking "debt forgiveness" must prepare a strategy paper that maps out the road map for addressing poverty (International Monetary Fund, 2016b). Specifically, the road map begins with the formulation of an interim poverty reduction strategy paper that is anchored on the following major pillars:

1. A summary of the current knowledge and analysis of a country's poverty situation;
2. A description of the existing poverty reduction strategy;
3. A mapping out of the process for producing a fully developed poverty reduction strategy paper (PRSP) (International Monetary Fund, 2016a:1).

Further, there is the stipulation that the process for formulating the PRS must be participatory "involving domestic stakeholders as well as development partners, including the World Bank and the International Monetary Fund" (International Monetary Fund, 2016b:1). As Ademujobi (2006:13) observes,

> … PRSPs … emphasize the importance of dialogue on development strategies. The approach and emphasis in the PRSPs is about the process through which development policies are developed, implemented and monitored. The underlying assumption is that for policies to be meaningful and realizable the process through which they are formulated must be inclusive with popular participation in them.

Another major pillar is the formulation of a full PRSP. Essentially, this entails the analysis of the poverty situation in a country, prioritizing poverty reduction programs and projects, and the undertaking of costing (Newborne, 2004). Importantly, the full PRSP is supposed to be "comprehensive: integrating macro-economic, sectoral, structural and social dimensions of poverty… [and] long-term: reforming institutions and building capacity based on a long-term perspective of poverty reduction" (Newborne, 2004: 2).

The PRSPS are then subjected to an approval process that consists of two major steps:

1. The staffs of the IMF and World Bank review both the interim and full PRSP. Thereafter, the staffs of the two major international financial institutions then provide feedback to the countries. In turn, the feedback is used to revise both documents.

2. The revised and approved PRSPs are then submitted to the executive committees of the IMF and World Bank for approval. Thereafter, the country then receives "debt forgiveness."

In addition, an African country that is receiving "debt forgiveness" must update its PRSP every three years, and provide annual progress report to the IMF and World Bank.

Although the PRS has placed poverty reduction on the global policy agenda, it has several major weaknesses. Characteristically, like all of the externally-imposed strategies of the neo-liberal development model, the PRS lacks domestic accountability. That is, an African country that receives "debt forgiveness" is not accountable to its citizens, but to the IMF and the World Bank—what Newborne (2004: 4) refers to as "donor-recipient relationships rather than government-citizen accountability."

Another major shortcoming of the PRS is that it does not link poverty reduction to the budgeting, broader resource allocation, and other major decision-making process as within an African state that receives "debt forgiveness" (Newborne, 2004). For example, there is no surety that an African state that is receiving "debt forgiveness" will allocate funds in its national budget to poverty alleviation programs and projects. So, the PRS, notwithstanding, a "debt forgiveness" receiving African state could make the decision to allocate national resources through the budgetary and other processes to programs and projects that do not improve the material conditions of its citizens, thereby reducing poverty.

Also, there is the problem of the lack of local ownership of the PRS (Newborne, 2004; Ademujobi, 2006). That is, the terms of reference and related elements of the PRS are not formulated domestically by "debt forgiveness" seeking African states. Instead, based on the usual formulaic approach, the IMF and World Bank have developed the key components of the PRS, and imposed them on African states that are seeking "debt forgiveness." Hence, the PRS reflects the views, interests, agendas and orientation of the IMF and the World Bank. Further, these twin institutions have the final authority to approve the PRS.

As well, the PRS fails to take cognizance of the prevalence of non-democratic governance systems in Africa (Freedom House, 2016b). According to Freedom House (2016b:), in 2015, there were 43 non-democratic states in Africa—21 authoritarian states, and 22 hybrid ones. Therefore, it is not possible for the PRS to be formulated in a participatory manner. In short, political participation and inclusion are antithetical to non-democratic governance systems. So, this means that the PRS process in these non-democratic African states that have received "debt forgiveness" was non-participatory and inclusive.

Even in some of the African states that are democratizing, the formulation of the PRS is not done through a participatory and inclusive process (Ademujobi, 2006). For example, the government selects the civil society organizations (CSOs) that participate in the process (Ademujobi, 2006). This means that only those CSOs that are deemed favorable to the government get selected to participate in the process. On the other hand, those CSOs that the government determines are critical of its policies do not get selected to participate in the process (Ademujobi, 2006). This means that critical voices that provide alternate viewpoints are not included in the process. Moreover, usually, the government drafts the PRS, and then invites the selected CSOs to review it. Hence, the process is one of consultation with the chosen CSOs, rather than participation, since the latter do not participate in the drafting of the PRS (Ademujobi, 2006).

A related weakness of the PRS process is that the poor, the professed beneficiaries of poverty reduction, are marginalized. This is because the CSOs that are supposed to represent them are elitist in nature, "mostly dependent on external funding and can rarely claim to be the voices of the poor" (Ademujobi, 2006:21). Anyang' Nyong'o (2002:48) provides a poignant critique of the CSOs that claim to be the representatives of the poor thus: "... [CSOs] are rarely in the position to mobilize the poor to speak for themselves.... The poor therefore remain largely unorganized, powerless, and marginalized in terms of raising their voices in public policy making, or in terms of participation in public affairs."

The lack of the democratic reconstitution of the state makes it impossible to reduce poverty in African states. This is because a state that has visited mass abject poverty on the subaltern classes, while privileging the ruling classes cannot shepherd the process of poverty reduction. So, poverty reduction is taking place in a state construct whose portrait—nature, mission, character and political economy—is anti-poor people (Kieh, 2008a, 2008b, 2009a, 2009b, 2012b, 2015). Even in those African states that are experiencing liberal democratization, the overarching emergent effect is the opening up of the political space, rather than the transformation of the material well-being of ordinary Africans. So, only the democratic reconstitution of the state that is comprehensive and transformative can create the enabling environment for successful poverty reduction (Kieh, 2009a).

Linked to the problem of the absence of democratic state reconstitution is the lack of the structural transformation of the peripheral capitalist economies of African states. Basically, African states have monocrop economies and lack industrial base. Hence, they are primarily producers of raw materials within the context of the "global division of labor" and its attendant "system of unequal exchange." In addition, African states have marginal roles in the "international division of power." In this vein, the global political economy imposes major structural constraints on African states that undermine poverty reduction. For example, African states receive less for their primary products, but are required to pay more for manufactured goods from the "global north." One of the major resulting consequences is that African states usually experience terms of trade problems and the consequent adverse impact on their foreign exchange earnings. So, even with the best intention of reducing poverty, the unjust global political economy undermines this effort.

The State of Human Development in Africa, 2015

Country	Human Development Index (HDI)	Global Rank
Algeria	0.736	83
Angola	0.532	149
Benin	0.480	166
Botswana	0.698	106
Burkina Faso	0.402	183
Burundi	0.400	184
Cape Verde	0.646	122
Cameroon	0.512	153
Central African Republic	0.350	187
Chad	0.392	185
Comoros	0.503	159
Congo, Republic of the	0.591	136

Country	Human Development Index (HDI)	Global Rank
Congo, Democratic Republic of the	0.433	176
Côte d'Ivoire	0.462	172
Djibouti	0.470	168
Egypt	0.690	108
Equatorial Guinea	0.587	138
Eritrea	0.391	186
Ethiopia	0.442	174
Gabon	0.684	110
Gambia	0.441	175
Ghana	0.579	140
Guinea	0.411	182
Guinea-Bissau	0.420	178
Kenya	0.548	145
Lesotho	0.497	161
Liberia	0.430	177
Libya	0.724	94
Madagascar	0.510	154
Malawi	0.445	173
Mali	0.419	179
Mauritania	0.506	156
Mauritius	0.777	63
Morocco	0.628	126
Mozambique	0.416	180
Namibia	0.628	126
Niger	0.348	188
Nigeria	0.514	152
Rwanda	0.483	163
São Tomé and Principe	0.556	143
Senegal	0.466	170
Seychelles	0.772	64
Sierra Leone	0.413	181
Somalia	–	
South Africa	0.660	116
South Sudan	0.467	169
Sudan	0.479	167
Swaziland	0.531	150
Tanzania	0.521	151
Togo	0.484	162
Tunisia	0.721	96
Uganda	0.483	163
Zambia	0.586	139
Zimbabwe	0.509	155

NOTE: Scores: =High Level of Human Development; Medium Level of Human Development; Low Level of Human Development.

NOTE: Score: Very High = 0.800 and above; High = 0.700–0.799; Medium = 0.550–0.699; and Low = Less than 0.550.

Source: Adapted from the United Nations Development Program, Human Development Report, 2016 (New York: United Nations Development Program, 2016), pp. 208–210.

An Overall Assessment
of Neo-Liberal Development in Africa

So, what have been some of the major effects of neo-liberal development on the continent? A major one is that the African Continent experienced an annual growth rate of more than 5 percent, from 2000–2015 (Zamfir, 2016). However, these high growth rates have not translated into improvement in the material conditions of ordinary Africans. Essentially, it has been "growth without development" (Ayelazuno, 2014:80).

Overall, the neoliberal development strategy has not addressed Africa's crises of socio-economic underdevelopment, especially the vagaries of mass abject poverty, bourgeoning unemployment, inadequate health care, sanitation and clean drinking water, and the broad gamut of social malaise. In 2015, the state of human development in the overwhelming majority of African states was poor. Specifically, 36 African states were ranked in the lowest stratum. Even the IMF, one of the leading architects of the neo-liberal development model has admitted the framework's failure. For example, IMF Deputy Director Jonathan Ostry and Division Chief David Fuceri argued in their interesting paper "Neo-Liberalism: Oversold?" that "neoliberal economic policies have resulted in inequality and stunted economic growth" (Grier, 2016:1).

Toward an Alternative Development Trajectory for Africa

The Foundation: The Democratic Reconstitution
of the Neo-Colonial African State

The critically important initial step in rethinking development in Africa should involve the democratic reconstitution of the neo-colonial African state that has asphyxiated human-centered development on the continent, since the post-independence era. This is because the neo-colonial state that has adorned the African landscape since the post-independence era is incapable of being the agency for human-centered development. As Samatar and Samatar (2002:5) argued, "The failure of the state in Africa is so uncontested that both scholarly discussions and policy concerns have increasingly shifted to what is 'civil society.'"

The democratic reconstitution of the state should be anchored on two major sets of interlocking processes. One should focus on the transformation of the portrait—the nature, mission, character and political economy—of the neo-colonial state. Specifically, they should entail changing the nature of the

African state from an externally-imposed construct that is not reflective of the historical-cultural experiences of the various ethnicities that constitute African states to one that does. Also, the mission of the state should be changed from the creation of propitious conditions for the accumulation of wealth by metropolitan-based multinational corporations and other business and their African compradors to a construct that accords primacy to human development. Further, the state's character should be transformed from being negligent, among others, to serviceable to the needs and aspirations of the people of Africa, especially the subaltern classes. As for the political economy, its relations of production and power relationships, among others, should be transformed so that they promote human development based on the principles of equity, equality and social justice.

The other process should seek to transform the various sectors of African societies. For example, in the cultural sector, the emphasis should be on the promotion of ethnic pluralism and peaceful co-existence. As Mbaku (2001:95) argues, "The reconstituted African states should provide mechanisms that do not place any individual or group at a competitive disadvantage or advantage in the competition for resources on the basis of ethnicity."

In the economic domain, the peripheral capitalist mode of production should be transformed through industrialization, intersectoral linkages, addressing poverty, combating corruption, the creation of wealth, and the resistance to externally imposed economic remedies that have deleterious effects on human needs. In terms of the environmental sector, the democratically reconstituted state should formulate and implement policies that address the issues of the depletion of arable land, over population, pollution, deforestation, and the disposal of toxic wastes.

As for the political sector, the reconstituted state would shepherd the process of establishing a democratic constitutional order that ensures the protection of political rights and civil liberties, and promotes pluralism, the rule of law, "checks and balances," the establishment of a vibrant multiparty system, the holding of competitive elections at regular time intervals, transparency, accountability, decentralization, and a vibrant civil society. In terms of religious issues, the reconstituted state would promote secularism, freedom of religion, pluralism, tolerance and peaceful co-existence. As for the security sector, the reconstituted state will ensure the protection of persons and properties, stability, and the constitutional and democratic control of the military, police and security establishments. Socially, attention will be paid to education, health care, public housing public transportation, the availability and access to clean drinking water and acceptable sanitation, and food security. As well, the reconstituted state would promote gender equity by dismantling the vestiges of patriarchy, so that women can be empowered and participate meaningfully in national development.

The New Development Model:
The Social Democratic Development State

THE NATURE OF THE CONSTRUCT

Then social democratic developmental state links democracy and development as two mutual reinforcing phenomena: A sustainable democracy requires sustainable development and vice versa (Kieh, 2015:8). In essence, one cannot be sustained without the other. As Sen (2000:3) argues, "Development can be seen ... as a process of expanding the real freedoms that people enjoy.... Development required the removal of the major sources of unfreedom: poverty as well as tyranny, poor economic opportunities as well as systematic social deprivation, neglect of public facilities as well as intolerance or overactivity of repressive states."

Importantly, the thrust of the social democratic development trajectory is to address human needs within a context in which citizens can simultaneously exercise and enjoy their political rights and civil liberties. For example, a premium will be placed on "ending both relative and absolute poverty" (Kieh, 2015:9). At the same time, citizens would be freed to participate in the political process by, among other things, joining organizations of their choice, including interest groups and political parties. Overall, the construct seeks to create what Marshall (1950: 1) aptly refers to as "social citizenship"—citizens enjoying economic, political and social rights.

THE FUNDAMENTS

Several major interrelated elements provide the base of the social democratic developmental state. A key one is the importance of leadership, particularly servants-leaders, who are honest, committed and patriotic. Essentially, these leaders must be primarily driven by the desire to serve the interests of the citizens first, rather than theirs. As Habisse (2010:1) observes, "the leadership must be strongly committed to the development goals, and [must place] national development ahead of personal enrichment and/or short-term political gains."

Another major element is development ideology. The state through its leadership must have a clear vision that frames the development agenda. At the core must be the postulate that "the ideological underpinning of the state [is] developmental" (Mkandawire, 1998:2). Specifically, the ideology must shape and condition the processes of the formulation of the development agenda, including the objectives, targets, costs and timelines, the articulation of the agenda particularly to the citizens, and the implementation of development projects. Based on the development ideology, the aforementioned processes must be inclusive by involving all of the major stakeholders in the state, including women and youth organizations.

Also, the state must be embedded in the society (Evans, 1995). This would mean that the state must develop cooperative and collaborative relationships with various groups in the society. The ostensible purpose should be to involve them in the development process as both stakeholders and partners. Importantly, the process of choosing the groups must be inclusive, taking into consideration the social composition of a particular African state. Overall, state embeddedness is indispensable to the gaining of legitimacy from the citizens.

Further, the state must be autonomous. That is, the state must be freed from the control of any particular individual or group in the domestic arena. Similarly, the state must also exercise independence in its relations with external actors, including other states, as well as international organizations and businesses. The rationale, as Seddon and Belton-James (1995:326) note, "Effective insulation from immediate pressures of special interests enables policy-makers to respond swiftly and effectively to new circumstances..."

Moreover, the state would have institutional capacity. Specifically, this would entail three major assets. A key one is the careful designing of state agencies that would provide the organizational architecture. Linked to this is the establishment of a professional civil service in which people get their positions through merit, and have the security of tenure, among other things. The professional civil service will serve as the corps of technocrats who will provide the technical, managerial and administrative skills that are required for development governance. As well, financial, logistical and material resources should be available for the formulation and implementation of various development programs and projects.

Another major tenet is the funding of development. This would entail the generation of revenues through, for example, taxes, investments, the prudent management of natural resources, trading in manufactured goods, capital formation through domestic savings. These financial resources would then be prudently used to fund the various development projects, including the construction of schools, hospitals, roads, electrical grid, water system, and public housing.

A mixed system based on both public and private ownership of the major means of production will anchor the economic system. In addition, the state would foster co-operative relations with domestic businesses. One of the major ways will be through the provision of tax breaks, tax holidays, and duty free privileges. As Musamba (2010:24) suggests, "The state[must utilize] a wide range of institutional instruments to poke and prod domestic firms to meet domestic and international business standards, productivity levels, and organizational and technical capacities."

DEMOCRACY

The democratic plank would be based on several mutually reinforcing planks. Among them are the protection and promotion of political rights and civil liberties, a system of "checks and balances" to militate against autocracy (Persson eta al, 1997), the establishment and operation of a vibrant multiparty system, the holding of free and fair elections at regular time intervals (Lindberg, 2014), the establishment of both "horizontal and vertical accountability" (O'Donnell, 1998), transparency, the rule of law, an independent judiciary, and a vibrant civil society.

DEVELOPMENT

Linked to the democratic dimension would the development one. In this domain, the focus will be on the structural transformation of the economy through industrialization and economic diversification, the importance of development planning, the creation of a domestic entrepreneurial class, the building of the physical infrastructure, the formulation and implementation of industrial strategies, the state controlling the "market," so that the latter can conformed to the development agenda, and the provision of "public goods," such as health care, education, jobs, public housing, and public transportation. Overall, development will be centered on the promotion of the material well-being of the citizens. The United Nations Development Program (1990:1) provides an excellent summation of human-centered development thus:

> [Human development] is about people—how development enlarges their choices. It is more than GNP growth ... more than producing commodities and accumulating capital ... the most critical of these wide ranging choices are to live a long and healthy life, to be educated and to have access to resources needed for s decent standard of living.

Conclusion

The essay has attempted to weave the common major threads that run through the various contributions to this volume spanning from democracy to food security. A major one is that while it is true that African states have made appreciable progress since the post-independence era, considerable work remains to be done in terms of promoting development. Another is that meaningful and sustainable development must focus on the advancement of the material well-beings of all Africans, irrespective of their ethnicities, classes, genders, religions, and other cultural, economic, political and social backgrounds. Further, the neoliberal development model, which has been imposed on African states, has failed to set into motion the process of human-centered development.

Against this background, it is imperative that development on the African Continent be rethought. Essentially, this should focus on the rejection of the neoliberal development model and the adaption of the social democratic developmental state model. The rationale for the suggesting the latter is that it focuses on human development by seeking to combine democracy and development as mutually reinforcing processes. Specifically, the pathway would entail the democratic reconstitution of the state, a transformative process that transcends political liberalization, and seeks to integrate the various sector of society—cultural, economic, and environmental, gender, political, religious, security and social. Subsequently, the social democratic development state model would be set into motion with its emphasis on integrating democracy and development.

REFERENCES

Ademujobi, Said. 2006. *Governance and Poverty Reduction in Africa: A Critique of Poverty Reduction Strategy Papers.* Paper presented at the Inter-Regional Conference on Social Policy and Welfare Regimes in Comparative Perspectives. Held at the University of Texas at Austin. April 20–23.

Agbese, Pita Ogaba, and George Klay Kieh, Jr. 2007. "Introduction: Democratizing States and State Reconstitution in Africa." In Pita Ogaba Agbese and George Klay Kieh, Jr. (eds.). *Reconstituting the State in Africa.* New York: Palgrave, pp. 3–29.

Agbese, Pita Ogaba, and George Klay Kieh, Jr. (eds.). 2015. "Introduction: The Pedigree of the Post-Colonial State in Africa." In Pita Ogaba Agbese and George Klay Kieh, Jr. (eds.). *The State in Africa: Beyond False Starts.* Ota, Nigeria: Third World Publishers, pp. 1–22.

Amable, Bruno. 2011. "Morals and Politics in the Ideology of Neo-Liberalism." *Socio-Economic Review.* 9(1), pp. 3–30.

Amahazion, Fikrejesus, 2015. "Neoliberalism and African Development." *MADOTE.* September. www.madote.com/2015/09/neoliberlaism-and-african-development.html. Accessed September 4, 2017.

Ayang Nyong'o, Peter. 2002. "Governance, Poverty and Sustainable Development in Africa." In Heinrich Boll Foundation(ed.). *Sustainable Development, Governance and Globalization: African Perspectives.* Nairobi, Kenya: Heinrich Boll Foundation, pp. 38–48.

Ayelazuno, Jasper Abembia. 2014. "Neo-liberalism and Growth Without Development in Ghana: A Case for State-led Industrialization." *Journal of Asian and African Studies.* 49(1), pp. 80–99.

Belton-James, Tim, and David Seddon. 1995. "The Political Determinants of Economic Flexibility With Special Reference to the East Asian 'NICs.'" In Killick Tony(ed.). *The Flexible Economy: Causes and Consequences of the Adaptability of National Economics.* Abingdon-on-Thames: Routledge, pp. 325–364.

Cheru, Fantu. 2002. "Debt, Adjustment and the Politics of Effective Response to HIV/AIDS in Africa." *Third World Quarterly.* 23(2), pp. 299–312.

Evan, Peter. 1995. *Embedded Autonomy.* Princeton: Princeton University Press.

Freedom House. 2017 *Freedom in the World: Comparative and Historical Data, 1972–2016.* Washington, D.C.: Freedom House.

Grier, Ben. 2016. "Even the IMF Now Admits Neo-Liberalism Has Failed." *Fortune.* June 3, p.1.

Habisse, Tesfaye. 2010. The Challenge of Building the Democratic Developmental State. *TIGRI Online,* pp. 1–2.

Herrera, Remy. 2006. "The Neoliberal 'Rebirth' of Development Economics." *Monthly Review.* 58(1), pp. 38–50.

International Monetary Fund. 2016a. *Debt Relief Under the Heavily Indebted Poor Countries Initiative.* September 20.

International Monetary Fund. 2016b. *Poverty Reduction Strategy Papers (PRSPs).* November.

Kieh, George Klay, Jr. 2015. "Constructing the Social Democratic Developmental State in Africa: Lessons from the Global South." *Bandung: The Journal of the Global South.* 2(2), pp. 1–14.

Kieh, George Klay, Jr. 2008a. *The First Liberian Civil War: The Crises of Underdevelopment.* New York: Peter Lang Publishing.

Kieh, George Klay, Jr. 2008b. "The State in Africa." In George Klay Kieh, Jr. (ed.). *Africa and the New Millennium.* Trenton, NJ: Africa World Press, pp. 53–85.

Kieh, George Klay, Jr. 2009a. "Reconstituting the Neo-Colonial State in Africa." *Journal of Third World Studies.* 24(1), pp. 41–55.

Kieh, George Klay, Jr. 2009b. "The State and Political Instability in Africa." *Journal of Developing Societies.* 25(1), pp. 1–25.

Kieh, George Klay, Jr. 2012a "The Hegemonic Presidency and Post-Conflict Peacebuilding in Liberia." *Africa Peace and Conflict Journal.* 5(2), pp. 14–26.

Kieh, George Klay, Jr. 2012b. *Liberia's State Failure, Collapse and Reconstitution.* Cherry Hill, NJ: Africana Homestead Legacy Publishers.

Kieh, George Klay, Jr., and Pita Ogaba Agbese. 2015. "Introduction: The Tragedies of the Authoritarian State in Africa." In George Klay Kieh, Jr., and Pita Ogaba Agbese (eds.). *Reconstructing the Authoritarian State in Africa.* Abingdon-on-Thames: Routledge, pp. 1–17.

Krasner, Stephen. 2009. "The Sovereign State is Just About Dead." *Foreign Policy.* November 20, pp. 1–4.

Marshall, T.H. 1950. *Citizenship and Social Class.* Cambridge: Cambridge University Press.

Mbaku, John Mukum. 1999. *Making the State Relevant in African Societies.* In John Mukum Mbaku(ed.). *Preparing Africa for the Twenty-First Century.* Aldershot, UK: Ashgate Publishing, pp. 299–333.

Mbaku, John Mukum. 2001. *Ethnicity, Constitutionalism and Governance in Africa.* In John Mukum Mbaku et al. (eds.). *Ethnicity and Governance in the Third World.* Aldershot, UK: Ashgate Publishing, pp. 59–95.

Meredith, Martin. 2011. *The State of Africa: A History of the Continent Since Independence.* New York: Simon & Schuster.

Mkandawire, Thandika. 1998. *Thinking About Developmental States in Africa.* Paper presented at the UN-AERC Workshop on Institutions and Development in Africa. Tokyo, Japan: United Nations University.

Monbiot, George. 2016. "Neoliberalism—The Ideology at the Root of All Our Problems." *The Guardian (UK).* April 15, pp. 1–3.

Munever, Daniel, and Eric Toussaint. 2013. "The Debt of Developing Countries: The Devastating Impacts of IMF-World bank 'Economic Medicine.'" *Global Research.* October 11, pp. 1–2.

Musamba, Charity. 2010. "The Developmental State Concept and its Relevance to Africa." In P. Meyns and C. Musamba (eds.). *The Developmental State in Africa: Problems and Prospects.* Duisburg, Germany: Duisburg Institute for Development and Peace, University of Duisburg–Essen, pp. 11–41.

Newbourne, Peter. 2004. *Background Information on Poverty Reduction Strategy Papers and the Water Sector.* Working and Discussion Papers Series. London: Overseas Development Institute.

O'Donnell, Guillermo. 1998. "Horizontal Accountability in New Democracies." *Journal of Democracy.* 9(3), pp. 112–126

Olukoshi, Adebayo. 2005. Changing Patterns in African Politics." In A. Atilio and Gladys Lechini(eds). *Politics and Social Movements in A Hegemonic World: Lessons from Africa, Asia, and Latin America.* Buenos Aires, Argentina: CLACSO, pp. 177–201.

Panapress. 2016. Africa Debt: Reinforcing the Can't Pay, Won't Pay Argument. February, p.1.

Persson, Torsten, et al. 1997. "Separation of Powers and Political Accountability." *The Quarterly Journal of Economics*. 1/2(4), pp. 1163–1202.

Prempeh, H. Kwasi. 2008. "Presidential Power in Comparative Perspective: The Puzzling Persistence of Imperial Presidency in Post-Authoritarian Africa." *Hastings Constitutional Law Quarterly*. 35(4), pp. 761–834.

Ramsay, Jeffress. 1993. "Introduction: Africa: The Struggle for Development." In Jeffress Ramsay(ed.). *Global Studies: Africa*. Guilford, CT: McGraw-Hill/Dushkin, pp. 1–3.

Samatar, Abdi, and Ahmed Samatar. 2002. "Introduction." In Abdi Samatar and Ahmed Samatar (eds.). *The African State: Reconsideration*. Portsmouth, NH: Heinemann, pp.1–16.

Sen, Amarya. 2000. *Development As Freedom*. New York: Anchor Books.

Turner, Rachel. 2008. *Neo-Liberal Ideology: History, Concepts and Policies*. Edinburg: University of Edinburg Press.

United Nations Development Program. 1990. *Human Development Report, 1990*. New York: Oxford University Press.

United Nations Development Program. 2016. *Human Development Report, 2016*. New York: Oxford University Press.

Welch, Carol. "Structural Adjustment Programs and Poverty Reduction Strategy." *Foreign Policy in Focus*. October 12, pp. 1–5.

Welch, Carol, and Jason Oringer. 1998. "Structural Adjustment Programs." *Foreign Policy in Focus*. April 1, pp. 1–3.

Zamfir, Lonel. 2016. *Africa's Economic Growth*. Brussels: European Parliamentary Research Service, European Union.

About the Contributors

George Klay **Kieh,** Jr., is a professor of political science at the University of West Georgia. He earned his Ph.D. in political science at Northwestern University in Illinois. His research interests include security studies, American foreign policy, the state, democratization and democracy, development studies, political economy, regional and global institutions.

Samuel Wai **Johnson,** Jr., is a visiting instructor of economics at Eastern Mennonite University in Harrisonburg, Virginia. His research interests include development finance, economic development (poverty reduction strategies, food security and economic security), and the economic dimensions of conflict and post-conflict peace building.

Johnson W. **Makoba** is a professor of sociology at the University of Nevada, Reno. His research interests include organizations and bureaucracies, and alternative African development strategies. He has published two books on development in Africa, as well as several book chapters and articles in numerous scholarly journals.

David N.P. **Mburu** was a lecturer of Kiswahili language and culture at the University of Kansas. Prior to that, he taught at several universities in Kenya. His research interests were comparative education, curriculum and instruction, and gender and education.

Emmanuel O. **Oritsejafor** is chair of the Department of Political Science at North Carolina Central University. He is coeditor of the *Liberian Studies Journal* and the *African Social Science Review*, and senior fellow at the United Negro College Fund. His research interests include political economy, public policy and public administration. He has published numerous articles in various journals.

E. Ike **Udogu** is a professor of political science at Appalachian State University in North Carolina. His research interests include human rights, conflict resolution, ethnic politics, and minority politics. His has published numerous books and articles on leadership and politics in Africa and around the world.

Samuel **Zalanga** is a professor of sociology at Bethel University in Minnesota. He has served as the associate editor for Africa for the *Journal of Third World Studies.* His interests include social justice and a more just and egalitarian society at the global, national, and community levels. He has published numerous book chapters and articles on these topics.

Index

www.ingramcontent.com/pod-product-compliance
Lightning Source LLC
Chambersburg PA
CBHW022312280326
41932CB00010B/1068